Experience
RPG IV Tutorial

2nd Edition

Heather Rogers, Julie Santilli
& Maha Masri

Experience RPG IV Tutorial

2nd Edition

*Heather Rogers, Julie Santilli
& Maha Masri*

ADVICE Press
366 Cambridge Avenue
Palo Alto, CA 94306

Experience RPG IV Tutorial - 2nd Edition
by Heather Rogers, Julie Santilli & Maha Masri

IBM Centre for Advanced Studies, Dr. Gabriel Silberman, Program Director

IBM Consulting Editor: Sheila Richardson

Published by   ADVICE Press, 366 Cambridge Avenue, Palo Alto, CA 94306.
            Phone: (650) 321-2197 Fax: (650) 321-2199 info@advice.com

Printing History:

          May 1998:   First Book Edition

AS/400, C/400, Experience RPG IV, IBM, ILE, Integrated Language Environment, OS/400, RPG IV, RPG/400, Visual Age, Visual Age for Java and the IBM logo are trademarks of IBM Corporation in the US and/or other countries,

This edition applies to Version 4, Release 2, Modification Level 0, of IBM Integrated Language Environment RPG for AS/400 (Program 5769-RG1), RPG/400 (Program 5716-RG1) and to all subsequent releases and modifications until otherwise indicated in new editions. Makre sure you are using the correct edition for the level of the product.

Windows and Windows95 are registerered trademark of Microsoft Corporation.

Many of the designations used by manufactureers and sellers to distinguish their products are claimed as trademarks or service marks. All such trademarks and service marks are the property of their respective holders and the Publisher and Authors make no claim of any kind on these trademarks.

While every precaution has been taken in the preparation of this book, the authors and publisher assume no responsibility for errors or ommissions, or for damages resulting from the use of the information contained herein.

This book is printed on acid-free paper with 85% recycled content, 15% post-consumer waste. ADVICE Press is committed to using and selecting paper, printers and other suppliers in a fashion consistent with a sustainable environment.

ISBN: 1-889671-22-3   [5/98]

Author Dedications

Heather Rogers: To my incredible husband Andy, and my wonderful children, Benjamin, Alaina, and Joshua, thank you so much for your love, support, and encouragement, and for putting up with all the late nights and weekends I had to work on this project. I love you all!

Julie Santilli: To my family and friends whose love, support and enthusiasm gave me the energy to meet my aspirations and challenges on this publication.

Maha Masri: To my mother and father Hiyam and Juma, my sisters Ghada, Lina and Diana, and a special dedication to Jason Shayer who helped me get through it all, thank you for being there.

Author Acknowledgements

The authors would like to thank the following people for their valuable contributions to this project: Denise Eng, for sharing your time and your excellent Java coding skills. Barbara Morris, for all your great technical feedback and help in reviewing the tutorial. Karen Carlyle, Joe Chang, Anne James, Sheila Richardson, and Jamie Roberts for your work on the first version of this tutorial; your hard work made this second edition possible. Jon Paris and Hans Boldt for your support and help reviewing the first version of the tutorial. And a special thank you to Susan Gantner, for providing the technical base for the original tutorial, and generously agreeing to let us use your likeness. Thanks!

Contents

Notices

Any reference to an IBM product, program, or service is not intended to state or imply that only that IBM product, program, or service may be used. Any functionally equivalent product, program, or service that does not infringe any IBM intellectual property right may be used instead. However, it is the user's responsibility to evaluate and verify the operation of any non-IBM product, program, or service.

IBM may have patents or pending patent applications covering subject matter described in this document. The furnishing of this document does not give you any license to these patents. You can send license inquiries, in writing, to:

IBM Director of Licensing
IBM Corporation
500 Columbus Avenue
Thornwood, NY 10594
U.S.A.

Licensees of this program who wish to have information about it for the purpose of enabling: (i) the exchange of information between independently created programs and other programs (including this one) and (ii) the mutual use of the information which has been exchanged, should contact:

IBM Canada Ltd.
Department 071
1150 Eglinton Avenue East
Toronto, Ontario
M3C 1H7
Canada

This information contains examples of data and reports used in daily business operations. To illustrate them as completely as possible, the examples include the names of individuals, companies, brands, and products. All of these names are fictitious and any similarity to the names and addresses used by an actual business enterprise is entirely coincidental.

This publication contains small programs that are furnished by IBM as simple examples to serve as exercises. These examples have not been thoroughly tested under all conditions. IBM, therefore, cannot guarantee or imply reliability, serviceability, or function of these programs. All programs contained herein are provided to you "AS IS." THE IMPLIED WARRANTIES OF MERCHANTABILITY AND FITNESS FOR A PARTICULAR PURPOSE ARE EXPRESSLY DISCLAIMED.

Programming Interface Information

This publication is intended to help you create programs using RPG IV source. This publication documents general-use programming interfaces and associated guidance information provided by the ILE RPG for AS/400 compiler. General-use programming interfaces allow you to write programs that request or receive services of the ILE RPG for AS/400 compiler.

Trademarks and Service Marks

The following terms are trademarks of the International Business Machines Corporation in the United States, other countries, or both:

400	Operating System/400
AS/400	OS/400
C/400	RPG/400
IBM	System/38
Integrated Language Environment	VisualAge

Microsoft and Windows are registered trademarks of Microsoft Corporation.

UNIX is a registered trademark in the United States and other countries licensed exclusively through X/Open Company Limited.

Netscape and Netscape Navigator are registered trademarks of Netscape Communications Corporation.

Other company, product, and service names may be trademarks or service marks of others.

About Experience RPG IV

Welcome to Experience RPG IV, your self-study guide to programming in RPG IV. This educational package can help you move forward to the latest version of the RPG IV language and will walk you through the changes and additions from RPG III to RPG IV. Learning about these changes can help RPG III programmers prepare for the future AS/400 market and new RPG IV programmers understand and maintain existing code. This tutorial will enable you to explore all the new functions in RPG IV, write your own functions using subprocedures, create modular programs within the Integrated Language Environment (ILE), and much more.

The package includes an easy to use HTML tutorial and an accompanying workbook. The tutorial has fourteen stages of key RPG IV and ILE topics. After completing each stage of the tutorial, you will have a chance to answer multiple-choice questions in the checkpoint sections, then you can go to the workbook and work through exercises related to the stage you just completed. The workbook gives you additional computer exercises in which you can code and compile programs.

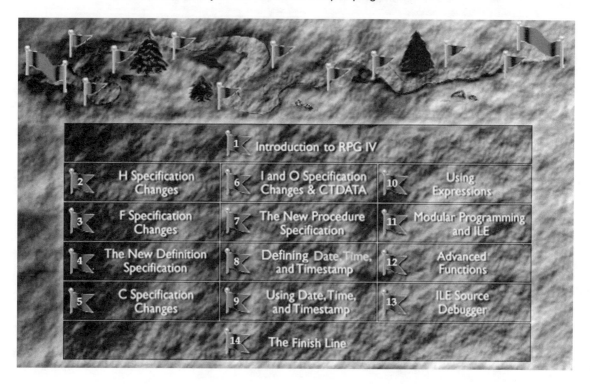

The Experience RPG IV package includes this workbook and a CD-ROM with two sets of files: one set with everything you will need to run the tutorial and the RPG IV sample programs, and another complementary set of files for you to explore the latest version of ADTS CS (see "About the Application Development ToolSet Client Server for AS/400

Evaluation CD-ROM" on page xvii). Each component of the Experience RPG IV package is described in more detail in the following sections.

Who Should Use Experience RPG IV

If you have experience working with RPG III, and want to move into programming with RPG IV, this tutorial is for you. It focuses on the differences between RPG III and the new features and functions of RPG IV. It is also a great way for new RPG programmers to learn RPG IV.

Before using this product, you should know how to:

- Use basic Programming Development Manager (PDM) and Source Entry Utility (SEU) functions to edit, compile and debug programs

  or

- Use basic CODE/400 features to edit, compile, and debug programs (see "About the Application Development ToolSet Client Server for AS/400 Evaluation CD-ROM" on page xvii).

Experience RPG IV Requirements

The minimum hardware requirements to run the Experience RPG IV Tutorial are:

- 80486 or greater processor
- IBM-compatible PC with VGA display
- 8 MB memory
- 4MB free disk space
- CD-ROM drive

The minimum software requirements to run the Experience RPG IV Tutorial are:

- Netscape Navigator 3.0 or higher (Netscape 4.0 is highly recommended and is provided with this tutorial for your convenience)

About the Experience RPG IV Tutorial

Through text, graphics, and animation, you will be led through a roadmap of topics, including:

- How to create modules using ILE
- The differences between static and dynamic binding (also called linking)
- The changes in H, F, I, O, and C specifications
- How to use the new D specification
- How to use the new P specification and write your own functions using subprocedures
- How to use Free-Format Expressions in RPG IV
- How to use the ILE source debugger

- How to use the new functions of RPG IV

    - Specification input by keywords
    - New Source type
    - DBCS data type
    - Date, time, and timestamp data types
    - New integer and float data types
    - New variable-length character and graphic fields
    - RPG IV built-in functions including %ERROR, %STATUS, %EQUAL, and more
    - Compile options in your source
    - Pointer data types and APIs

Start-up Instructions for Experience RPG IV Tutorial

The following instructions tell you how to run the *Experience RPG IV Tutorial* using the CD provided with the tutorial package.

Note: JavaScript must be enabled in your Netscape browser for the tutorial navigation to work correctly. To ensure that JavaScript is enabled, do the following:

- For Netscape 3.x, select Options → Network Preferences and select the Languages tab. If the Enable JavaScript box is not already checked, click in the box to check it. Click OK.

- For Netscape 4.x, select Edit → Preferences, then single-click on Advanced in the navigation tree on the left side of the window. If the Enable JavaScript box is not already checked, click in the box to check it. Click OK.

1. Insert the Experience RPG IV CD in your CD-ROM drive.

2. If you are running Windows 95 or Windows NT and Netscape is your primary browser you can start Experience RPG IV from Windows Explorer. Double-click on the Startup.htm file in the root directory of the CD.

   Or

3. If you are not running Windows 95 or Windows NT, start your Netscape browser and select File → Open Page (Netscape 4) or File → Open File (in Netscape 3) and enter the following:

   `x:\rpgweb\intro\index.htm` (where x is the drive letter of your CD-ROM drive)

   Use the arrow buttons on the Dashboard to navigate through the tutorial.

Note: You may use the score sheet in the back of this workbook to tally your rally points as you work through the tutorial.

Here's a tip to get you off on the right track:

This tutorial is optimized for Netscape 4.0, so we highly recommend that you use Netscape 4.0 to view it. We also recommend that you check your browser font settings before viewing the tutorial, so that you can get the most out of the code samples that you will find throughout Experience RPG IV.

To check your font settings in Netscape 3, do the following:

1. Select Options → General Preferences and select the Font tab.

2. In the Use the Fixed Font field, select the Choose Font button.

3. Ensure that Courier New is selected, and that 12 is selected for the size.

4. Click OK to close the Choose Base Font window, and then OK again to close the Preferences Notebook.

To check your font settings in Netscape 4, do the following:

1. Select Edit → Preferences and select the Fonts item under the Appearance heading in the tree view.

2. Ensure that Courier New is selected for the Fixed Width Font, and that 12 is selected for the size.

3. Click OK to close the Preferences Notebook.

About this Workbook

This workbook is a component of the Experience RPG IV package. The workbook complements and supplements the lessons in the *Experience RPG IV Tutorial*. After you have completed one of the fourteen stages of the tutorial, you can turn to the workbook to complete the exercise pertaining to that stage.

details to purge

Sales Orders

...d summarizes key points of the rele-
...luded in this workbook. The first type,

...ires a userid to an AS/400 system,
...ercises generally involve coding a
... program. The coding part of the
...xercise if you are unable to access a

... for many of the new features of ILE
...mation on:

...PG IV
...RPG IV

...phy" on page 297.

About the Sample Code

Included on the Experience RPG IV CD-ROM is sample code containing:

- A save file, WKBKLIB, which contains source files needed for the exercises as well as source for the solutions in this workbook.

- A save file, TUTORIAL, which contains source files for the sample code from the *Experience RPG IV Tutorial*.

  The source from the tutorial represents the source used to test the online samples. You may find the samples useful when writing RPG IV programs later.

- A text file, README, which contains some suggested procedures on how to upload the above save files from your PC onto your AS/400 system.

Note: You will need a communications link between your PC and your AS/400 system to upload these files.

About the Application Development ToolSet Client Server for AS/400 Evaluation CD-ROM

The Experience RPG IV CD includes the latest Application Development ToolSet Client Server for AS/400 (ADTS CS) product.

ADTS CS (for Windows) is a workstation product that includes two server access programs:

- CoOperative Development Environment/400 (CODE/400)

- VisualAge for RPG

CODE/400 contains features to help edit, compile, and debug: RPG, ILE RPG, COBOL, ILE COBOL, Control Language (CL), ILE C, and ILE CL host source programs; design display, printer, and database host files; and manage the components that make up your application. This enhances program development and moves the program development workload off the host. The application, when built, runs on an AS/400. For RPG and ILE RPG application development and maintenance, CODE/400 provides:

- Language sensitive editing — includes token highlighting, format lines, a full suite of prompts, and online help.
- Incremental syntax checking — provides immediate error feedback as each line of source is entered
- Program verification — performs, at the workstation, the full range of syntax and semantic checking that the compiler does, without generating object code
- Program conversion — performs, at the workstation, an OPM to ILE RPG conversion
- A windowed environment for submitting host compiles and binds
- Source-level debugging
- A DDS design utility — allows you to easily change screens, reports, and database files
- Access to Application Dictionary Services.

VisualAge for RPG offers a visual development environment on the workstation platform for RPG application developers to develop, maintain, and document client/server applications. Applications can be edited, compiled, and debugged on your workstation. The applications, when built, are started on a workstation and can access AS/400 host data and other AS/400 objects. Its integrated components allow application developers to preserve their current skills and easily develop AS/400 RPG applications with graphical user interfaces.

If you want to learn more about CODE/400 and VisualAge for RPG, see the most current information available on the World Wide Web at:

`http://www.software.ibm.com/ad/varpg/`

Start-up Instructions for ADTS CS Evaluation CD-ROM

The following instructions tell you how to run the ADTS CS Evaluation front end using the CD provided with the tutorial package.

1. Insert the Experience RPG IV CD in your CD-ROM drive.

2. If you are running Windows 95 or Windows NT you can start the ADTS CS Evaluation front end from Windows Explorer. Double-click on the adtscs.exe file in the **adtscs** directory of the CD.

   Or

3. From a DOS session enter the following:

   `x:\adtscs\adtscs` (where x is the drive letter of your CD-ROM drive)

Exercises

This part contains the exercises that accompany Stages 1-14 of the Experience RPG IV kit. There are 25 exercises in total.

You will find for each stage:

- A summary of the stage
- One or more exercises to reinforce the key points of the stage

Appendix A contains solutions to the exercises. For the most part, the solutions represent just one of many possible approaches, because coding exercises often have more than one solution.

Before you begin

You will need to make a library available to use with the computer exercises. You may use an existing library or create a new one for purposes of the tutorial. You will also need to create a source file into which you can copy the RPG IV source code provided on the sample-code diskette. You should copy the code *before* you begin to make your changes.

To create the source file, issue the following command, where *YourFile* is the name of your source file and *YourLib* is the name of your library. Please note the record length (112) of the source file is NOT the default.

```
CRTSRCPF FILE(YourLib/YourFile) RECLEN(112) TEXT(RPG IV Source File)
```

After you have created the library and source file, you can copy the contents of the computer exercise library, WKBKLIB, onto your system. It has been stored on the diskette as a save file. The contents of WKBKLIB are listed in an appendix.

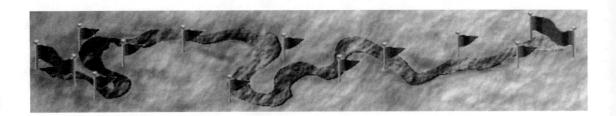

Stage 1. Exercises — Introduction to RPG IV

Now that you have finished Stage 1 of the Tutorial, you should be ready for the Stage 1 exercises in this workbook.

Stage 1 focuses on the overall changes in RPG from the RPG III language definition to the RPG IV definition. The most visible changes to RPG IV include:

- New Definition specification
- New Procedure specification
- Keyword-oriented specifications
- Free-format expressions
- Expanded fields and other limit changes (see below)
- Mixed-case entry

Summary of How Limits Have Changed from RPG III

The following table lists changes in limits from RPG III to RPG IV. In some cases, the limits have expanded; in others, no practical limit exists. In revising these limits, many changes have been made to the RPG specifications. For example, field names can now be defined with names that are up to 4096 character long. However, the practical limit is determined by the size of the entry in which the field is used and by the readability of your program.

Fixed-format entries, where a field name is allowed, are now all at least 14 positions long to accommodate longer field names or to allow for an array name and an index. Free-format fields allow even longer field names, because the fields can be continued on multiple lines.

Table 1. Changed Limits

Function	RPG III Limit	RPG IV Limit
Length of field name	6 characters	4096 characters
Length of named constant	256 bytes	1024 bytes
Length of character variable	256	32767
Number of elements in an array or table	9999	32767
Length of a single-occurrence data structure	9999	32767
Number of occurrences of a multiple-occurrence data structure	9999	32767
Input record length for compile-time arrays or tables	80	100
Number of decimal positions	9	30
Number of files per program	50	No limit
Number of subroutines	254	No limit
Record length for SPECIAL file	32767	99999

Exercise 1 — RPG Enhancements

This exercise focuses on the main enhancements of RPG IV. It is a desk exercise; you will not be compiling any source.

Objectives

At the end of this exercise, you should be familiar with the general enhancements of RPG IV.

Instructions

Circle at least *five* enhancements of RPG IV that are reflected in the following RPG IV source member.

```
*-----------------------------------------------------------------------*
* DESCRIPTION:  This program creates a printed output of employee's pay  *
*               for the week.                                            *
*-----------------------------------------------------------------------*
H DATEDIT(*DMY/) DFTACTGRP(*NO) ACTGRP('MyActGrp')
*-----------------------------------------------------------------------*
* File Definitions                                                      *
*-----------------------------------------------------------------------*
FTRANSACT  IP  E          K DISK
FEMPMST    IF  E          K DISK
FQSYSPRT   O   F   80       PRINTER
*-----------------------------------------------------------------------*
* Variable Declarations                                                 *
*-----------------------------------------------------------------------*
D Pay           S            8P 2


*-----------------------------------------------------------------------*
* Prototype Definition for subprocedure CalcPay                        *
*-----------------------------------------------------------------------*
D CalcPay       PR           8P 2
D   Rate                     5P 2 VALUE
D   Hours                   10U 0 VALUE
D   Bonus                    5P 2 VALUE
*-----------------------------------------------------------------------*
* For each record in the transaction file (TRANSACT), if the employee  *
* is found, compute the employee's pay and print the details.          *
*-----------------------------------------------------------------------*
C     TRN_NUMBER   CHAIN(E)  EMP_REC                           99
C                  IF        %FOUND AND NOT %ERROR
C                  EVAL      PAY = CalcPay(EMP_RATE : TRN_HOURS :
C                                      TRN_BONUS)
C                  ENDIF
```

Figure 1 (Part 1 of 3). Sample RPG IV Source

```
     *-------------------------------------------------------------------*
     * Report Layout                                                     *
     *  -- print the heading lines if 1P is on                           *
     *  -- if the record is found (indicator 99 is off) print the payroll *
     *     details otherwise print an exception record                   *
     *  -- print 'END OF LISTING' when LR is on                          *
     *-------------------------------------------------------------------*
OQSYSPRT   H    1P                      2  3
O                                           35 'PAYROLL REGISTER'
O                        *DATE          Y    60
O          H    1P                      2
O                                           60 'NUMBER  NAME            -
O                                              RATE    HOURS   -
O                                              BONUS   PAY          '
O          H    1P                      2
O                                           60 '_____  _____ -
O                                                 _____ ____    -
O                                                 _____ _____ '
O          D    N1PN99                  2
O                       TRN_NUMBER           5
O                       EMP_NAME            24
O                       EMP_RATE        L   33
O                       TRN_HOURS       L   40
O                       TRN_BONUS       L   49
O                       Pay                 60 '$     0. '
O          D    N1P 99                  2
O                       TRN_NUMBER           5
O                                           35 '** NOT ON EMPLOYEE FILE **'
O          T    LR
O                                           33 'END OF LISTING'
```

Figure 1 (Part 2 of 3). Sample RPG IV Source

```
         *-------------------------------------------------------------------*
         * Subprocedure  -- calculates overtime pay.                         *
         *-------------------------------------------------------------------*
P CalcPay        B
D CalcPay        PI            8P 2
D   Rate                       5P 2 VALUE
D   Hours                     10U 0 VALUE
D   Bonus                      5P 2 VALUE

D Overtime       S             5P 2 INZ(0)
 * Determine any overtime hours to be paid.
C                IF        Hours > 40
C                EVAL      Overtime = (Hours - 40) * Rate * 1.5
C                EVAL      Hours = 40
C                ENDIF
 * Calculate the total pay and return it to the caller
C                RETURN    Rate * Hours + Bonus + Overtime

P CalcPay        E
```

Figure 1 (Part 3 of 3). Sample RPG IV Source

Stage 2. Exercises — H Specification

Now that you have finished Stage 2 of the Tutorial, you should be ready for the Stage 2 exercises in this workbook.

Stage 2 focuses on the changes to the H specification. The most notable change is in the use of keywords. In particular, the H spec now consists entirely of keywords. It is not position dependent.

In addition, compile options, specified throught the CRTBNDRPG and CRTPGMOD commands, can now be specified using control specification keywords. This identifies the compile options to be used on every compile of the program.

Refer to the following tables for more information on the H spec:

Table No.	Description
2	RPG III H spec
3	RPG IV H spec

Each of these tables provides a comparison of the RPG III and RPG IV specs.

Table 2 (Page 1 of 2). RPG III Control Specification Summary Chart (H)			
Positions	**Name**	**Entry**	**RPG IV**
6	Form type	H	6
7-14		Blank	n/a
15	Debug	Blank 1	DEBUG
16-17		Blank	n/a
18	Currency symbol	Blank Currency symbol	CURSYM
19	Date format	Blank M D Y	DATEDIT
20	Date edit (Y edit code)	Blank any character	DATEDIT

Table 2 (Page 2 of 2). RPG III Control Specification Summary Chart (H)

Positions	Name	Entry	RPG IV
21	Decimal Notation	Blank I J D	DECEDIT DATEDIT
22-25		Blank	n/a
26	Alternate collating sequence	Blank S	ALTSEQ
27-40		Blank	n/a
41	Forms alignment	Blank 1	FORMSALIGN
42		Blank	n/a
43	File translation	Blank F	FTRANS
44-56		Blank	n/a
57	Transparency check	Blank 1	n/a
58-74		Blank	n/a
75-80	Program identification		DFTNAME

Positions or Keyword	Name	Entry	RPG III
		Table 3 (Page 1 of 2). RPG IV Control Specification Summary Chart (H)	
6	Form type	H	6
7-80	Keywords		n/a
ACTGRP	Activation group	*NEW I *CALLER I 'activation-group-name'	n/a
ALTSEQ	Alternate collating sequence	{*NONE I *SRC I *EXT}	26
ALWNULL	Allow null-capable fields	*NO I *INPUTONLY I *USRCTL	n/a
AUT	Authority	*LIBRCRTAUT I *ALL I *CHANGE I *USE I *EXCLUDE I 'authorization-list-name'	n/a
BNDDIR	Binding directories	'binding-directory-name' {:'binding-directory-name'...}	n/a
COPYNEST	Maximum nesting level	1-2048	n/a
COPYRIGHT	Copyright string	'string'	n/a
CURSYM	Currency symbol	'symbol'	18
CVTOPT	Convert options	*{NO}DATETIME *{NO}GRAPHIC *{NO}VARCHAR *{NO}VARGRAPHIC	n/a
DATEDIT	Date edit (Y edit code)	fmt{separator}	19,20,21
DATFMT	Date format	fmt{separator}	n/a
DEBUG	Debug	{*NO I *YES}	15
DECEDIT	Decimal notation	*JOBRUN I 'value'	21
DFTACTGRP	Default activation group	*YES I *NO	n/a
DFTNAME	Default name	rpg_name	75-80
ENBPFRCOL	Enable performance collection	*PEP I *ENTRYEXIT I *FULL	n/a
EXPROPTS	Expression options	*MAXDIGITS I *RESDECPOS	n/a
EXTBININT	Integer format for externally-described binary fields	{*NO I *YES}	n/a
FIXNBR	Fix decimal data	*{NO}ZONED *{NO}INPUTPACKED	n/a
FLTDIV	Floating point division	{*NO I *YES}	n/a
FORMSALIGN	Forms alignment	{*NO I *YES}	41
FTRANS	File Translation	{*NONE I *SRC}	43
GENLVL	Generation level	0-20	n/a

Table 3 (Page 2 of 2). RPG IV Control Specification Summary Chart (H)

Positions or Keyword	Name	Entry	RPG III
INDENT	Indent in source listing	*NONE I 'character-value'	n/a
LANGID	Language identifier	*JOBRUN I *JOB I 'language-identifier'	n/a
NOMAIN	Module without main procedure		n/a
OPTIMIZE	Optimization level	*NONE I *BASIC I *FULL	n/a
OPTION	Options	*{NO}XREF *{NO}GEN *{NO}SECLVL *{NO}SHOWCOPY *{NO}EXPDDS *{NO}EXT *{NO}SHOWSKP	n/a
PRFDTA	Profiling data	*NOCOL I *COL	n/a
SRTSEQ	Sort sequence table	*HEX I *JOB I *JOBRUN I *LANGIDUNQ I *LANGIDSHR I 'sort-table-name'	n/a
TEXT	Program information text	*SRCMBRTXT I *BLANK I 'description'	n/a
TIMFMT	Time format	fmt{separator}	n/a
TRUNCNBR	Move truncated value	*YES I *NO	n/a
USRPRF	User profile	*USER I *OWNER	n/a

Exercise 2 — H Spec

In this exercise, you focus on the new layout of the RPG IV H spec and the use of keywords to code it. This exercise is a desk exercise; you will not be compiling any source.

Objectives

At the end of this exercise, you should be able to describe the new H spec layout and list its keywords.

Instructions

With the help of the tables in the the previous section, write an RPG IV H spec that can do the following:

- Specify a comma as a decimal separator for edited decimal numbers
- Allow for forms alignment
- Specify a default program name of TEST
- Specify the named activation group TESTAG and the DFTACTGRP parameter for use with the CRTBNDRPG command.

```
*.. 1 ...+... 2 ...+... 3 ...+... 4 ...+... 5 ...+... 6 ...+... 7 ...+... 8 ...+... 9 ...+... 10
HKeywords+++++++++++++++++++++++++++++++++++++++++++++++++++++++++++++++++++++Comments++++++++++++
```

Figure 2. RPG IV H Spec

Stage 3. Exercises — F Specification

Now that you have finished Stage 3 of the Tutorial, you should be ready for the Stage 3 exercises in this workbook.

Stage 3 focuses on the changes to the F specification. The most notable change is in the use of keywords. The F spec still has positions, and many of these keywords have changed. However, a coded F spec is now easier to read because of the use of keywords.

The F spec also has a new function. It handles all of the RPG III L spec function as well as the record-address file (RAF) function of the RPG III E spec.

Refer to the following tables for more information on the F specs:

Table No.	Description
4	RPG III Main F spec
5	RPG IV F spec fixed form
6	RPG III F spec continuation line
7	RPG III F spec continuation line options
8	RPG IV F spec keywords
9	Correspondence of RPG III L spec to RPG IV F spec

Each of these tables provides a comparison of the RPG III and RPG IV specs.

Main File Description Line Summary Chart

Positions	Name	Entry	RPG IV
Table 4 (Page 1 of 2). RPG III Main File Description Line Summary Chart (F, FK)			
6	Form type	F	6
7-14	File name	Valid file name	7-16
15	File type	I O U C	17
16	File designation	Blank P S R T F	18
17	End of file	E Blank	19
18	Sequence	A or Blank D	21
19	File format	F E	22
20-23		Blank	n/a
24-27	Record length	1-9999	23-27
28	Limits processing	L Blank	28
29-30	Length of key field or record address field	1-99 Blank	29-33
31	Record address type	Blank A P K	34
32	Type of file organization	Blank I T	35
33-34	Overflow indicators	Blank OA-OG, OV 01-99	OFLIND
35-38	Key field starting location	Blank 1-9999	KEYLOC
39	Extension code	Blank E L	n/a

Table 4 (Page 2 of 2). RPG III Main File Description Line Summary Chart (F, FK)

Positions	Name	Entry	RPG IV
40-46	Device	PRINTER DISK WORKSTN SPECIAL SEQ	36-42
47-52		Blank	n/a
53	Continuation lines	Blank K	n/a
54-59	Name of routine	Name of user-supplied routine	SPECIAL
60-65		Blank	n/a
66	File addition/unordered	Blank A	20
67-70		Blank	
71-72	File condition	Blank U1-U8 UC	EXTIND USROPN
73-74		Blank	n/a
75-80	Comments	Optional	81-100

Table 5 (Page 1 of 2). RPG IV File Description Fixed Form Summary Chart (F)

Positions or Keyword	Name	Entry	RPG III
6	Form type	F	6
7-16	File name	Valid file name	7-14
17	File type	I O U C	15
18	File designation	Blank P S R T F	16
19	End of file	E Blank	17
20	File addition/unordered	Blank A	66
21	Sequence	A or Blank D	18

Positions or Keyword	Name	Entry	RPG III
22	File format	F E	19
23-27	Record length	1-32766	24-27
28	Limits processing	L Blank	28
29-33	Length of key field or record address field	1-2000 Blank	29-30
34	Record address type	Blank A P K G D T Z F	31
35	Type of file organization	Blank I T	32
36-42	Device	PRINTER DISK WORKSTN SPECIAL SEQ	40-46
43	Reserved	Blank	n/a
44-80	Keywords		n/a
81-100	Comments	Optional	75-80

Table 5 (Page 2 of 2). RPG IV File Description Fixed Form Summary Chart (F)

Continuation Line Summary Chart

Table 6. RPG III Continuation Line Summary Chart (FC)			
Positions	**Name**	**Entry**	**RPG IV**
6	Form type	F	6
7-18		Blank	n/a
19-28		External name of record format	RENAME IGNORE
29-46		Blank	n/a
47-52	Record number field for SFILE	Numeric field name	SFILE
53	Continuation line	K	n/a
54-59, 60-67[1]			n/a
68-74		Blank	n/a
75-80	Comments	Optional	81-100

Notes:

1. These positions are used together. Positions 54 through 59 specify the option, while positions 60 through 67 provide further explanation of the option.

Continuation Line Options Summary Chart

The valid entries for positions 54 through 67 are:

Table 7 (Page 1 of 2). RPG III Continuation Line Options

Option (54-59)	Entry (60-67)	Explanation	RPG IV
COMIT	Blank	This file is specified for commitment control.	COMMIT
ID	Field name	Positions 60-65 contain the left-justified name of a 10-character alphanumeric field, which does not need to be further defined. This field contains the name of the program device that supplied the record being processed in the file.	DEVID
IGNORE	Blank	This option lets you ignore a record format from an externally-described file.	IGNORE
IND	Indicator number	Indicators from 01 to the number specified are saved and restored for each device attached to a mixed or multiple device file.	SAVEIND
INFDS	Data structure name	This entry lets you define and name a data structure to contain the exception/error information. The data structure name is entered in positions 60 through 65 and left justified. If INFDS is specified for more than one file, each associated data structure must have a unique name.	INFDS
INFSR	Subroutine name	The file exception/error subroutine named (left justified) in positions 60 through 65 may receive control following file exceptions/errors. The subroutine name may be *PSSR, which indicates the user-defined program exception/error subroutine is to be given control for errors on this file.	INFSR
NUM	Maximum number of devices	The number specified must be greater than zero and right justified in positions 60 through 65.	MAXDEV
PASS	*NOIND	Specify PASS *NOIND on the file-description specification continuation line for a program described WORKSTN file if you are taking responsibility for passing indicators on input and output.	PASS
PLIST	Parameter list name	This entry is valid only when the device specified in positions 40 through 46 of the main file description line is SPECIAL. Positions 60 through 65 give the left-justified name of the parameter list that is to be passed to the special routine.	PLIST
PRTCTL	Data structure name	The dynamic printer control option is being used. The data structure specified left justified in positions 60 through 65 refers to the forms control information and line count value.	PRTCTL

Table 7 (Page 2 of 2). RPG III Continuation Line Options			
Option (54-59)	Entry (60-67)	Explanation	RPG IV
RECNO	Field name	This entry is optional for disk files to be processed by relative record number. A RECNO field must be specified for output files processed by relative record number, output files that are referenced by a random WRITE calculation operation, or output files that are used with ADD on the output specifications.	RECNO
RENAME	Record format name	This entry, which is optional, allows you to rename record formats in an externally described file. Positions 19 through 28 of the continuation line specify the external name of the record format that is to be renamed. Positions 60 through 67 specify the left-justified name of the record as it is used in the program.	RENAME
SAVDS	Data structure name	Positions 60-65 contain the left-justified name of the data structure that is saved and restored for each device.	SAVEDS
SFILE	Record format name	Positions 60 through 67 must specify, left-justified, the RPG name of the record format to be processed as a subfile. Positions 47 through 52 must specify the name of the relative record number field for this subfile.	SFILE
SLN	Field name	Positions 60-65 contain the left-justified name of a start line number (SLN) field. The SLN field determines where a record format will be written to a display file.	SLN

Table 8 (Page 1 of 2). RPG IV File Description Specification Keywords (F)			
RPG IV Keyword	Name	Entry	RPG III
BLOCK	Record blocking	*YES | *NO	n/a
COMMIT	Commitment control	{rpg_name}	COMIT
DATFMT	Date format	fmt{separator}	n/a
DEVID	Program device	fieldname	ID
EXTIND	External indicator	*INU1-*INU8	71-72
FORMLEN	Form length of printer file	number	(L) 15-17, 18-19
FORMOFL	Overflow line number	number	(L) 20-22, 23-24
IGNORE	Ignore record format	recformat	IGNORE
INCLUDE	Include record format	recformat	n/a
INDDS	Name an indicator data structure	data structure name	n/a
INFDS	Name a feedback data structure	data structure name	INFDS
INFSR	File exception/error subroutine	subroutine name	INFSR
KEYLOC	Key field location	number	35-38

RPG IV Keyword	Name	Entry	RPG III
MAXDEV	Maximum number of devices for WORKSTN file	*ONLY | *FILE	NUM
OFLIND	Overflow indicator	*INOA-*INOG, *INOV, *IN01-*IN99	33-34
PASS	Do not pass indicators	*NOIND	PASS
PGMNAME	SPECIAL device	program name	54-59
PLIST	Name of parameter list to be passed to program for SPECIAL file	plist name	PLIST
PREFIX	Prefix, partial rename	prefix string{:number}	n/a
PRTCTL	Dynamic printer control	PRTCTL	
RAFDATA	Name of raf data file	filename	(E) 11-18
RECNO	Processed by relative record number	fieldname	RECNO
RENAME	Rename record format from externally described file	external_format_name : internal_format_name	RENAME
SAVEDS	Save data structure	data structure name	SAVDS
SAVEIND	Save indicators	number	IND
SFILE	Subfiles	recformat : rrnfield	SFILE
SLN	Start line number	number	SLN
TIMFMT	Time format	fmt{separator}	n/a
USROPN	User-controlled open		71-72

Line Counter Specifications

Positions	Name	Entry	RPG IV
Table 9. RPG III Line Counter Specification Summary Chart (L)			
Positions	**Name**	**Entry**	**RPG IV**
6	Form type	L	n/a
7-14	File name	Valid file name	(F) 7-16
15-17	Number of lines per page	2-112	(F) FORMLEN
18-19	Form length	FL	(F) FORMLEN
20-22	Overflow line number	2-112	(F) FORMOFL
23-24	Overflow line	OL	(F) FORMOFL
25-74		Blank	n/a
75-80	Comments	Optional	(F) 81-100

Exercise 3 — Specifying a Record-Address File

In this exercise, you focus on the new layout of the RPG IV F spec and some of its new function. This exercise is a desk exercise; you will not be compiling any source.

Objectives

At the end of this exercise, you should be able to:

- Describe the new F spec layout
- List some of its keywords
- Code an F spec
- Specify a Record-Address File

Instructions

Rewrite the following RPG III specs as their RPG IV equivalent.

```
     FRAF      IR  F              T      EDISK
     FCTLD     IP  F        30           DISK
     E     RAF      CTLD
```

Figure 3. RPG III Specs to Be Rewritten

```
*.. 1 ...+... 2 ...+... 3 ...+... 4 ...+... 5 ...+... 6 ...+... 7 ...+... 8 ...+... 9 ...+... 10
FFilename++IPEASFRlen+LKlen+AIDevice+.Keywords++++++++++++++++++++++++++++++Comments++++++++++++
F...................................Keywords++++++++++++++++++++++++++++++Comments++++++++++++
```

Figure 4. RPG IV Equivalent

Exercise 4 — Print Overflow

In this exercise, you focus on the RPG IV F spec keywords pertaining to print overflow. This exercise is a desk exercise; you will not be compiling any source.

Objectives

At the end of this exercise, you should be able to code an RPG IV F spec that specifies print overflow function.

Instructions

Rewrite the following RPG III specs as their RPG IV equivalent.

```
FQSYSPRT O   F    132     OF   LPRINTER
LQSYSPRT  60FL 560L
```

Figure 5. RPG III Specs to Be Rewritten

```
*.. 1 ...+... 2 ...+... 3 ...+... 4 ...+... 5 ...+... 6 ...+... 7 ...+... 8 ...+... 9 ...+... 10
FFilename++IPEASFRlen+LKlen+AIDevice+.Keywords+++++++++++++++++++++++++++++++++Comments+++++++++++
F................................Keywords+++++++++++++++++++++++++++++++++Comments+++++++++++
```

Figure 6. RPG IV Equivalent

Stage 4. Exercises — New Definition Specification

Now that you have finished Stage 4 of the Tutorial, you should be ready for the Stage 4 exercises in this workbook.

Stage 4 focuses on the new Definition specification type. The new D spec allows you to define all types of program data in a simpler and easier manner than you could in RPG III. The key features of the D spec are:

- Field name definitions can be continued to define long names
- Name-entry field is 15 characters wide and a continued-name line is 80 characters wide, so you can float, indent, or continue names for enhanced readability
- Field length can be defined using absolute or length notation
- New definition types have been added for user-defined functions
- Several new internal data types have been added.

The following table provides a breakdown by position of the RPG IV D spec in comparison to the corresponding positions in RPG III.

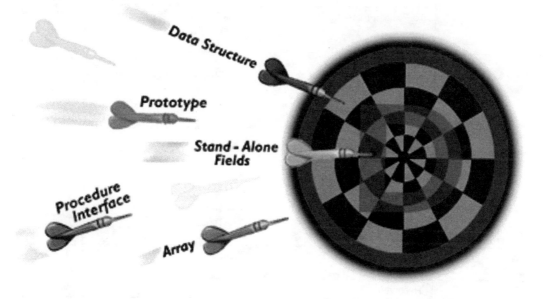

Positions or Keyword	Name	Entry	RPG III
Table 10 (Page 1 of 3). RPG IV Definition Specification (D)			
6	Form type	D	n/a
7-21	Name	Symbolic name	(I) 7-12, 53-58 (E) 27-32, 46-51
22	External Description	Blank E	(I) 17
23	Type of Data Structure	Blank S U	(I) 18
24-25	Type of Definition	Blank C DS PI PR S	(I) 19-20, 43
26-32	From Position	Blank nnnnn	(I) 44-47
33-39	To Position / Length	Blank nnnnn +l-nnnnn	(I) 48-51 (E) 40-42, 52-54
40	Internal Data Type	Blank A — Character B — Binary D — Date F — Float G — Graphic I — Integer N — Indicator P — Packed decimal S — Zoned T — Time U — Unsigned Z — Timestamp * — Pointer	(I) 43
41-42	Decimal Positions	Blank 0-30	(I) 52 (E) 44, 56
43	Reserved		n/a
44-80	Keywords		n/a
ALIGN	Align integer, unsigned, and float subfields		n/a
ALT	Alternating array	main array_name	(E) 27-32
ALTSEQ	Alternate sequence options for field	*NONE	n/a

Table 10 (Page 2 of 3). RPG IV Definition Specification (D)

Positions or Keyword	Name	Entry	RPG III
ASCEND	Sort sequence		(E) 45, 57
BASED	Basing pointer	basing_pointer_name	n/a
CONST	Constant name	constant value	(I) 21-42, 43
CONST	Read-only parameter		n/a
CTDATA	Compile time data		n/a
DATFMT	Date format	format{separator}	n/a
DESCEND	Sort sequence		(E) 45, 57
DIM	Number of elements in array	numeric constant	(E) 36-39
DTAARA	Data area name	{data area name}	n/a
EXPORT	Field can be exported	{external name}	n/a
EXTFLD	Rename an externally described subfield	field name	(I) 21-30
EXTFMT	External data type	B F I L P R S U	(E) 43, 55
EXTNAME	External file with field descriptions	file_name {:format_name}	(I) 21-30
EXTPGM	External prototyped program name	program name	n/a
EXTPROC	External prototyped procedure name	procedure name	n/a
FROMFILE	File pre-run time array is loaded from	file_name	(E) 11-18
IMPORT	Field can be imported	{external name}	n/a
INZ	Initialize data	{constant}	(I) 21-42
LIKE	Define a field like another	rpg_name	n/a
NOOPT	No optimization		n/a
OCCURS	Number of occurrences in multiple occurrence data structure	numeric_constant	(I) 44-47
OPDESC	Operational descriptor		n/a
OPTIONS	Parameter passing options for prototyped parameters	*NOPASS *OMIT *VARSIZE *STRING	n/a
OVERLAY	Overlay data structure subfield	name{:pos}	n/a

Table 10 (Page 3 of 3). RPG IV Definition Specification (D)

Positions or Keyword	Name	Entry	RPG III
PACKEVEN	Packed field has an even number of digits		n/a
PERRCD	Number of elements per record	numeric constant	(E) 33-35
PREFIX	Add, replace a prefix to externally described fields	prefix string{:number}	n/a
PROCPTR	Field is a procedure pointer		n/a
STATIC	Data item uses static storage		n/a
TIMFMT	Time format	format{separator}	n/a
TOFILE	File to which to write array or table data	file_name	(E) 19-26
VALUE	Pass prototyped parameter by value		n/a
VARYING	Varying length character or graphic field		n/a

The next table shows how the RPG III E spec maps to the D spec.

Table 11 (Page 1 of 2). RPG III Extension Specification Summary Chart (E)

Positions	Name	Entry	RPG IV
6	Form type	E	n/a
7-10		Blank	n/a
11-18	From file name	Blank Record-address file name Array or table file name	(F) RAFDATA (D) FROMFILE
19-26	To file name	Blank Name of an input or update file containing data records Name of an output or combined file	(D) TOFILE
27-32	Table or array name	Table or array name	(D) 7-21
33-35	Number of entries per record	Blank 1-999	(D) PERRCD
36-39	Number of entries per array or table	1-9999	(D) DIM

Table 11 (Page 2 of 2). RPG III Extension Specification Summary Chart (E)			
Positions	**Name**	**Entry**	**RPG IV**
40-42	Length of entry	1-256	(D) 33-39
43	Data format	Blank P B I R	(D) EXTFMT
44	Decimal positions	Blank 0-9	(D) 41-42
45	Sequence	Blank A D	(D) ASCEND DESCEND
46-51	Table or array name (alternating format)	Table or array name (alternating format)	(D) ALT (D) 7-21
52-54	Length of entry	1-256	(D) 33-39
55	Data format	Blank P B L R	(D) EXTFMT
56	Decimal positions	Blank 0-9	(D) 41-42
57	Sequence	Blank A D	(D) ASCEND DESCEND
58-80	Comments	Optional	(D) 81-100

The next three tables show how the RPG III I spec maps in part to the D spec.

Table 12. RPG III Data Structure Statement Specifications (DS)

Positions	Name	Entry	RPG IV
6	Form type	I	(D) 6
7-12	Data structure name	Blank Data structure name	(D) 7-21
13-16		Blank	n/a
17	External description	Blank E	(D) 22
18	Option	Blank I S U	(D) 23
19-20	Record identifying indicators	DS	(D) 24-25
21-30	External file name	External name of data struc-ture	(D) EXTNAME
31-43		Blank	n/a
44-47	Occurrences	Blank 1-9999	(D) OCCURS
48-51	Data structure length	Blank 1-9999	(D) 33-39
52-74		Blank	n/a
75-80	Comments	Optional	81-100

Table 13 (Page 1 of 2). RPG III Data Structure Subfield Specifications (SS)

Positions	Name	Entry	RPG IV
7		Blank	n/a
8	Initialization option	Blank I	(D) INZ
9-20		Blank	n/a
21-30	External field name	External name of subfield	(D) EXTFLD
21-42	Initialization value	Initial value	(D) INZ
31-42		Blank	n/a
43	Data format	Blank P B	(D) 40
44-47	From	1-9999	(D) 26-32
48-51	To	1-9999	(D) 33-39
52	Decimal position	Blank 0-9	(D) 41-42
53-58	Subfield name	Subfield name	(D) 7-21

Table 13 (Page 2 of 2). RPG III Data Structure Subfield Specifications (SS)			
Positions	**Name**	**Entry**	**RPG IV**
59-74		Blank	n/a
75-80	Comments	Optional	81-100

Table 14. RPG III Named Constant Specifications (N)			
Positions	**Name**	**Entry**	**RPG IV**
6	Form type	I	(D) 6
7-20		Blank	n/a
21-42	Constant	Constant value	(D) CONST
43	Data type	C Blank	(D) 24
44-52		Blank	n/a
53-58	Constant name	Name	(D) 7-21
59-74		Blank	n/a

D Spec Keywords and Associated Definition Type

There are different types of D specs, depending on the kind of field you are defining. (The layout of the D spec is the same for each definition type.) The definition type is identified by the entry in positions 24-25. The types allowed are:

Pos. 24-25	Definition Type
Blank	A data structure subfield or a parameter
C	Named constant
DS	Data structure
PR	Prototype
PI	Procedure interface
S	Stand-alone field

Subfields must immediately follow the data structure definition. Subfields of a data structure are associated with the preceding data structure definition. Arrays and tables can be defined as either a data-structure subfield or a stand-alone field. Definitions of data structures, prototypes, and procedure interfaces end with the next definition that is nonblank (or when the D specs end). Parameter of a subprocedure or program are associated with the preceding prototype or procedure interface definition.

Procedure interface, prototype, and parameter definitions are discussed in more detail in Stage 7 of this workbook.

Table 15 on page 33 lists the required and allowed entries for each definition specification type.

Table 16 on page 33 and Table 17 on page 35 give a listing of the keywords allowed for each definition specification type.

Note: An **R** indicates that an entry in these positions is **required** and an **A** indicates that an entry in these positions is **allowed**.

Table 15. Required/Allowed Entries for Each D Spec Type									
Type	Pos. 7-21 Name	Pos. 22 External	Pos. 23 DS Type	Pos. 24-25 Defn. Type	Pos. 26-32 From	Pos. 33-39 To / Length	Pos. 40 Data-type	Pos. 41-42 Decimal Pos.	Pos. 44-80 Key-words
Data Structure	A	A	A	R		A			A
Data Structure Subfield	A				A	A	A	A	A
External Subfield	A	R							A
Stand-alone Field	R			R		A	A	A	A
Named Constant	R			R					R
Prototype	R			R		A	A	A	A
Prototype Parameter	A					A	A	A	A
Procedure Interface	A			R		A	A	A	A
Procedure Interface Parameter	R					A	A	A	A

Table 16 (Page 1 of 2). Data Structure, Stand-alone Fields, and Named Constants Keywords					
Keyword	Data Structure	Data Structure Subfield	External Subfield	Stand-alone Field	Named Constant
ALIGN	A				
ALT		A	A	A	
ALTSEQ	A	A	A	A	
ASCEND		A	A	A	
BASED	A			A	
CONST[1]					R
CTDATA[2]		A	A	A	
DATFMT		A		A	
DESCEND		A	A	A	
DIM		A	A	A	
DTAARA[2]	A	A		A	
EXPORT[2]	A			A	

Table 16 (Page 2 of 2). Data Structure, Stand-alone Fields, and Named Constants Keywords

Keyword	Data Structure	Data Structure Subfield	External Subfield	Stand-alone Field	Named Constant
EXTFLD			A		
EXTFMT		A	A	A	
EXTNAME[4]	A				
FROMFILE[2]		A	A	A	
IMPORT[2]	A			A	
INZ	A	A	A	A	
LIKE		A		A	
NOOPT	A			A	
OCCURS	A				
OVERLAY		A			
PACKEVEN		A			
PERRCD		A	A	A	
PREFIX[4]	A				
PROCPTR		A		A	
STATIC[3]	A			A	
TIMFMT		A		A	
TOFILE[2]		A	A	A	
VARYING		A		A	

Notes:

1. When defining a named constant, the keyword is optional, but the parameter to the keyword is required. For example, to assign a named constant the value '10', you could specify either CONST('10') or '10'.

2. This keyword applies only to global definitions.

3. This keyword applies only to local definitions.

4. This keyword applies only to externally described data structures.

Keyword	Prototype (PR)	Procedure Interface (PI)	PR or PI Parameter
Table 17. Prototype, Procedure Interface, and Parameter Keywords			
ASCEND			A
CONST			A
DATFMT	A	A	A
DESCEND			A
DIM	A	A	A
EXTPGM	A		
EXTPROC	A		
LIKE	A	A	A
NOOPT			A
OPDESC	A	A	
OPTIONS			A
PROCPTR	A	A	A
TIMFMT	A	A	A
VALUE			A
VARYING	A	A	A

Exercise 5 — D Spec

In this exercise, you focus on the new Definition specification that is part of RPG IV. This exercise is a desk exercise; you will not be compiling any source.

Objectives

At the end of this exercise, you should be able to:

- describe the D spec layout
- list some of the keywords
- code an array, data structure, and stand-alone fields.

Instructions

Write RPG IV D specs that define the same data that is defined in the following RPG III specs.

```
     E                   ARY      100  5
     IDS1        DS
     I                               1 500 ARY
     I I                             501 531 NAME
     I                               501 515 FIRST
     I                               517 531 LAST
     I                               516 516 MI
     C                   Z-ADD0      TEMP      30
     C           *LIKE   DEFN NAME   SAVENM
     C                   SETON                 LR
```

Figure 7. RPG III Specs to Be Rewritten Using the RPG IV D Spec

```
*.. 1 ...+... 2 ...+... 3 ...+... 4 ...+... 5 ...+... 6 ...+... 7 ...+... 8 ...+... 9 ...+... 10
DContinuedName++++++++++++++++++++++++++++++++++++++++++++++++++++++++Comments++++++++++++
DName+++++++++++ETDsFrom+++To/L+++IDc.Keywords+++++++++++++++++++++++++Comments++++++++++++
D.............................Keywords+++++++++++++++++++++++++++++++++Comments++++++++++++
```

Figure 8. RPG IV D Spec Equivalent

Exercise 6 — Defining Subfield Length

In this exercise, you focus on the two ways of defining subfield length: positional, and length notation. With positional (absolute) notation, you must specify a value in both the From and To entries on the D spec. This is similar to how you code a subfield on an RPG III I spec. With length notation, you specify only a value in the To entry. This exercise is a desk exercise; you will not be compiling any source.

Objectives

At the end of this exercise, you should be able to define a subfield using either positional or length notation.

Instructions

1. Write a set of D specs to define the following data structure using positional notation.

   a. A data structure called Address1

   b. A packed numeric subfield 5 digits long (with no decimals) named StreetNo1

   c. A character subfield 20 bytes long named StreetNam1

   d. A character subfield 15 bytes long named City1

   e. A character subfield 15 bytes long named State1

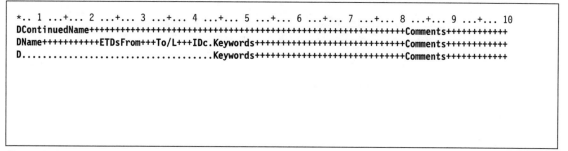

```
*.. 1 ...+... 2 ...+... 3 ...+... 4 ...+... 5 ...+... 6 ...+... 7 ...+... 8 ...+... 9 ...+... 10
DContinuedName++++++++++++++++++++++++++++++++++++++++++++++++++++++++Comments++++++++++++
DName++++++++++ETDsFrom+++To/L+++IDc.Keywords++++++++++++++++++++++++++++++++Comments++++++++++++
D..................................Keywords++++++++++++++++++++++++++++++++Comments++++++++++++
```

Figure 9. Data Structure Defined Using the Positional Notation

2. Write another set of D specs to define the preceding data structure using length notation. This time, name the data structure and subfields with '2' rather than '1' (for example, Address2, StreetNo2, and so on).

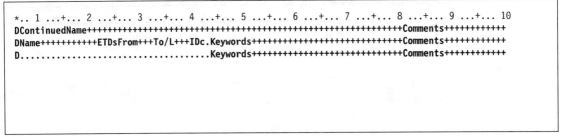

```
*.. 1 ...+... 2 ...+... 3 ...+... 4 ...+... 5 ...+... 6 ...+... 7 ...+... 8 ...+... 9 ...+... 10
DContinuedName+++++++++++++++++++++++++++++++++++++++++++++++++++++++++++++++Comments++++++++++++
DName++++++++++++ETDsFrom+++To/L+++IDc.Keywords+++++++++++++++++++++++++++++++Comments++++++++++++
D...................................Keywords+++++++++++++++++++++++++++++++++Comments++++++++++++
```

Figure 10. Data Structure Defined Using the Length Notation

Stage 5. Exercises — C Specification

Now that you have finished Stage 5 of the Tutorial, you should be ready for the Stage 5 exercises in this workbook.

The RPG IV Calculation specifications have undergone several significant changes since RPG III. Enhancements include:

- Factor 1, Factor 2, and Result Field entries are now 14 characters long
- Opcode field expanded to 10 characters
- Opcode extenders moved to follow opcode in opcode field, making them easier to use
- Free-format expressions in extended Factor 2 field
- New opcodes: ADDDUR, ALLOC, CALLB, CALLP, DEALLOC, DOU, DOW, EVAL, EXTRCT, IF, REALLOC, SUBDUR, TEST, and WHEN
- Simplification of conditioning indicators to allow only one

Note: The expanded opcode field has resulted in the renaming of some of the existing opcodes. For example, LOKUP is now LOOKUP. Also, the DEBUG and FREE opcodes are not supported in RPG IV. These RPG III opcodes are shown in Table 18 on page 40 with dark shading. Light shading refers to new RPG IV opcodes.

Table 18 on page 40 provides a summary of the RPG IV operation codes. Note that required fields are shown with underlined descriptions. More detailed information on the new opcodes is provided in "New Operation Codes" on page 165.

Table 18 (Page 1 of 4). Operation Code Specifications Summary

Codes	Factor 1	Factor 2	Result Field	Resulting Indicators
ACQ (e[8])	Device name	WORKSTN file		_ ER _
ADD (h)	Addend	Addend	Sum	+ – Z
ADDDUR (e)	Date/Time	Duration: Duration Code	Date/Time	_ ER _
ALLOC (e)		Length	Pointer	_ ER _
ANDxx	Comparand	Comparand		
BEGSR	Subroutine name			
BITOFF (BITOF)		Bit numbers	Character field	
BITON		Bit numbers	Character field	
CABxx	Comparand	Comparand	Label	HI LO EQ
CALL (e)		Program name	Plist name	_ ER LR
CALLB (d e)		Program name	Plist name	_ ER LR
CALLP (e m/r)		NAME{ (Parm1 {:Parm2...}) }		
CASxx	Comparand	Comparand	Subroutine name	HI LO EQ
CAT (p)	Source string 1	Source string 2:number of blanks	Target string	
CHAIN (e n)	Search argument	File name or Record name	Data structure	NR[2] ER _
CHECK (e)	Comparator string	Base string:start	Left-most position(s)	_ ER FD[2]
CHECKR (e) (CHEKR)	Comparator string	Base string:start	Right-most position(s)	_ ER FD[2]
CLEAR	*NOKEY	*ALL	Structure, Variable, or Record name	
CLEAR	*NOKEY	Structure, Variable, or Record name		
CLOSE (e)		File name		_ ER _
COMMIT (e) (COMIT)	Boundary			_ ER _
COMP[1]	Comparand	Comparand		HI LO EQ
DEALLOC(e/n)			Pointer	_ ER _
DEBUG	Identifier	Output file	Debug info	
DEFINE (DEFN)	*LIKE	Referenced field	Defined field	
DEFINE (DEFN)	*DTAARA or *NAMVAR	External data area	Internal program area	
DELETE (e) (DELET)	Search argument	File name		NR[2] ER _
DIV (h)	Dividend	Divisor	Quotient	+ – Z
DO	Starting value	Limit value	Index value	
DOU (m/r)		Indicator expression		
DOUxx	Comparand	Comparand		
DOW (m/r)		Indicator expression		

Table 18 (Page 2 of 4). Operation Code Specifications Summary

Codes	Factor 1	Factor 2	Result Field	Resulting Indicators
DOWxx	Comparand	Comparand		
DSPLY (e)[4]	Message identifier	Output queue	Response	_ ER _
DUMP	Identifier			
ELSE				
END		Increment value		
ENDCS				
ENDDO		Increment value		
ENDIF				
ENDSL				
ENDSR	Label	Return point		
EVAL (h m/r)		Result = Expression		
EXCEPT (EXCPT)		EXCPT name		
EXFMT (e)		Record format name		_ ER _
EXSR		Subroutine name		
EXTRCT (e)		Date/Time :Duration Code	Target field	_ ER _
FEOD (e)		File name		_ ER _
FORCE		File name		
FREE		Program name		_ ER _
GOTO		Label		
IF (m/r)		Indicator expression		
IFxx	Comparand	Comparand		
IN (e)	*LOCK	Data area name		_ ER _
ITER				
KFLD		Indicator	Key field	
KLIST	KLIST name			
LEAVE				
LOOKUP[1] (LOKUP)				
(array)	Search argument	Array name		HI LO EQ[7]
(table)	Search argument	Table name	Table name	HI LO EQ[7]
MHHZO		Source field	Target field	
MHLZO		Source field	Target field	
MLHZO		Source field	Target field	
MLLZO		Source field	Target field	
MOVE (p)	Date/Time format	Source field	Target field	+ – ZB
MOVEA (p)		Source	Target	+ – ZB
MOVEL (p)	Date/Time format	Source field	Target field	+ – ZB
MULT (h)	Multiplicand	Multiplier	Product	+ – Z
MVR			Remainder	+ – Z

Table 18 (Page 3 of 4). Operation Code Specifications Summary

Codes	Factor 1	Factor 2	Result Field	Resulting Indicators
NEXT (e)	Program device	File name		_ ER _
OCCUR (e) OCUR	Occurrence value	Data structure	Occurrence value	_ ER _
OPEN (e)		File name		_ ER _
ORxx	Comparand	Comparand		
OTHER				
OUT (e)	*LOCK	Data area name		_ ER _
PARM	Target field	Source field	Parameter	
PLIST	PLIST name			
POST (e)[3]	Program device	File name or Record name	INFDS name	_ ER _
READ (e n)[5]		File name or Record name	Data structure	_ ER EOF[6]
READC (e)		Record name		_ ER EOF[6]
READE (e n)[5]	Search argument	File name or Record name	Data structure	_ ER EOF[6]
READP (e n)[5]		File name or Record name	Data structure	_ ER BOF[6]
READPE(e n)[5] (REDPE(n))	Search argument	File name or Record name	Data structure	_ ER BOF[6]
REALLOC (e)		Length	Pointer	_ ER _
REL (e)	Program device	File name		_ ER _
RESET	*NOKEY	Structure or Variable or Record name		_ ER _
RESET (e)	*NOKEY	*ALL	Structure or Variable or Record name	_ ER _
RETRN				
RETURN (h m/r)		Expression		
ROLBK (e)				_ ER _
SCAN (e)	Comparator string:length	Base string:start	Left-most position(s)	_ ER FD[2]
SELECT (SELEC)				
SETGT (e)	Search argument	File name or Record name		NR[2] ER _
SETLL (e)	Search argument	File name or Record name		NR[2] ER EQ[7]
SETOFF[1] (SETOF)				OF OF OF
SETON[1]				ON ON ON
SHTDN				ON _ _
SORTA		Array name		
SQRT (h)		Value	Root	
SUB (h)	Minuend	Subtrahend	Difference	+ – Z

Table 18 (Page 4 of 4). Operation Code Specifications Summary

Codes	Factor 1	Factor 2	Result Field	Resulting Indicators
SUBDUR (e) (duration)	Date/Time/ Timestamp	Date/Time/ Timestamp	Duration: Duration Code	_ ER _
SUBDUR (e) (new date)	Date/Time/ Timestamp	Duration: Duration Code	Date/Time/ Timestamp	_ ER _
SUBST (e p)	Length to extract	Base string:start	Target string	_ ER _
TAG	Label			
TEST (e)[9]			Date/Time/ Timestamp Field	_ ER _
TEST (e d/t/z)[9]	Date/Time/ Timestamp Format		Character/ Numeric field	_ ER _
TESTB[1]		Bit numbers	Character field	OF ON EQ
TESTN[1]			Character field	NU BN BL
TESTZ[1]			Character field	AI JR XX
TIME			Numeric/ Date/Time/ Timestamp	
UNLOCK (e) (UNLCK)		Data area or file name		_ ER _
UPDATE (e)[5] (UPDAT)		File name or Record name	Data structure	_ ER _
WHEN (m/r)		Indicator expression		
WHENxx (WHxx)	Comparand	Comparand		
WRITE (e)[5]		File name or Record name	Data structure	_ ER EOF[6]
XFOOT (h)		Array name	Sum	+ – Z
XLATE (e p)	From:To	String:start	Target string	_ ER _
Z-ADD (h)		Addend	Sum	+ – Z
Z-SUB (h)		Subtrahend	Difference	+ – Z

Notes:

1. At least one resulting indicator is required.

2. The %FOUND built-in function can be used as an alternative to specifying an NR or FD resulting indicator. Note that in RPG III, the NR indicator is required on the CHAIN operation.

3. You must specify factor 2 or the result field. You may specify both.

4. You must specify factor 1 or the result field. You may specify both.

5. A data structure is allowed in the result field only when factor 2 contains a program-described file name.

6. The %EOF built-in function can be used as an alternative to specifying an EOF or BOF resulting indicator. Note that in RPG III, the EOF and BOF indicators are required.

7. The %EQUAL built-in function can be used to test the SETLL and LOOKUP operations.

8. For all operation codes with extender 'E', either the extender 'E' or an ER error indicator can be specified, but not both.

9. You must specify the extender 'E' or an error indicator for the TEST operation.

Exercise 7 — C Specs

In this exercise, you focus on changes to the C spec. This exercise is a desk exercise; you will not be compiling any source.

Objectives

At the end of this exercise, you should be able to code an RPG IV C spec.

Instructions

Write RPG IV C specs that perform the same logic shown in the following RPG III specs.

```
     C                     READEFILE1              N    10
     C                     MOVE ARR3,3   FIELD1
```

Figure 11. RPG III Specs to Be Rewritten Using the RPG IV D Spec

```
*.. 1 ...+... 2 ...+... 3 ...+... 4 ...+... 5 ...+... 6 ...+... 7 ...+... 8 ...+... 9 ...+... 10
CL0N01Factor1+++++++Opcode(E)+Factor2+++++++Result++++++++Len++D+HiLoEq....Comments++++++++++++
CL0N01Factor1+++++++Opcode(E)+Extended-factor2+++++++++++++++++++++++++++++Comments++++++++++++
```

Figure 12. RPG IV C Spec Equivalent

Stage 6. Exercises — I and O Specifications and Program Data

Now that you have finished Stage 6 of the Tutorial, you should be ready for the Stage 6 exercises in this workbook.

Stage 6 examines the changes to the I and O specs, and the specification of program data. The RPG IV I spec is used only to describe input records. Data structures and named constants are defined on the RPG IV D spec.

Both the I and O specs have undergone field expansion, where file names are now 10 characters and field name entries are 14 characters. The 14-character field name entry allows for a full 14-character field name or a field name plus array subscript that are 14 characters long in total.

In addition, the Skip Before/After and Space Before/After have been expanded to allow a maximum of three positions, which allows a maximum value of 255.

Changes pertaining to program data include:

- CTDATA keyword on D spec to identify compile-time arrays or tables
- FTRANS keyword on H spec to specify file translation
- ALTSEQ keyword on H spec to specify use of special collating sequence

To indicate the type of program data that follows the **, use any of these keywords as required: CTDATA <data name>, FTRANS, or ALTSEQ. By associating the program data with the appropriate keyword, you can place the groups of program data in any order after the source records.

I SPEC   D SPEC

The following tables show how the RPG III I spec maps to the RPG IV specs.

Table 19. RPG III Externally Described Files, Record Identification Entries (IX)

Positions	Name	Entry	RPG IV
6	Form type	I	6
7-14	Record name	Record format name	7-16
15-18		Blank	17-20
19-20	Record identifying indicators	Blank 01-99 L1-L9, LR H1-H9 U1-U8 RT	21-22
21-74		Blank	23-80
75-80	Comments	Optional	81-100

Table 20. RPG III Externally Described Files, Field Entries (JX)

Positions	Name	Entry	RPG IV
7-20		Blank	7-20
21-30	External field name	Field name	21-30
31-52		Blank	31-48
53-58	RPG field name	Field name	49-62
59-60	Control level	Blank L1-L9	63-64
61-62	Match fields	Blank M1-M9	65-66
63-64		Blank	67-68
65-70	Field indicators	Blank 01-99 H1-H9 U1-U8 RT	69-74
71-74		Blank	75-80
75-80	Comments	Optional	81-100

Table 21. RPG III Program Described Files, Record Identification Entries (I)

Positions	Name	Entry	RPG IV
6	Form type	I	6
7-14	File name	Valid file name	7-16
14-16	Logical relationship	AND or OR	16-18
15-16	Sequence	Any two alphabetic characters Any two-digit number	17-18
17	Number	Blank 1 N	19
18	Option	Blank O	20
19-20	Record identifying indicators	01-99 L1-L9, or LR H1-H9 U1-U8 RT * *	21-22
21-24, 28-31, 35-38	Position	Blank 1-9999	23-27, 31-35, 39-43,
25, 32, 39	Logical relationship	Blank N	28, 36, 44
26, 33, 40	Code part	C Z D	29, 37, 45
27, 34, 41	Character	Any character	30, 38, 46
42-74		Blank	47-80
75-80	Comments	Optional	81-100

Table 22. RPG III Program Described Files, Field Description Entries (J)			
Positions	**Name**	**Entry**	**RPG IV**
7-42		Blank	7-30
43	Data format	Blank B L P R	36
44-47	From	1-9999	37-41
48-51	To	1-9999	42-46
52	Decimal positions	Blank 0-9	47-48
53-58	Field name	Symbolic name	49-62
59-60	Control Level	Blank L1-L9	63-64
61-62	Match fields	Blank M1-M9	65-66
63-64	Field record relation	Blank 01-99 L1-L9 MR U1-U8 H1-H9 RT	67-68
65-70	Field indicators	Blank 01-99 H1-H9 U1-U8 RT	69-74
71-74		Blank	75-80
75-80	Comments	Optional	81-100

Table 23. RPG IV Externally Described Files, Record Identification Entries (IX)

Positions	Name	Entry	RPG III
6	Form type	I	6
7-16	Record name	Record format name	7-14
17-20		Blank	15-18
21-22	Record identifying indicators	Blank 01-99 L1-L9, LR H1-H9 U1-U8 RT	19-20
23-80		Blank	21-74
81-100	Comments	Optional	75-80

Table 24. RPG IV Externally Described Files, Field Entries (JX)

Positions	Name	Entry	RPG III
6	Form type	I	6
7-20		Blank	7-20
21-30	External field name	Field name	21-30
31-48		Blank	31-52
49-62	RPG field name	Field name	53-58
63-64	Control level	Blank L1-L9	59-60
65-66	Match fields	Blank M1-M9	61-62
67-68		Blank	63-64
69-74	Field indicators	Blank 01-99 H1-H9 U1-U8 RT	65-70
75-80		Blank	71-75
81-100	Comments	Optional	75-80

Table 25. RPG IV Program Described Files, Record Identification Entries (I)

Positions	Name	Entry	RPG III
6	Form type	I	6
7-16	File name	Valid file name	7-14
16-18	Logical relationship	AND or OR	14-16
17-18	Sequence	Any two alphabetic characters Any two-digit number	15-16
19	Number	Blank 1 N	17
20	Option	Blank O	18
21-22	Record identifying indicators	Blank 01-99 L1-L9, or LR H1-H9 U1-U8 RT * *	19-20
23-27, 31-35, 39-43,	Position	Blank 1-32766	21-24, 28-31, 35-38
28, 36, 44	Logical relationship	Blank N	25, 32, 39
29, 37, 45	Code part	C Z D	26, 33, 40
30, 38, 46	Character	Any character	27, 34, 41
47-80		Blank	42-74
81-100	Comments	Optional	75-80

Table 26. RPG IV Program Described Files, Field Description Entries (J)

Positions	Name	Entry	RPG III
6	Form type	I	6
7-30		Blank	7-42
31-34	Data attributes	*VAR or Date/Time external format	n/a
35	Date/Time separator	Any character	n/a
36	Data format	Blank A B D F G I L N P R S T U Z	43
37-41	From	1-32766	44-47
42-46	To	1-32766	48-51
47-48	Decimal positions	Blank 0-30	52
49-62	Field name	Symbolic name	53-58
63-64	Control level	Blank L1-L9	59-60
65-66	Match fields	Blank M1-M9	61-62
67-68	Field record relation	Blank 01-99 L1-L9 MR U1-U8 H1-H9 RT	63-64
69-74	Field indicators	Blank 01-99 H1-H9 U1-U8 RT	65-70
75-80		Blank	71-74
81-100	Comments	Optional	75-80

The following tables show the relationship of the O specs in RPG III and RPG IV.

Table 27. RPG IV Externally Described Files, Record Identification Entries (IX)

Positions	Name	Entry	RPG III
6	Form type	I	6
7-16	Record name	Record format name	7-14
17-20		Blank	15-18
21-22	Record identifying indicators	Blank 01-99 L1-L9, LR H1-H9 U1-U8 RT	19-20
23-80		Blank	21-74
81-100	Comments	Optional	75-80

Table 28. RPG IV Externally Described Files, Field Entries (JX)

Positions	Name	Entry	RPG III
6	Form type	I	6
7-20		Blank	7-20
21-30	External field name	Field name	21-30
31-48		Blank	31-52
49-62	RPG field name	Field name	53-58
63-64	Control level	Blank L1-L9	59-60
65-66	Match fields	Blank M1-M9	61-62
67-68		Blank	63-64
69-74	Field indicators	Blank 01-99 H1-H9 U1-U8 RT	65-70
75-80		Blank	71-75
81-100	Comments	Optional	75-80

Positions	Name	Entry	RPG III
6	Form type	I	6
7-16	File name	Valid file name	7-14
16-18	Logical relationship	AND or OR	14-16
17-18	Sequence	Any two alphabetic characters Any two-digit number	15 16
19	Number	Blank 1 N	17
20	Option	Blank O	18
21-22	Record identifying indicators	Blank 01-99 L1-L9, or LR H1-H9 U1-U8 RT * *	19-20
23-27, 31-35, 39-43,	Position	Blank 1-32766	21-24, 28-31, 35-38
28, 36, 44	Logical relationship	Blank N	25, 32, 39
29, 37, 45	Code part	C Z D	26, 33, 40
30, 38, 46	Character	Any character	27, 34, 41
47-80		Blank	42-74
81-100	Comments	Optional	75-80

Table 29. RPG IV Program Described Files, Record Identification Entries (I)

Table 30. RPG IV Program Described Files, Field Description Entries (J)

Positions	Name	Entry	RPG III
6	Form type	I	6
7-30		Blank	7-42
31-34	Data attributes	*VAR or Date/Time external format	n/a
35	Date/Time separator	Any character	n/a
36	Data format	Blank A B D F G I L N P R S T U Z	43
37-41	From	1-32766	44-47
42-46	To	1-32766	48-51
47-48	Decimal positions	Blank 0-30	52
49-62	Field name	Symbolic name	53-58
63-64	Control level	Blank L1-L9	59-60
65-66	Match fields	Blank M1-M9	61-62
67-68	Field record relation	Blank 01-99 L1-L9 MR U1-U8 H1-H9 RT	63-64
69-74	Field indicators	Blank 01-99 H1-H9 U1-U8 RT	65-70
75-80		Blank	71-74
81-100	Comments	Optional	75-80

Exercise 8 — I Specs

In this exercise, you focus on changes to the I spec. This exercise is a desk exercise; you will not be compiling any source.

Objectives

At the end of this exercise, you should be able to code an RPG IV I spec.

Instructions

Write RPG IV I specs that define the same information as the following RPG III specs.

```
IFILE1   NS  01
I                                     1   5 FIELD1
I                                     6  102BIN1
IDS1        DS
I                               P   1  50F1
I                               B  11 120F2
I                               B  21 240F3
I                                  31 350F4
I                                   1  80 F5
I I            '*****'             76  80 ZZZ1
  * ZZZ1 is a dummy name so we can initialize the last 5 bytes
```

Figure 13. RPG III Specs to Be Rewritten Using the RPG IV D Spec

```
*.. 1 ...+... 2 ...+... 3 ...+... 4 ...+... 5 ...+... 6 ...+... 7 ...+... 8 ...+... 9 ...+... 10
```

Figure 14. RPG IV Equivalent

Exercise 9 — O Specs

In this exercise, you focus on changes to the O spec. This exercise is a desk exercise; you will not be compiling any source.

Objectives

At the end of this exercise, you should be able to code an O spec and be more familiar with several of the other RPG IV specs.

Instructions

Write RPG IV I specs that define the same information as the following RPG III specs.

```
FQSYSPRT O   F    80    OA    PRINTER
C                       EXCPT
C                       SETON                        LR
OQSYSPRT H 32A0    1PNOA
O                              24 'THIS IS AN RPG TESTCASE '
O                              36 'DATE:'
O                  UDATE Y     45
O        E 2
O                              24 'RECORD NUMBER 1 HAS BEEN'
O                              48 ' IDENTIFIED AS CORRUPTED'
O                              65 'CHECK YOUR FILE'
```

Figure 15. RPG III Specs to Be Rewritten Using the RPG IV D Spec

```
*.. 1 ...+... 2 ...+... 3 ...+... 4 ...+... 5 ...+... 6 ...+... 7 ...+... 8 ...+... 9 ...+... 10
```

Figure 16. RPG IV Spec Equivalent

Exercise 10 — Compile-Time Array

In this exercise, you focus on changes to program data. This exercise is a desk exercise; you will not be compiling any source.

Objectives

At the end of this exercise you should be able to code an RPG IV compile-time array, and an RPG IV do loop.

Instructions

Write RPG IV specs that define the same information as the following RPG III specs.

```
FOUT      O  F     80          DISK
E            OUT    PAR    1   4 50
I            4                  C       PAR#
I            '00000Unknown'     C       DFTADR
C            1       DO    PAR#    X    50
C            PAR,X   IFEQ  *BLANKS
C                    MOVELDFTADR    PAR,X
C                    ENDIF
C                    ENDDO
C                    SETON                    LR
**
00003Cowslip Street    Toronto       Ontario
01150Eglinton Avenue   North York    Ontario
00012Jasper Avenue     Edmonton      Alberta
00027Avenue Road       Sudbury       Ontario
```

Figure 17. RPG III Specs to Be Rewritten Using the RPG IV D Spec

```
*.. 1 ...+... 2 ...+... 3 ...+... 4 ...+... 5 ...+... 6 ...+... 7 ...+... 8 ...+... 9 ...+... 10




```

Figure 18. RPG IV Spec Equivalent

Stage 7. Exercises — New Procedure Specification

Now that you have finished Stage 7 of the Tutorial, you should be ready for the Stage 7 exercises in this workbook.

Stage 7 focuses on the new Procedure specification type. The new P spec allows you to define prototyped procedures that are specified after the main source section, otherwise known as subprocedures.

Before defining the subprocedure, you must define its prototype in the main source section of the module containing the subprocedure definition. The prototype specifies parameters passed to the procedure and a return value, if any.

The subprocedure is a procedure specified after the main source section and includes the following parts:

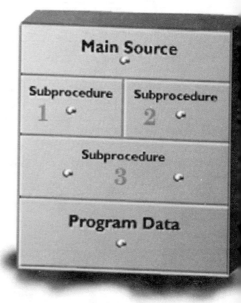

1. A begin-procedure specification (B in position 24 of a procedure specification), including the subprocedure name and optionally the EXPORT keyword.

2. A procedure-interface definition, which specifies parameters passed to the procedure and a return value, if any. If there are no parameters or return value the procedure-interface is optional. The procedure interface must match the corresponding prototype.

3. Local definitions, including variables, constants, and prototypes needed by the subprocedure. Names defined within the subprocedure are not accessible outside the subprocedure, that is, the storage is local to the subprocedure or has local scope.

4. Any calculations that are needed to perform the task of the procedure. The RETURN opcode must be coded if the subprocedure returns a value. A subprocedure that returns a value is essentially a user-defined function.

5. An End-Procedure specification (E in position 24 of a procedure specification)

Except for a procedure-interface definition, which may be placed anywhere within the definition specifications, a subprocedure must be coded in the order shown above.

The following table provides a breakdown by position of the RPG IV P spec.

Table 31. RPG IV Procedure Specification (PR)

Positions or Keyword	Name	Entry
6	Form type	P
7-21	Name	Symbolic name
24	Begin/End procedure	B E
44-80	Keywords	
81-100	Comments	Optional
EXPORT	Procedure can be exported	

Exercise 11 — P Spec

In this exercise, you focus on the new Procedure specification that is part of RPG IV. This exercise is a desk exercise; you will not be compiling any source.

Objectives

At the end of this exercise, you should be able to:

- describe the P spec layout
- code a procedure interface, prototype, and parameter definitions
- code a subprocedure with a return value.

Instructions

1. Write the prototype for the following subprocedure.

   a. A subprocedure called FmtCust

   b. A parameter named FirstName that is a character field of length 10

   c. A parameter named LastName that is a character field of length 15

   d. A parameter named Indicator that is an indicator field

   e. A return value that is a character field of length 25.

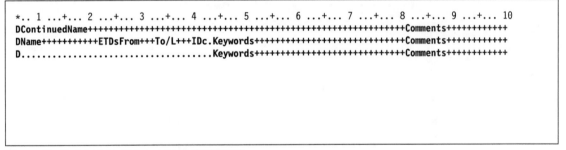

```
*.. 1 ...+... 2 ...+... 3 ...+... 4 ...+... 5 ...+... 6 ...+... 7 ...+... 8 ...+... 9 ...+... 10
DContinuedName++++++++++++++++++++++++++++++++++++++++++++++++++++++++++Comments++++++++++++
DName++++++++++ETDsFrom+++To/L+++IDc.Keywords+++++++++++++++++++++++++++++Comments++++++++++++
D.................................Keywords+++++++++++++++++++++++++++++++Comments++++++++++++
```

Figure 19. Prototype for Subprocedure CUSTFILE

2. Write the corresponding procedure interface and Begin- and End-P specs that are used to define the subprocedure CUSTFILE.

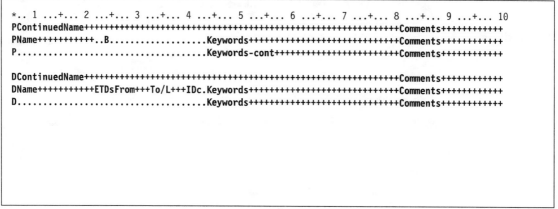

```
*.. 1 ...+... 2 ...+... 3 ...+... 4 ...+... 5 ...+... 6 ...+... 7 ...+... 8 ...+... 9 ...+... 10
PContinuedName++++++++++++++++++++++++++++++++++++++++++++++++++++++++++++Comments+++++++++++++
PName++++++++++++..B..................Keywords+++++++++++++++++++++++++++++++++Comments+++++++++++++
P...............................Keywords-cont+++++++++++++++++++++++++++++++Comments+++++++++++++

DContinuedName++++++++++++++++++++++++++++++++++++++++++++++++++++++++++++Comments+++++++++++++
DName+++++++++++ETDsFrom+++To/L+++IDc.Keywords+++++++++++++++++++++++++++++++++Comments+++++++++++++
D...............................Keywords+++++++++++++++++++++++++++++++++Comments+++++++++++++
```

Figure 20. Data Structure Defined Using the Length Notation

Stage 8. Exercises — Defining Date, Time, and Timestamp Fields

Now that you have finished Stage 8 of the Tutorial, you should be ready for the Stage 8 exercises in this workbook.

Stage 8 focuses on the new date, time, and timestamp data types and how to define them. Date, time and timestamp fields have an internal format that is independent of the external format. The internal format is the way the field is stored in the program. You need to be aware of the internal format when passing parameters or when overlaying subfields in data structures. The external format is the way the field is stored in files.

In general, it is recommended that you use the default ISO internal format, especially if you have a mixture of external format types. You can use the DATFMT and TIMFMT keywords on the H spec to change the default internal format, if desired, by specifying a new format. In addition, you can use the D spec to:

- Override the default internal format by using the DATFMT and TIMFMT keywords

- Specify an initial value for a date, time, or timestamp field that is different than the default by using the INZ keyword

If you have date, time, and timestamp fields in program-described files, then you must specify their external format. You can use the F spec to specify the default external format for date, time, and timestamp fields in a program-described file by using the DATFMT and TIMFMT keywords. You can use the I and O specs to specify an external format for a particular field.

Exercise 12 — Defining Date and Time Fields

In this desk exercise, you focus on defining date, time, and timestamp fields using D specs.

Objectives

At the end of this exercise, you should be able to code date, time, and timestamp fields on the H and D specs.

Instructions

Assuming the RPG IV H spec shown below, write D specs for the following fields:

1. A date field, MyDate, that is in YY/MM/DD format and has an initial value of Feb 1, 1998

2. A date field, CurDate, that is in MM/DD/YYYY format and initialized to *JOB

3. A date field, ThisDate, that is in MM/DD/YY format

4. A time field, MyTime, that is in HH:MM:SS format with an initial value of noon

```
*.. 1 ...+... 2 ...+... 3 ...+... 4 ...+... 5 ...+... 6 ...+... 7 ...+...
8 ...+... 9 ...+... 10
HKeywords+++++++++++++++++++++++++++++++++++++++++++++++++++++++++++++Comments++++++++++++
    H DATFMT(*MDY) TIMFMT(*HMS) DATEDIT(*MDY/)

DContinuedName+++++++++++++++++++++++++++++++++++++++++++++++++++++++++Comments++++++++++++
DName++++++++++++ETDsFrom+++To/L+++IDc.Keywords+++++++++++++++++++++++++Comments++++++++++++
D...................................Keywords++++++++++++++++++++++++++++Comments++++++++++++
```

Figure 21. D specs for Date, Time, and Timestamp Fields

Exercise 13 — Using Dates in a Program

This exercise provides an opportunity to define and use dates in an RPG IV program.

The RPG program used in this exercise prints a list of all *PGM objects in a library. The list includes the attributes of the program and the last used date for each. You will manually create a database file that can contain the information included here. After you have created the file and entered the data in it, (using the CL command, DSPOBJD), you may call the RPG program to print the report.

Objectives

The main objective is to replace the old mechanism for converting the date format and to edit the date on the report by using the new date data type features of RPG IV.

At the end of this computer exercise, you should be able to:

- Define date data types in RPG IV
- Convert a date format from MMDDYY to YYMMDD
- Edit, compile, and run an RPG IV program

Instructions

The WKBKLIB library contains an RPG IV source program called PRTOBJ. This program is currently written to read a file that contains the programs from a specific library as well as information about those programs. It then prints a report with each program listed and the date it was last used. PRTOBJ reads from a file, which you will create and fill with data using the DSPOBJD command.

For the purposes of this exercise, you are concerned with the following pieces of information for the program objects:

- Program name
- Program type
- Attribute
- Date program was last used

Follow these instructions to change this program to use RPG IV date data types and duration support:

1. Change your job's current library to the library you are using for these exercises. Enter the following command and substitute your library name for *YourLib*.

   ```
   CHGCURLIB Yourlib
   ```

2. Create the file that will be the input to this program by using the following command:

   ```
   CRTDUPOBJ OBJ(QADSPOBJ) FROMLIB(QSYS) OBJTYPE(*FILE) TOLIB(YourLib)
   NEWOBJ(DSPOBJ) DATA(*NO)
   ```

3. After creating the file, you may want to display the format and field descriptions in the file to help understand how some of the fields are used in the RPG program. You do this by issuing the Display File Field Description command:

```
DSPFFD FILE(DSPOBJ)
```

Note especially the input field format for ODUDAT, which contains the date each object was last used.

4. Add data to the file you just created using the following command:

```
DSPOBJD OBJ(Alib/*ALL) OBJTYPE(*PGM) OUTPUT(*OUTFILE)
   OUTFILE(DSPOBJ)
```

Substitute for the name *ALib* the name of a library that contains some program objects. This may be the same library you are using for the workbook exercises or it may be a different library, so long as it is a library that contains program objects.

5. The source for PRTOBJ is shown on Figure 22 on page 67. Copy the source member for the PRTOBJ program from the original library and source file (WRKBKLIB/WKBKSRC) to your own library and source file.

6. Edit the source member PRTOBJ and make the appropriate source code changes to accomplish the following:

   a. Use an RPG IV date data type and a MOVE operation to replace the CVTDAT subroutine currently in the program. CVTDAT reformats a field representing a date from the MMDDYY format to the YYMMDD format.

   b. It is possible that some of the dates from the input file (in the field named ODUDAT) will contain blanks, indicating that an object has never been used since its creation. Ensure your code considers this possibility and places the words "Not Used" in the Last used column for programs that have not been used (that is, that have blanks in the ODUDAT field).

   c. Use the date field formatted in YYMMDD format in the O spec that produces the printed output.

7. Compile your source code using PDM option 14 (CRTBNDRPG). Accept the defaults for the CRTBNDRPG command.

8. Test your program. It should produce printed output that looks similar to this:

```
                    Objects in Library
    Object     Obj type   Attribute   Last used

    PGM1       *PGM       CLLE        98/01/08
    PGM2       *PGM       RPGLE       Not Used
    PGM3       *PGM       RPG         98/02/08
```

```
* PRTOBJ  - RPG Program to Print Objects and Date Last Used
*
* DSPOBJ is the outfile from DSPOBJD - Create it manually
FDSPOBJ    IF   E           DISK
FQPRINT     O   F  132      PRINTER OFLIND(*INOF)
*********************************************************
C                      EXCEPT  HDG                                Prt heading
*********************************************************
* Read a record
* QLIDOBJD is the format name of the QADSPOBJ file
C                      READ    QLIDOBJD                       20  Read
* Continue reading until EOF
C     *IN20            DOWEQ   '0'                                Not EOF
*********************************************************
* Use a subroutine to convert the date from MMDDYY to YYMMDD
C                      MOVE    ODUDAT    MMDDYY    6              MMDDYY fmt
C                      EXSR    CVTDAT                             Convert date
C                      MOVE    YYMMDD    LSTUSD    6 0            Last used dt
C                      EXCEPT  DETAIL                             Print detail
C     OF               EXCEPT  HDG                                Prt heading
C                      READ    QLIDOBJD                       20  Read
C                      ENDDO                                      Loop Back
* End the program
C                      SETON                              LR      Set LR
*********************************************************
C     CVTDAT           BEGSR
* Convert date from MMDDYY to YYMMDD format
C                      MOVE    MMDDYY    WORK2     2              Move YY
C                      MOVEL   WORK2     YYMMDD    6              Move YY
C                      MOVEL   MMDDYY    WORK4     4              Move MMDD
C                      MOVE    WORK4     YYMMDD                   Move MMDD
C                      ENDSR
*********************************************************
OQPRINT    E          HDG        2 06
O                                       25 'Objects '
O                                          'in Library'
O          E          HDG        2
O                                        6 'Object'
O                                       18 'Obj type'
O                                       30 'Attribute'
O                                       42 'Last used'
O          E          DETAIL     1
O                     ODOBNM              10
O                     ODOBTP              19
O                     ODOBAT              33
O                     LSTUSD     Y        41
```

Figure 22. Original Source Code for PRTOBJ

Stage 9. Exercises — Using Date, Time, and Timestamp Fields

Now that you have finished Stage 9 of the Tutorial, you should be ready for the Stage 9 exercises in this workbook.

A real advantage to having native date, time, and timestamp data types is the ability to add or subtract date and time fields directly, and to calculate durations.

You can use the following opcodes with date, time, and timestamp fields:

ADDDUR   Allows you to add durations to date, time, and timestamp fields

SUBDUR   Allows you to subtract dates and times and to calculate durations

EXTRCT   Allows you to extract logical portions of date, time, and timestamp fields

MOVE, MOVEL

Allow you to move data to and from date, time, and timestamp fields. When moving to numeric fields, separators are removed

TEST   Allows you to test character or numeric fields to see if they have a valid date, time, or timestamp

Exercise 14 — Calculating Durations

In this desk exercise, you will practice using the fields you defined in Exercise 12.

Objectives

At the end of this exercise, you should be able to calculate durations.

Instructions

Using the H and D specs from Exercise 12, write the C spec logic to determine how many days have passed since Feb 1, 1998.

```
*.. 1 ...+... 2 ...+... 3 ...+... 4 ...+... 5 ...+... 6 ...+... 7 ...+... 8 ...+... 9 ...+... 10
CL0N01Factor1+++++++Opcode(E)+Factor2+++++++Result++++++++Len++D+HiLoEq....Comments++++++++++++
CL0N01Factor1+++++++Opcode(E)+Extended-factor2++++++++++++++++++++++++++++++Comments++++++++++++
```

Figure 23. C Spec for Determining a Duration

Exercise 15 — Calculating Duration from Current Date

In this computer exercise, you practice using the fields you defined in Exercise 13, PRTOBJ. Copy PRTOBJ to another member if you want to save the results of that exercise.

Objectives

At the end of this exercise, you should be able to calculate durations.

Instructions

1. Make additional changes to PRTOBJ to add a column to the report that represents the number of days from the current date since the object was last changed.

2. Compile this program using PDM option 14 (CRTBNDRPG) and take the defaults for the compile.

3. Run your program. Using the WRKSPLF command, you should see a report that looks similar to this:

```
                 Objects in Library

Object    Obj type   Attribute   Last used   Days Since Used

PGM1      *PGM       CLLE        98/01/08          20
PGM2      *PGM       RPGLE       Not Used    Not Used
PGM3      *PGM       RPG         98/02/08          50
```

Stage 10. Exercises — Using Expressions

Now that you have finished stage 10 of the Tutorial, you should be ready for the stage 10 exercises in this workbook.

One of the key features of RPG IV is the ability to code free-form expressions. Expressions are simply groups of operands and operators. For example:

```
A + B * C
STRINGA + STRINGC
D = %ELEM(ARRAYNAME)
```

You code expressions on the extended factor 2 field of the C spec.

An important aspect of expressions is the precedence rules. Precedence rules determine the order in which operations are performed within expressions. High precedence operations are performed before lower precedence operations. This list indicates the precedence of operators from highest to lowest:

1. ()
2. Built-in functions, user-defined functions
3. unary +, unary -, NOT
4. **
5. *, /
6. binary +, binary -
7. =, <>, >, >=, <, <=
8. AND
9. OR

Because parentheses have the highest precedence, operations within parentheses are always performed first. Operators of the same precedence are evaluated in left to right order.

Any data field, named constant, literal, or procedure call can be used as an operand. However, the data type of the operand must match that allowed by the operator. (This is the basic idea behind the classification of expressions as arithmetic, conditional, or string.)

Table 32 describes the type of operand allowed for each unary operator and the type of the result. Table 33 on page 75 describes the type of operands allowed for each binary operator and the type of the result.

Table 32. Types Supported for Unary Operations

Operation	Operand Type	Result Type
- (negation)	Numeric	Numeric
+	Numeric	Numeric
NOT	Indicator	Indicator

Table 33. Operands Supported for Binary Operations

Operator	Operand 1 Type	Operand 2 Type	Result Type
+ (addition)	Numeric	Numeric	Numeric
- (subtraction)	Numeric	Numeric	Numeric
* (multiplication)	Numeric	Numeric	Numeric
/ (division)	Numeric	Numeric	Numeric
** (exponentiation)	Numeric	Numeric	Numeric
+ (concatenation)	Character	Character	Character
+ (concatenation)	Graphic	Graphic	Graphic
+ (add offset to pointer)	Basing Pointer	Numeric	Basing Pointer
- (subtract pointers)	Basing Pointer	Basing Pointer	Numeric
- (subtract offset from pointer)	Basing Pointer	Numeric	Basing Pointer
Note: For the following operations, the operands may be of any type, but the two operands must be of the same type.			
= (equal to)	Any	Any	Indicator
>= (greater than or equal to)	Any	Any	Indicator
> (greater than)	Any	Any	Indicator
<= (less than or equal to)	Any	Any	Indicator
< (less than)	Any	Any	Indicator
<> (not equal to)	Any	Any	Indicator
AND (logical and)	Indicator	Indicator	Indicator
OR (logical or)	Indicator	Indicator	Indicator

Exercise 16 — Arithmetic and Conditional Expressions

In this computer exercise, you use RPG IV's free-form expressions.

The RPG program that you will be starting with calculates:

- The weekly pay for hourly employees
- The tax to be withheld
- The new pay resulting from subtracting the tax from the earnings

Your mission is to replace the old-style calculations for the earnings and the tax calculations. The program prints a report so you can check the accuracy of your calculations.

Objectives

At the end of the exercise, you should be able to code arithmetic and logical free-form expressions.

Instructions

1. Copy the source members RPGPAY and PAYROLL to your own source file (See Figure 24 on page 77 for the original source for the program RPGPAY and Figure 25 on page 78 for the DDS for PAYROLL.)

2. Make the necessary source code changes to rewrite the two subroutines PayCalc and TaxCalc so that they use RPG IV expression support. Be sure to use both conditional and arithmetic expressions. Remember that you may need to define Result fields on the D spec, because you do not have a Result field on the expanded Factor 2 field of the C spec.

3. Compile your source code using PDM option 14 (CRTBNDRPG command).

4. Test your program. It should produce printed output that looks similar to this:

```
Pay and tax calculation    01/09/98
First and Last name        Earned   Pay tax   Net pay

Jerry     Anderson         1299.38   241.86   1057.52
Eddy      Wheeler           816.90   197.41    619.49
Arthur    Misner            820.31   111.66    708.65
Doris     Hattenberger      950.25   195.07    755.18
Kevin     Sachow            784.00   163.52    620.48
```

```
 * RPGPAY   - Pay check program
 *
FPAYROLL   IF  E             DISK
FQPRINT    O   F  132        PRINTER OFLIND(*INOF)
 *
D NET           S            +2   LIKE(RATE)
 *
C                 EXCEPT    Heading                              Prt Heading
 * Read a record
C    *IN20        DOWEQ     '0'
C                 READ      PAYREC                        20     EOF
 *
C    *IN20        IFEQ      '0'                                  If not EOF
***
 * Calculate pay and tax
C                 EXSR      PayCalc                              Calc pay
C                 EXSR      TaxCalc                              Calc tax
C    PAY          SUB       TAX         NET                      Net pay
C                 EXCEPT    Detail                               Prt record
C    OF           EXCEPT    Heading                              Prt Heading
C                 ENDIF                                          EndIf EOF
C                 ENDDO                                          Loop back
***
C                 SETON                               LR         Set LR
C                 RETURN                                         Return

C    PayCalc      BEGSR
 *
 * Calculate payment - hours over 35 get additional 50 %
 *
C    HOURS        IFLE      35                                   Hours <= 35
C    HOURS        MULT      RATE        PAY                      Total pay
C                 ELSE                                           -else-
C    RATE         MULT      35          PAY        7 2           Full 35 hrs
C    HOURS        SUB       35          OTIME      3 0           Overtime hours
C    RATE         MULT      1.75        OTRATE     9 4           Find rate
C    OTRATE       MULT(H)   OTIME       OTPAY      7 2           Overtime pay
C                 ADD       OTPAY       PAY                      Total pay
C                 END
C                 ENDSR

C    TaxCalc      BEGSR
 *
 * Calculate Tax - the first 200 are tax free.
 *
C    PAY          IFLE      200                                  Pay < 200
C                 Z-ADD     0           TAX        7 2           no tax
C                 ELSE                                           -else-
C    PAY          SUB       200         TXABLE     7 2           200 tax free
C    TXABLE       MULT      TAXD        TXWRK      9 2           calc %
C    TXWRK        DIV(H)    100         TAX                      Tax to pay
C                 END
C                 ENDSR
```

Figure 24 (Part 1 of 2). Original Source Code for RPGPAY

```
OQPRINT      E           Heading       2 06
O                                         25 'Pay and tax calculation '
O                        UDATE        Y  36
O            E           Heading       2
O                                         19 'First and Last name'
O                                         36 'Earned'
O                                         46 'Pay tax'
O                                         56 'Net pay'
O            E           Detail        1
O                        FNAME            10
O                        LNAME            26
O                        PAY          3   36
O                        TAX          3   46
O                        NET          3   56
```

Figure 24 (Part 2 of 2). Original Source Code for RPGPAY

```
A*   Payroll
A         R PAYREC                   TEXT('Payroll record')
A           FNAME       10A          TEXT('First name')
A                                    COLHDG('First' 'name')
A           LNAME       15A          TEXT('Last name')
A                                    COLHDG('Last' 'name')
A           BORN         L           TEXT('Date born - *ISO form
A                                    COLHDG('Date' 'born')
A           HOURS       3P 0         TEXT('Hours worked')
A                                    COLHDG('Hours')
A           RATE        5P 2         TEXT('Hourly rate')
A           TAXD        3P 0         TEXT('Tax deduction percent
A                                    COLHDG('Tax' ' % ')
```

Figure 25. DDS for File PAYROLL

Exercise 17 — Procedure Calls in an Expression

In this computer exercise, you will rewrite the two subroutines PayCalc and TaxCalc defined in Exercise 16 so that RPG IV subprocedures are used instead. Copy RPGPAY to another member if you want to save the results of that exercise.

Objectives

At the end of this exercise, you should be able to write an expression to call a subprocedure.

Instructions

1. Make additional changes to RPGPAY to change the subroutines PayCalc and TaxCalc into subprocedures.

2. Subprocedure PayCalc should return Pay and has no parameters.

3. Subprocedure TaxCalc should return Tax and has no parameters.

4. Specify DFTACTGRP(*NO) ACTGRP('MyActGrp') on the H spec.

5. Compile this program using PDM option 14 (CRTBNDRPG) and take the defaults for the compile.

6. Run your program. Using the WRKSPLF command, you should see a report that looks similar to this (same as Exercise 16):

```
                   Objects in Library

   Object    Obj type   Attribute   Last used   Days Since Used

   PGM1      *PGM       CLLE        98/01/08          20
   PGM2      *PGM       RPGLE       Not Used      Not Used
   PGM3      *PGM       RPG         98/02/08          50
```

Exercise 18 — String Expressions

Now that you have successfully used RPG IV arithmetic and logical expressions, try your hand at writing expressions that manipulate strings.

Objectives

At the end of this computer exercise, you should be able to code string expressions.

Instructions

1. Using the EVAL opcode, concatenate the first name (FNAME) and last name (LNAME) fields with one space between them. *Hint:* You might want to use the built-in function %TRIMR. See "New Built-In Functions" on page 189 for more information.

2. Compile your source code using option 14 (CRTBNDRPG).

3. Test your program. It should produce printed output that looks similar to this:

```
                      Pay and tax calculation   01/09/98
        First and Last name        Earned   Pay tax   Net pay

        Jerry Anderson            1299.38    241.86   1057.52
        Eddy Wheeler               816.90    197.41    619.49
        Arthur Misner              820.31    111.66    708.65
        Doris Hattenberger         950.25    195.07    755.18
        Kevin Sachow               784.00    163.52    620.48
```

Stage 11. Exercises — Modular Programming and ILE

Now that you have finished stage 11 of the Tutorial, you should be ready for the stage 11 exercises in this workbook.

One of the main benefits of ILE is the ability to have static binding or bind by copy. With bind by copy you can make greater use of modular programming.

There are three common strategies for creating ILE programs using bind by copy.

1. Create a program using CRTBNDRPG to maximize OPM compatibility.
2. Create an ILE program using CRTBNDRPG.
3. Create an ILE program using CRTRPGMOD and CRTPGM.

The first strategy is recommended as a temporary one. It is intended for users who have OPM applications and who, perhaps due to lack of time, cannot move their applications to ILE all at once. The second strategy can also be a temporary one. It allows you time to learn more about ILE, but also allows you to immediately use some of its features. The third strategy is more involved, but offers the most flexibility.

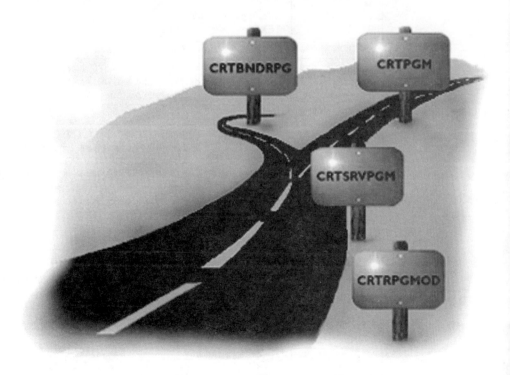

Both the first and second strategies make use of the one-step program creation process, namely, CRTBNDRPG. The third strategy uses the two-step program creation process, namely, CRTRPGMOD followed by CRTPGM.

For additional information on program creation, see Stage 18, "Creating an ILE Program" on page 147.

Understanding the New Create Commands

To help you relate the new program creation command CRTBNDRPG to CRTRPGPGM, the following table compares the two commands.

Table 34 (Page 1 of 2). Parameter Comparison of CRTRPGPGM to CRTBNDRPG

CRTRPGPGM	CRTBNDRPG	Status
PGM	PGM	Same
SRCFILE	SRCFILE	Same
SRCMBR	SRCMBR	Same
GENLVL	GENLVL	Similar; CRTBNDRPG has values 0-20 only; default is 10
TEXT	TEXT	Same
OPTION	OPTION	Similar; there are some differences in the keywords
GENOPT	OPTIMIZE	Changed; OPTIMIZE supports three values, *BASIC, *FULL, and *NONE. All other similar GENOPT keywords are not supported.
INDENT	INDENT	Same
CVTOPT	CVTOPT	Similar; CRTBNDRPG CVTOPT(*NONE) means use the RPG IV native date, time, and timestamp data types. Also, CRTBNDRPG allows keywords *GRAPHIC, *VARGRAPHIC, *VARCHAR for converting graphic, and variable-length length graphic and character fields to fixed length graphic fields.
SRTSEQ	SRTSEQ	Same
LANGID	LANGID	Same
SAAFLAG	N/A	Not supported
PRTFILE	N/A	Assumes QSYSPRT as a default printer file
REPLACE	REPLACE	Same
TGTRLS	TGTRLS	Same
USRPRF	USRPRF	Same
AUT	AUT	Same
PHSTRC	N/A	Not supported
ITDUMP	N/A	Not supported
SNPDUMP	N/A	Not supported

Table 34 (Page 2 of 2). Parameter Comparison of CRTRPGPGM to CRTBNDRPG

CRTRPGPGM	CRTBNDRPG	Status
CODELIST	N/A	Not supported
IGNDECERR	FIXNBR	Similar; default for CRTBNDRPG is to fix zoned decimal data errors that occur upon conversion to packed
ALWNULL	ALWNULL	Same

The CRTBNDRPG command also has the following new parameters:

ACTGRP   Allows you to specify which activation group the created program will run in.

BNDDIR   Allows you to identify any binding directory to be used when creating the program.

DBGVIEW   Specifies the type of debug information, if any, that is to be associated with the object when the module or program is created.

DFTACTGRP
              Specifies whether the created program is to run only in the OPM default activation group.

OUTPUT   OUTPUT(*PRINT) corresponds to CRTRPGPGM OPTION(*SOURCE *XREF).

TRUNCNBR
              Specifies if a truncated value is moved to the Result field or if an error is generated when numeric overflow occurs.

ENBPFRCOL
              Specifies whether performance collection is enabled and how performance statistics are gathered.

PRFDTA   Specifies the program profiling data attribute for the program.

DEFINE   Specifies condition names that are defined before the compilation begins. Using the parameter DEFINE(condition-name) is equivalent to coding the /DEFINE condition-name directive on the first line of the source file.

Note: The CRTRPGMOD command has most of the same parameters as the CRTBNDRPG command except that it does not have the following parameters:

- ACTGRP
- DFTACTGRP
- USRPRF

The ILE create commands Create Program (CRTPGM) and Create Service Program (CRTSRVPGM) are very similar to each other. Their parameters and default values are listed below.

Table 35. Parameters for CRTPGM and CRTSRVPGM Commands and their Default Values

Parameter Group	CRTPGM Command (Default Value)	CRTSRVPGM Command (Default Value)
Identification	PGM(*library name/program name*) MODULE(*PGM)	SRVPGM(*library name/service program name*) MODULE(*SRVPGM)
Program access	ENTMOD(*FIRST)	EXPORT(*SRCFILE) SRCFILE(*LIBL/QSRVSRC) SRCMBR(*SRVPGM)
Binding	BNDSRVPGM(*NONE) BNDDIR(*NONE)	BNDSRVPGM(*NONE) BNDDIR(*NONE)
Run time	ACTGRP(*NEW)	ACTGRP(*CALLER)

Miscellaneous	OPTION(*GEN *NODUPPROC *NODUPVAR
	      *WARN *RSLVREF)
	DETAIL(*NONE)
	ALWUPD(*YES)
	ALWRINZ(*NO)
	REPLACE(*YES)
	AUT(*LIBCRTAUT)
	TEXT(*ENTMODTXT)
	TGTRLS(*CURRENT)
	USRPRF(*USER)
		OPTION(*GEN *NODUPPROC *NODUPVAR
		      *WARN *RSLVREF)
		DETAIL(*NONE)
		ALWUPD(*YES)
		ALWRINZ(*NO)
		REPLACE(*YES)
		AUT(*LIBCRTAUT)
		TEXT(*ENTMODTXT)
		TGTRLS(*CURRENT)
		USRPRF(*USER)

Exercise 19 — Creating an ILE Program

This computer exercise allows you to become more familiar with ILE program creation. It is based on the exercises you did for Stages 8 and 9 (printing the days since an object was last used). However, in this case the application has been written in a more modular fashion. It contains the following components:

1. The 'days from today' calculation has been moved to a separate source member, DAYSSINCE. This member.

   - accepts a date as an input parameter
   - returns in a second parameter the number of days between that date and today

2. A CL program has been created to fill DSPOBJ with the object descriptions. This source is found in member DSPOBJMOD.

3. The RPG program that reads the DSPOBJ file and prints the report is found in member PRTOBJILE. It has been modified to call DAYSSINCE.

Your mission is to modify two of the modules so that they make procedure calls instead of program calls. Then to create all the modules needed from the source code provided to you, and to bind the modules together using bind by copy.

Objectives

At the end of the exercise, you should be able to:

- Create RPG IV and CL modules
- Understand how to code a procedure call in RPG or CL
- Create a multi-module ILE program using bind by copy

Instructions

Follow these instructions to modify the source members and then create an ILE program from the respective modules.

1. Find the source member for the CL module, DSPOBJMOD, in the file WKBKSRC in the library WKBKLIB.

   Note the statement that calls the RPG routine PRTOBJILE. As currently written, it is a program call, rather than a procedure call. Modify the source to make the statement a procedure call. *Hint:* Use the CALLPRC command.

2. Compile the DSPOBJMOD member using the option 15 from PDM or the CRTCLMOD command. Take the defaults for the compile.

3. Find the source member for the RPG module, PRTOBJILE, in the file WKBKSRC in the library WKBKLIB.

   The call statement in this source member (to DAYSSINCE) is also currently a program call. Modify the source to make the statement a procedure call.

4. Compile the PRTOBJILE module using option 15 from PDM or the CRTRPGMOD command. Take the defaults for the compile.

5. Find the source member for DAYSSINCE. Compile it using option 15 from PDM or CRTRPGMOD, taking the defaults.

6. After all modules have compiled successfully, create a bound program using bind by copy.

   a. Issue a CRTPGM command at the command line and press F4 for prompting

   b. Name this program PRTOBJPGM

   c. Include in the list of modules to be bound (the Module parameter) the DSPOBJMOD, PRTOBJILE, and DAYSSINCE modules

   Take the defaults for the remaining parameters.

7. Call your new program, PRTOBJPGM, and specify as the parameter the name of the library you used in the date exercises. (It may be any library that contains some *PGM objects.)

8. Look at the spooled file created by your program. It should look similar to the results from the date exercises you did earlier.

```
         PGM        PARM(&LIB)
         DCL        VAR(&LIB) TYPE(*CHAR) LEN(10) VALUE('*CURLIB')
         MONMSG     MSGID(CPD2104 CPF2130)
         DSPOBJD    OBJ(&LIB/*ALL) OBJTYPE(*PGM) DETAIL(*BASIC) +
                      OUTPUT(*OUTFILE) OUTFILE(*CURLIB/DSPOBJ) +
                      /* CL Command to put all program objects +
                      from requested library into DSPOBJ for +
                      input to PRTOBJILE */
         CALL       PGM(PRTOBJILE)
                      endpgm
```

Figure 26. Source Code for CL Module DSPOBJMOD

```
         HDATEDIT(*YMD) DATFMT(*YMD)
         DCurDate      S          D    INZ(*JOB)
         DDateIn       S          D
         DNoDays       S          5 0
         DError        C              99999                99999 meanserr
         C    *ENTRY    PLIST                              Convert date
         C              PARM              DateIn
         C              PARM              NoDays
         C              TEST              DateIn          10
         C              IF      NOT *IN10
         C    CurDate   SubDur  DateIn    NoDays:*D
         C              ELSE
         C              EVAL    NoDays = Error
         C              ENDIF
         C              RETURN
```

Figure 27. Source Code for RPG Module DAYSSINCE

```
 * PRTOBJ   - Print program modified to use a date field
 *
 * DSPOBJ is the outfile from DSPOBJD - Create it manually
FDSPOBJ    IF   E              DISK
FQPRINT    O    F  132         PRINTER OFLIND(*INOF)
DLSTUSD         S              D  DATFMT(*YMD)
DCvtFld         S              6  0
DNoDays         S              5  0
 ********************************************************************
 *               EXCEPT    HDG                                Prt heading
 ********************************************************************
 * Read a record
 * QLIDOBJD is the format name of the QADSPOBJ file
C               READ      QLIDOBJD                       20   Read
 * Continue reading until EOF
C    *IN20      DOWEQ     '0'                                 Not EOF
 ********************************************************************
 * Convert the date from MMDDYY to YYMMDD
C               MOVE      ODUDAT       CvtFld
C    *MDY       TEST(D)                CvtFld            10
C    *IN10      IFNE      '1'
C    *MDY       MOVE      CvtFld       LSTUSD
C               ENDIF
C               CALL      'DAYSSINCE'
C               PARM                   LstUsd
C               PARM                   NoDays
C               IF        NoDays <> 99999
C               EXCEPT    DETAIL                             Print detail
C    OF         EXCEPT    HDG                                Prt heading
C               ENDIF
C               READ      QLIDOBJD                       20   Read
C               ENDDO                                        Loop Back
 * End the program
C               SETON                                   LR   Set LR
OQPRINT    E         HDG          2 06
O                                       25 'Objects '
O                                          'in Library'
O          E         HDG          2
O                                        6 'Object'
O                                       18 'Obj type'
O                                       30 'Attribute'
O                                       42 'Last used'
 *  +++++                          Add the heading
O                                       60 'Days Since Used'
O          E         DETAIL       1
O                    ODOBNM          10
O                    ODOBTP          19
O                    ODOBAT          33
O          N10       LSTUSD          42
O          10                        42 'Not used'
O          N10       NoDays       L  56
O          10                        56 'Not used'
 *  +++++                          Add the field and edit
```

Figure 28. Source Code for RPG Module PRTOBJILE

Exercise 20 — Creating a Service Program

Now that you have successfully created a multi-module ILE program, try your hand at creating service programs. The DAYSSINCE procedure might be useful in some other programs. To take advantage of this, you will create a service program with that module and create a new program bound to this new service program.

Objectives

At the end of this exercise, you should be able to:

- Create a service program
- Create a multi-module ILE program using bind by copy and bind by reference

Instructions

1. Issue the CRTSRVPGM command on the command line and press F4 for prompting.

   Name the service program MYSRVPGM. Specify the module DAYSSINCE to be included and specify *ALL for the EXPORT parameter. (This indicates that all procedures in the service program can be called by other procedures.)

   Note: Service programs typically have many modules. For simplicity in this exercise, we are using a service program with only 1 module.

2.

   Now that the service program has been created, and assuming you have created the other modules in the previous exercise, you can create a new program that will use the DAYSSINCE procedure.

   Note: The new program will use the procedure from the service program rather than binding it by copy into the base program.

   Issue the CRTPGM command from the command line again and press F4 for prompting.

   a. Name this new program PRTOBJPGM2.

   b. List the CL module and the RPG mainline module in the module parameter (DSPOBJMOD and PRTOBJILE). However, do NOT include DAYSSINCE in the module list.

   c. Press F10 to see additional parameters and find the Bind Service Program parameter.

   d. Specify the name of your newly created service program, MYSRVPGM, there.

3. When the program is created, call the PRTOBJPGM2 program with the parameter of the library name you used in Exercise 15. Your spooled file report should look the same as for the previous exercise.

Stage 12. Exercises — Advanced Functions

Now that you have finished stage 12 of the Tutorial, you should be ready for the stage 12 exercises in this workbook.

This stage of the tutorial covers some of the more advanced features of RPG IV, including:

- Built-in functions: %ADDR, %ELEM, %PADDR, %SIZE, %SUBST, %TRIM, %TRIML, and %TRIMR

- Pointers for basing storage inside or outside a program

- Keywords EXPORT and IMPORT to enable sharing of data between modules

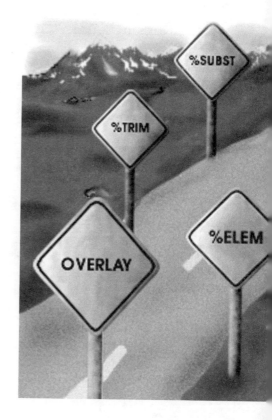

Built-In Functions

Built-in functions (BIFs) are similar to opcodes in that they perform operations on data you specify. However, unlike opcodes, BIFs return a value rather than place a value in a field. The syntax of BIFs is:

```
function-name(argument{:argument...})
```

Arguments for BIFs may be variables, constants, expressions, or other BIFs. An expression argument can include a BIF.

BIFs can be used in expressions on the extended-Factor-2 C spec and with keywords on the D spec. When used with D spec keywords, the value of the BIF must be known at compile time and the argument cannot have an expression.

The following table lists the built-in functions, their arguments, and the value they return.

Table 36 (Page 1 of 2). RPG IV Built-In Functions Summary

Built-in Function Name	Argument(s)	Value Returned
%ABS	Numeric expression	Absolute value of expression
%ADDR	Variable name	Address of variable
%CHAR	Graphic, date, time, or timestamp expression	Value in character data type
%DEC	Numeric expression {:digits:decpos}	Value in packed numeric format
%DECH	Numeric expression :digits:decpos	Half-adjusted value in packed numeric format
%DECPOS	Numeric expression	Number of decimal digits
%EDITC	Nonfloat numeric expression:edit code {:*CURSYM I *ASTFILL I currency symbol}	String representing edited value
%EDITFLT	Numeric expression	Character external display representation of float
%EDITW	Nonfloat numeric expression:edit word	String representing edited value
%ELEM	Array, table, or multiple-occurrence data structure name	Number of elements or occurrences
%EOF	{file name}	'1' if the most recent file input operation or write to a subfile (for a particular file, if specified) ended in an end-of-file or beginning-of-file condition
		'0' otherwise
%EQUAL	{file name}	'1' if the most recent SETLL (for a particular file, if specified) or LOOKUP operation found an exact match
		'0' otherwise
%ERROR		'1' if the most recent operation code with extender 'E' specified resulted in an error
		'0' otherwise
%FLOAT	Numeric expression	Value in float format
%FOUND	{file name}	'1' if the most recent relevant operation (for a particular file, if specified) found a record (CHAIN, DELETE, SETGT, SETLL), an element (LOOKUP), or a match (CHECK, CHECKR, SCAN)
		'0' otherwise
%INT	Numeric expression	Value in integer format
%INTH	Numeric expression	Half-adjusted value in integer format
%LEN	Any expression	Length in digits or characters

Table 36 (Page 2 of 2). RPG IV Built-In Functions Summary

Built-in Function Name	Argument(s)	Value Returned
%NULLIND	Null-capable field name	Value in indicator format representing the null indicator setting for the null-capable field
%OPEN	File name	'1' if the specified file is open
		'0' if the specified file is closed
%PADDR	Procedure name	Address of procedure
%PARMS	None	Number of parameters passed to procedure
%REPLACE	Replacement string: source string{:start position {:source length to replace}}	String produced by inserting replacement string into source string, starting at start position and replacing the specified number of characters
%SCAN	Search argument:string to be searched{:start position}	First position of search argument in string, or zero if not found
%SIZE	Variable, array, or literal {:* ALL}	Size of variable or literal
%STATUS	{file name}	0 if no program or file error occurred for the most recent operation code with extender 'E' specified
		Most recent value set for program or file status, if an error occurred
		If a file is specified, the value returned is the most recent status for that file
%STR	pointer{:maximum length}	Characters addressed by pointer argument up to but not including the first x'00'
%SUBST	string:start{:length}	Substring
%TRIM	String	String with left and right blanks trimmed
%TRIML	String	String with left blanks trimmed
%TRIMR	String	String with right blanks trimmed
%UNS	Numeric expression	Value in unsigned format
%UNSH	Numeric expression	Half-adjusted value in unsigned format

For more information on specific BIFs, see "New Built-In Functions" on page 189.

Exercise 21 — Coding BIFs

In this desk exercise, you are asked to answer a question that is based on a coding sample. Each code sample uses a built-in function, and the third question also includes a based field.

Objective

After answering these questions, you should be able to code built-in functions on RPG IV programs.

Questions

1. What will the value of X be following the EVAL?

```
D Question        S             25     INZ('Are BIFs Great?')
D Answer          S             15
D AnArray         S              5     DIM(5)
D X               S              3P 0
C                 EVAL       Answer = %Trim(%Subst(Question:4))
C           ' '   CHECKR     Answer        X
C                 EVAL       X = X + %Elem(AnArray)
C                              + %Size(AnArray:*ALL)
C                 SETON                                    LR
```

Figure 29. Sample Code for Question 1

X =

2. Given the same D specs from the previous question, code an EVAL string expression that would place the following value in the Answer field:

'BIFs Are Great!'

To accomplish this, use only built-in functions against the Question field.

```
D Question        S             25     INZ('Are BIFs Great?')
D Answer          S             15
D AnArray         S              5     DIM(5)
D X               S              3P 0
C                 EVAL
C
```

Figure 30. D Specs for Question 2

3. Given the following code, what will be the value of Result?

```
D Field1         S              4    INZ('ABCD')
D Field2         S             10    BASED(Pointer1)
D Result         S              3
C                EVAL      Pointer1 = %ADDR(Field1)
C                IF        Field1 = Field2
C                EVAL      Result = 'Yes'
C                ELSE
C                EVAL      Result = 'No'
C                ENDIF
C                RETURN
```

Figure 31. Sample Code for Question 3

Result =

4. Rewrite the code from Exercise 10 (Stage 6) to change the CONST keyword on the D spec for PAR# so that it uses the BIF %ELEM.

Exercise 22 — Using a Based Variable

In this exercise, you will have an opportunity to code a program that uses based variables to access data from a user space outside your program. Most of the source code for this program is provided for you. You need to supply the details surrounding defining and using the based variables.

This exercise involves the following objects:

FILLSPACE
> a program that puts data into a user space using two arrays based on pointers to the two user spaces.

PRODDISP
> a display file used by the program you'll create.

PRODINQ a program you will create which uses the data loaded by FILLSPACE. This program takes as input a product number entered on the screen and then displays the corresponding product description.

PRODFILE
> a physical file with data. It is supplied for you in the library WKBKLIB.

For more information on user spaces and the system APIs that apply to them, see the *System API Programming* manual.

Objectives

At the end of this exercise, you should be able to code and use based variables to make use of user spaces outside your RPG IV program.

Instructions

1. First, you must compile and run the program that will create and fill the user spaces. The program is written to create the user spaces in your current library, so be sure your work library name is the current library for your job. (Use CHGCURLIB if it is not.)

   Find the FILLSPACE source member. Copy it into your source file and compile it into your library using PDM option 14 or CRTBNDRPG (with defaults).

2. When FILLSPACE has successfully compiled, call it. You will not see any immediate evidence that the program was successful. However, you can look at the objects in your library and see if 2 user spaces were created.

3. Now find the source member for the display file, PRODDISP. Copy this member into your source file and compile the display into your library using PDM option 14 or CRTDSPF with the defaults. This display file will be used by the RPG program you will create.

4. Next find and copy the source for PRODINQ, the product inquiry program. This program will simply take as input from the screen a product number and display the product description. The product code and description will be retrieved from the data spaces created in the previous step.

5. In the PRODINQ source, you are responsible for ensuring that the variables that should be based on pointers are, that any pointers that are needed are defined, and that the pointers get the addresses to the data spaces properly. The code for this program is almost complete. You need only to properly code the pointers portions of the program. To help you, some question marks (???????) have been placed in some of the locations of the code where you will need to provide some code.

HINT: Use the FILLSPACE code as an example. Note the two parameters that need to be passed to the QUSPTRUS program to get the address of the user spaces.

6. Compile the changed source using PDM option 14 or CRTBNDRPG.

7. Call the PRODINQ program. Input product codes and see if the proper description appears. The following are the product codes and descriptions that were in the product file:

```
Code    Description
----    -----------
11111   Pencils (box)
22222   Pens
33333   Binders - Blue
44444   Binders - Red
55555   Foil Markers
```

If you key a product code other than those above, you should get an invalid product code response.

```
      *=================================================================
      * This program loads the product codes and the corresponding
      * product descriptions into separate user spaces
      *=================================================================

      * The file is keyed so the space gets filled with the product codes
      * in ascending order.  This ensures that the LOOKUP in the inquiry
      * program will not attempt to access the space beyond its bounds.
     FProdFile  IF   E           K DISK
     D ProdCode       S                   DIM(32767) BASED(ProdPtr)
     D                                    LIKE(PRDCOD)
     D ProdDesc       S                   DIM(32767) BASED(DescPtr)
     D                                    LIKE(PRDDSC)
      *
      * The following definitions of ProdPtr and DescPtr are optional.
      * If they were not coded, the compiler would generate them
      * because they are based fields.
      *
     D ProdPtr        S               *
     D DescPtr        S               *
      *
      * The following fields (Spacexxx) are fields that must be
      * passed to the system API that creates the user space.
      *
     D SpaceQName     DS
     D   SpaceName                   10
     D   SpaceLib                    10    INZ('*CURLIB')
     D SpaceAttr      S              10    INZ('DTA')
     D SpaceSize      S               5B 0 INZ(1024)
     D SpaceInit      S               1    INZ(X'00')
     D SpaceAuth      S              10    INZ('*ALL')
     D SpaceText      S              50    INZ('Product Data')

     D Ctr            S               3  0 INZ(1)
```

Figure 32 (Part 1 of 2). Source Code for RPG Program FILLSPACE

```
         * Now create the user spaces.
C     CrtPlist     PLIST
C                  PARM                    SpaceQname
C                  PARM                    SpaceAttr
C                  PARM                    SpaceSize
C                  PARM                    SpaceInit
C                  PARM                    SpaceAuth
C                  PARM                    SpaceText
         * Create User Space with System API QUSCRTUS with parms
C                  EVAL      SpaceName = 'PRODCODE'
C                  CALL      'QUSCRTUS'    CrtPlist
         * Now obtain a pointer (SpacePtr) to the newly created space
C                  CALL      'QUSPTRUS'
C                  PARM                    SpaceQname
C                  PARM                    ProdPtr

         * Create User Space with System API QUSCRTUS with parms
C                  EVAL      Spacename = 'PRODDESC'
C                  CALL      'QUSCRTUS'    CrtPlist
         * Now obtain a pointer (SpacePtr) to the newly created space
C                  CALL      'QUSPTRUS'
C                  PARM                    SpaceQname
C                  PARM                    DescPtr

         * It's now safe to reference fields in the space.
         * Loop through space moving product prices from record to space
         *    (PRDCOD and PRDDSC are field names from ProdFile)
         *
         * Note that the arrays are treated as if they are part of the
         * program, although the storage is actually outside of the
         * program in user spaces.
         *
         * Note the use of the %ELEM built-in function to control the
         * DOW loop.  This enhances maintainability.
         *
C                  DOW       (Ctr <= %elem(ProdCode)) AND
C                            (NOT *IN99)
C                  READ      PRODFILE                              99
C                  IF        NOT *IN99
C                  EVAL      ProdCode(Ctr) = PRDCOD
C                  EVAL      ProdDesc(Ctr) = PRDDSC
C                  EVAL      Ctr = Ctr + 1
C                  ENDIF
C                  ENDDO
C                  EVAL      ProdCode(Ctr) = *HiVal

C                  SETON                                 LR
```

Figure 32 (Part 2 of 2). Source Code for RPG Program FILLSPACE

```
     *
     * This program uses a lookup routine which locates the product code
     * and corresponding description from the user spaces without the
     * overhead of opening the product file and doing database I/O.
     *
FPRODDSP   CF   E              WORKSTN
D ProdCode      S              5      DIM(32767) ?????????????
D                                     ASCEND
D ProdDesc      S                     DIM(32767) ?????????????
D                                     LIKE(DESC)

D ProdSpcNam    DS
D   ProdName                  10      INZ('PRODCODE')
D   ProdLib                   10      INZ('*CURLIB')
D DescSpcNam    DS
D   DescName                  10      INZ('PRODDESC')
D   DescLib                   10      INZ('*CURLIB')
D Indx          S              5  0   INZ(1)
D Error         C                     'Invalid Product Code'

C* Obtain a pointer (ProdPtr) to the Product Code space
C               CALL      'QUSPTRUS'
C               PARM                   ProdSpcNam
C               PARM                   ??????????

C* Obtain a pointer (DescPtr) to the Product Description space
C               CALL      'QUSPTRUS'
C               PARM                   DescSpcNam
C               PARM                   ??????????
```

Figure 33 (Part 1 of 2). Source Code for RPG Program PRODINQ

```
C* Now Search ProdCode array for a product code and
C* display either the product's description (if found) or
C* "Invalid Product Code" if not found

C               DOW       NOT *IN03
C               EXFMT     ProdFmt
 * Exit loop if the user has pressed PF3
C               IF        *IN03
C               LEAVE
C               ENDIF

C               EVAL      Indx = 1
C     Prod      LookUp    ProdCode(Indx)                  12  10
C               IF        *IN10
C               EVAL      Desc = ProdDesc(Indx)
C               ELSE
C               EVAL      Desc = Error
C               ENDIF

C               ENDDO
C               SETON                                     LR
```

Figure 33 (Part 2 of 2). Source Code for RPG Program PRODINQ

```
A                               DSPSIZ(24 80 *DS3)
A          R PRODFMT
A                               CA03(03 'F3 = Exit')
A                             4 27'Product Description Inquiry'
A                               DSPATR(HI)
A                               DSPATR(UL)
A                               COLOR(WHT)
A                             8 27'Enter Product Code:'
A          PROD      R     B  8 48REFFLD(PRODREC/PRDCOD PRODFILE)
A   10
AO  12                       11 31'PRODUCT DESCRIPTION'
A                               DSPATR(HI)
A   10
AO  12     DESC      R     O 13 31REFFLD(PRODREC/PRDDSC PRODFILE)
A   12                          DSPATR(RI)
A                            23 29'Press PF3 to end Inquiry'
```

Figure 34. Source Code for Display File PRODDSP

Stage 13. Exercises — ILE Source Debugger

Now that you have finished Stage 13 of the Tutorial, you should be ready for the Stage 13 exercises in this workbook.

You debug ILE programs using the ILE source debugger. With the source debugger you can:

- Debug while viewing the actual source (if available)
- Add/remove breakpoints
- Step over or into programs and procedures
- Display the values of fields and expressions
- Change the values of fields

Interaction with the debugger occurs through using debug commands or PF keys that correspond to debug commands. The following debug commands are available with the source debugger.

Table 37 (Page 1 of 2). Debug Commands	
Command	**Description**
ATTR	Permits you to display the attributes of a variable. The attributes are the size and type of the variable as recorded in the debug symbol table on the system.
BREAK	Permits you to enter either an unconditional or conditional job breakpoint at a position in the program being tested. Use BREAK *line-number* WHEN *expression* to enter a conditional job breakpoint.
CLEAR	Permits you to remove conditional and unconditional breakpoints, or to remove one or all active watch conditions.
DISPLAY	Allows you to display the names and definitions assigned by using the EQUATE command. It also allows you to display a different source module than the one currently shown on the Display Module Source display. The module object must exist in the current program object.
EQUATE	Allows you to assign an expression, variable, or debug command to a name for shorthand use.
EVAL	Allows you to display or change the value of a variable or to display the value of expressions, records, structures, or arrays.
QUAL	Allows you to define the scope of variables that appear in subsequent EVAL or WATCH commands. Currently, it does not apply to ILE RPG.

Table 37 (Page 2 of 2). Debug Commands

Command	Description
SET	Allows you to change debug options, such as the ability to update production files, specify if find operations are to be case sensitive, or to enable OPM source debug support.
STEP	Allows you to run one or more statements of the program being debugged.
TBREAK	Permits you to enter either an unconditional or conditional breakpoint in the current thread at a position in the program being tested. Currently, it does not apply to ILE RPG.
THREAD	Allows you to display the Work with Debugged Threads display or change the current thread. Currently, it does not apply to ILE RPG.
WATCH	Allows you to request a breakpoint when the contents of a specified storage location is changed from its current value.
FIND	Searches forward or backward in the module currently displayed for a specified line number, string, or text.
UP	Moves the displayed window of source toward the beginning of the view by the amount entered.
DOWN	Moves the displayed window of source toward the end of the view by the amount entered.
LEFT	Moves the displayed window of source to the left by the number of columns entered.
RIGHT	Moves the displayed window of source to the right by the number of columns entered.
TOP	Positions the view to show the first line.
BOTTOM	Positions the view to show the last line.
NEXT	Positions the view to the next breakpoint in the source currently displayed.
PREVIOUS	Positions the view to the previous breakpoint in the source currently displayed.
HELP	Shows the online help information for the available source debugger commands.

Exercise 23 — Debugging a Multi-Module Program

In this exercise, you practice using the ILE source debugger using the source members from Stage 11 (Exercises 19 and 20).

Objectives

At the end of this exercise, you should know how to:

- Start the source debugger
- Change the module source
- Add and remove breakpoints
- Step into a procedure
- Display and change the values of fields

Instructions

Follow the instructions as you practice using the source debugger. Note that while there are many instructions in this exercise, it is not vital that you do all of them. To stop at any time, press F3 to end the program, then enter the ENDDBG command.

1. Enter the following command, where PRTOBJPGM2 is the program object you created for Stage 11, Exercise 20.

   `STRDBG YourLib/PRTOBJPGM2`

   What do you see on the screen? If you created PRTOBJPGM2 using the system-supplied defaults, then you should see the Display Module Source display containing a message that no source is available. This is because the default debug view used with PDM option 14 or 15 DBGVIEW(*STMT).

   Press F3 to leave the Display Module Source display and then enter ENDDBG on a system command line to end the debug session.

2. Recompile the source members DSPOBJMOD, PRTOBJLE, and DAYSSINCE specifying DBGVIEW(*SOURCE) for each compilation. Be sure to use the ones you modified to make use of procedure calls.

3. Recreate the programs PRTOBJPGM2 and MYSRVPGM using the same commands you used in Exercise 20.

4. Enter the following command to start the ILE source debugger.

   `STRDBG YourLib/PRTOBJPGM2 UPDPROD(*YES)`

   The parameter UPDPROD(*YES) is necessary because the module DSPOBJMOD will be writing to the file DSPOBJ when you call it.

   The first display should be a Display Module Source display showing the entry module of PRTOBJPGM2, which is the CL procedure DSPOBJMOD.

5. Set a breakpoint on the line with the procedure call so that you can make use of the step function later.

6. To change to one of the RPG modules, press F14 (Work with module list).

You should see a screen like the one shown below.

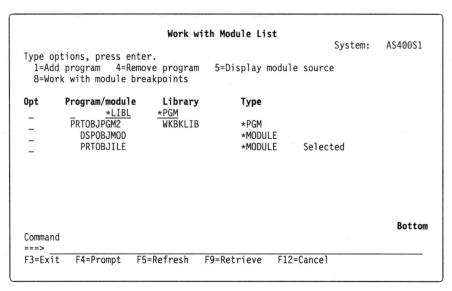

```
                        Work with Module List
                                                  System:   AS400S1
Type options, press enter.
  1=Add program   4=Remove program    5=Display module source
  8=Work with module breakpoints

Opt     Program/module     Library       Type
              *LIBL        *PGM
  _     PRTOBJPGM2         WKBKLIB       *PGM
  _       DSPOBJMOD                      *MODULE
  _       PRTOBJILE                      *MODULE       Selected




                                                              Bottom
Command
===> _____
F3=Exit    F4=Prompt    F5=Refresh    F9=Retrieve    F12=Cancel
```

Figure 35. Changing to a Different Module

As you'll recall, the program PRTOBJPGM2 was created by binding the two
modules DSPOBJMOD and PRTOBJILE to the service program MYSRVPGM.
Note that the service program is not included in the above list. Service programs
can only be added to a debug session after it has been started. (See Exercise 24.)

7. Select PRTOBJILE.

   You should now see a Display Module Source display for the PRTOBJILE procedure.

8. Now set a breakpoint in this procedure so that you can display some fields after
   calling the program. Move your cursor to one of the D specs and press F6.

   You will see that a breakpoint is added to the first C spec, not to the D spec. With
   the exception of the first statement in a program or procedure, breakpoints can
   only be set on an executable statement.

9. Move your cursor to the statement on which the breakpoint is currently set and
   press F6 again to remove the breakpoint. F6 is a toggle. If there is no breakpoint
   on the line in question, then a breakpoint is set; if there is a breakpoint, it is
   removed.

10. Now set a conditional breakpoint on the first MOVE statement such that the
    program will stop running when NoDays is greater than or equal to 0.

11. Press F3 to get a system command line and call the program, specifying the library
    of your choice. (Recall that the debug command line can only accept debug com-
    mands.)

You should see a display of the CL procedure with the line containing the procedure call highlighted.

12. Using F11, display the value of &LIB. The contents of &LIB should be the same as the library name passed on the call command.

13. Now step into PRTOBJILE by pressing F22. *Hint:* If you go past the CALLPRC statement by mistake, end the program by pressing F3, and then call the program from the command line.

    After you have stepped into the called procedure, the display will change to PRTOBJILE with the first line highlighted. (Line 1 is a default breakpoint when stepping into a procedure.)

14. Resume execution by pressing F12. Most likely, you will have the procedure stop again at line 20.

15. Display the values of CvtFld and LSTUSD. It is sometimes more convenient to use the Evaluate Expression display when working with fields. You can obtain this display at any time from a Display Module Source display by pressing Enter. Press Enter again to return to the source when you have finished.

16. Step forward to the CALLB statement and press F22 (Step Into) to step into the called procedure, DAYSSINCE. Because the service program was not added to the debug session previously, you cannot step into the procedure. Instead, the STEP INTO is treated as a STEP OVER, and the processing resumes in the calling procedure with the next executable statement following the procedure call.

17. End the program by pressing F3 and then enter ENDDBG on the system command line.

Exercise 24 — Debugging a Service Program

In this exercise, you practice changing the debug view that is displayed and adding a service program while debugging using the program you created for Exercises 19 and 20.

You will have to create a new debug view for this exercise. Rather than have you recreate the program PRTOBJPGM2 after you recompile the source specifying the new view, you are instructed to use the Update Program (UPDPGM) command. You can use this command to update one or more recompiled modules in a program after any change.

Objectives

At the end of this exercise, you should know how to:

- Create a different debug view
- Update a program
- Change the display to a different debug view
- Add a service program to a debug session

Instructions

This exercise uses the programs, PRTOBJPGM2 and MYSRVPGM, which you created for Exercises 19 and 20.

1. Recompile the module PRTOBJILE so that you will have all debug views possible. (Recall that the default is a statement view.)

2. Using the Update Program (UPDPGM) command, update the program PRTOBJPGM2 with the newly compiled module. For this command, you need only enter the name of the changed module, in this case PRTOBJILE, for the MODULE parameter.

3. Start the debugger specifying PRTOBJPGM2 and the appropriate option to allow the update of production files.

4. Set a breakpoint on the procedure call to PRTOBJILE.

5. Now add the service program MYSRVPGM to this debug session. Go to the Work with Module display and enter '1' to add a new item. Fill in the additional information to specify the service program.

6. Staying with the same display, change to PRTOBJILE.

7. Now change to a different debug view, such as the Listing view. Press F15 (Select view) and select the listing view.

8. Set a breakpoint on the procedure call to DAYSSINCE. (You may have to scroll a few screens.)

9. Call the program, PRTOBJPGM2, specifying the library of your choice.

10. Step into PRTOBJILE.

11. Step into DAYSSINCE. You should now see the source for the procedure DAYSSINCE.

   Note: If the Display Module Source display does not appear for DAYSSINCE, it may be because you used F21 to obtain a system command line rather than F3. Call the program again, making sure you are from the same command line as the one where you entered the STRDBG command.

12. Now for fun, have a look at the program stack. Use the WRKJOB command, specifying *PGMSTK for the OPTION parameter. From the Display Call Stack display you can press F11 to see the activation groups which the programs on the stack are associated with. Because you accepted the CRTPGM default when creating PRTOBJPGM2, the program is running in a new activation group. The number you see for PRTOBJPGM2 is the system-generated name of the new activation group.

13. End the program by pressing F3 and then enter ENDDBG on the system command line.

Experience RPG IV

World Car Rally Winner

Stage 14. Exercises — Finish Line

Stage 14 is a summary of the key differences between the RPG III and RPG IV definitions. Our final exercise tests your ability to incorporate all of these changes into a sample program.

Exercise 25 — Using RPG IV

Now that you have finished Stage 14 of the Tutorial, you should be ready for the Stage 14 exercises in this workbook.

This exercise revisits the source you looked at in Exercise 1, where you were asked to identify major enhancements. In this computer exercise, you are asked to modify and compile the source. The purpose is to reinforce some of the key enhancements of RPG IV.

Objectives

At the end of this exercise, you should be able to modify, compile, and debug an RPG IV program with ease!

Instructions

Follow these instructions as you change the program EMPPAY to:

1. Find the source in WKBKLIB for EMPPAY and copy it into your library.
2. Edit the program to:
   a. Compute overtime pay when the employee works more than 40 hours.
   b. Make sure that the report lists the number of hours for regular pay, overtime pay, and total pay.
   c. Handle overflow for QSYSPRT.
3. Create the program EMPPAY from the source using CRTBNDRPG, specifying DFTACTGRP(*NO) and DBGVIEW(*ALL).
4. Start the source debugger, specifying EMPPAY.
5. Enter STEP 1 on the debug command line and then call the program. (This will cause execution to stop immediately after the call so that you can display whatever variables you want.)
6. Let the program run to completion.
7. End the program and then the debug session.

The output for EMPPAY should resemble the output shown below.

```
                        PAYROLL REGISTER                         30/10/1994
         NUMBER  NAME          RATE  HOURS  REGULAR     OVERTIME     BONUS      TOTAL
         ─────   ─────────    ─────  ─────  ─────────   ─────────   ─────────   ─────
         101     Fred McAlister  7.50  40.0  $  300.00  $     .00  $ 300.00  $   60
         123     John Kline      7.00  35.5  $  248.50  $     .00  $ 275.00  $   52
         153     Peggy Langley   7.00  43.0  $  280.00  $   31.50  $ 550.00  $   86
         157     Melanie Jones   8.00  47.0  $  320.00  $   84.00  $ 430.00  $   83
```

```
     *----------------------------------------------------------------*
     * DESCRIPTION:  This program creates a printed output of employee's pay  *
     *               for the week.                                      *
     *----------------------------------------------------------------*

   H DATEDIT(*DMY/)


     *----------------------------------------------------------------*
     * File Definitions                                               *
     *----------------------------------------------------------------*
   FTRANSACT  IP  E          K DISK
   FEMPMST    IF  E          K DISK
   FQSYSPRT   O   F   80       PRINTER


     *----------------------------------------------------------------*
     * Variable Declarations                                          *
     *----------------------------------------------------------------*
   D Pay          S             8P 2


     *----------------------------------------------------------------*
     * Constant Declarations                                          *
     *----------------------------------------------------------------*
   D Heading1     C               'NUMBER  NAME            RATE   H-
   D                               OURS  BONUS    PAY        '
   D Heading2     C               '  _____   _____   _____  _-
   D                                 ___   _____   _____'


     *----------------------------------------------------------------*
     * For each record in the transaction file (TRANSACT), if the employee  *
     * is found, compute the employees pay and print the details.     *
     *----------------------------------------------------------------*
   C     TRN_NUMBER    CHAIN    EMP_REC                        99
   C                   IF       NOT *IN99
   C                   EVAL (H) Pay = EMP_RATE * TRN_HOURS + TRN_BONUS
   C                   ENDIF
```

Figure 36 (Part 1 of 2). RPG IV Source to Be Modified

```
*-------------------------------------------------------------------*
* Report Layout                                                     *
* -- print the heading lines if 1P is on                            *
* -- if the record is found (indicator 99 is off) print the payroll *
*    details otherwise print an exception record                    *
* -- print 'END OF LISTING' when LR is on                           *
*-------------------------------------------------------------------*
OQSYSPRT   H    1P                  2 3
O                                          35 'PAYROLL REGISTER'
O                      *DATE        Y       60
O          H    1P                  2
O                                          60 Heading1
O          H    1P                  2
O                                          60 Heading2
O          D    N1PN99             2
O                      TRN_NUMBER           5
O                      EMP_NAME            24
O                      EMP_RATE      L      33
O                      TRN_HOURS     L      40
O                      TRN_BONUS     L      49
O                      Pay                  60 '$     0. '
O          D    N1P 99             2
O                      TRN_NUMBER           5
O                                          35 '** NOT ON EMPLOYEE FILE **'
O          T    LR
O                                          33 'END OF LISTING'
```

Figure 36 (Part 2 of 2). RPG IV Source to Be Modified

```
A           R EMP_REC
A             EMP_NUMBER     5              TEXT('EMPLOYEE NUMBER')
A             EMP_NAME      16              TEXT('EXPLOYEE NAME')
A             EMP_RATE       5 2            TEXT('EXPLOYEE RATE')
A           K EMP_NUMBER
```

Figure 37. DDS for EMPMST

```
A           R TRN_REC
A             TRN_NUMBER     5              TEXT('EMPLOYEE NUMBER')
A             TRN_HOURS      4 1            TEXT('HOURS WORKED')
A             TRN_BONUS      6 2            TEXT('BONUS')
```

Figure 38. DDS for TRANSACT

This part summarizes the new features of ILE RPG/400 programming. It contains supplementary information on:

- How to move to RPG IV using the Conversion Aid

- How RPG IV differs in its behavior from RPG III

- The programming environment in which RPG IV operates

- How to create programs in the ILE environment

- New RPG IV opcodes and built-in functions

The first four sections are based on corresponding sections in the *ILE RPG for AS/400 Programming Guide*. The last one is based on information in the *ILE RPG for AS/400 Reference* .

Stage 15. Using the RPG III to RPG IV Conversion Aid

The RPG IV source specification layouts differ significantly from the System/38 environment RPG III and the OPM RPG/400 layouts. For example, the positions of entries on the specifications have changed and the types of specifications available have also changed. The RPG IV specification layouts are not compatible with the previous layouts. To take advantage of RPG IV features, you must convert RPG III and RPG/400 source members in your applications to the RPG IV source format.

Note: The valid types of source members you can convert are RPG, RPT, RPG38, RPT38, SQLRPG, and blank. The Conversion Aid does not support conversion of RPG36, RPT36, and other non-RPG source member types.

If you are in a hurry and want to get started, go to "Converting Your Source" on page 116 and follow the general directions.

Conversion Overview

You convert source programs to the RPG IV source format by calling the Conversion Aid through the CL command Convert RPG Source (CVTRPGSRC). The Conversion Aid converts:

- A single member
- All members in a source physical file
- All members with a common member-name prefix in the same file

To minimize the likelihood of conversion problems, you can optionally have the /COPY members included in the converted source code. For convenience in reading the code, you can also optionally include specification templates in the converted source code.

The Conversion Aid converts each source member on a line-by-line basis. After each member conversion, it updates a log file on the status of the conversion if you specified a log file on the command. You can also obtain a conversion report that includes information such as conversion errors, /COPY statements, CALL operations, and conversion status.

The Conversion Aid assumes that your source code is free of any compilation errors. If this is the case, then it will successfully convert most of your source code. In some cases, there may be a small amount of code that you may have to convert manually. Some of these cases are identified by the Conversion Aid. Others are not detected until you attempt to compile the converted source. To see which ones the Conversion Aid can identify, you can run the Conversion Aid using the unconverted member as input, and specify a conversion report but no output member. For information on the types of coding that cannot be converted, see "Resolving Conversion Problems" on page 129.

Conversion Aid Tool Requirements

To use the Conversion Aid, you need the following authority:

- *USE authority for the CVTRPGSRC command
- *USE authority to the library that contains the source file and source members
- *CHANGE authority to the new library that will contain the source file and converted source members
- Object management, operational, and add authority to the log file used by the Conversion Aid

In addition to object-authority requirements, there may be additional storage requirements. Each converted source program is, on average, about 25 percent larger than the size of the program before conversion. To use the Conversion Aid, you need sufficient storage to store the converted source files.

What the Conversion Aid Won't Do

- The Conversion Aid does not support conversion from the RPG IV format back to the RPG III or RPG/400 format.
- The RPG IV compiler does not support automatic conversion of RPG III or RPG/400 source members to the RPG IV source format *at compile time*.
- The Conversion Aid does not support converting RPG II source programs to the RPG IV source format.
- The Conversion Aid does not re-engineer source code, except where required (for example, the number of conditioning indicators).
- The Conversion Aid does not create files. The log file and the output file must exist prior to running the Conversion Aid.

Converting Your Source

This section explains how to convert source programs to the RPG IV format. It discusses the command CVTRPGSRC, which starts the Conversion Aid, and how to use it.

To convert your source code to the RPG IV format, follow these general steps:

1. If you use a data area as a control specification, you must create a new data area in the RPG IV format. Refer to the chapter on control specifications in *ILE RPG for AS/400 Reference* for more information.

2. Create a log file, if necessary.

   Unless you specify LOGFILE(*NONE), there must be a log file for the Conversion Aid to access. If you do not have one, then you can create one by using the CRTDUPOBJ command. For more information, see "Using the Log File" on page 129.

3. Create the file for the converted source members.

The Conversion Aid will not create any files. You must create the output file for the converted source prior to running the CVTRPGSRC command. The recommended name and record length for the output file is QRPGLESRC and 112 characters, respectively.

4. Convert your source using the CVTRPGSRC command.

   You need to enter the name of the file and member to be converted. If you accept the defaults, you will get a converted member in the file QRPGLESRC. The name of the member will correspond to the name of the unconverted source member. /COPY members will not be expanded in the converted source member, unless it is of type RPT or RPT38. A conversion report will be generated.

   See "The CVTRPGSRC Command" for more information.

5. Check the log file or the error report for any errors. For more information, see "Analyzing Your Conversion" on page 126.

6. If there are errors, correct them and go to step 4.

7. If there are no errors, create your program. For information on how to create ILE RPG programs, see "Creating a Program Using CRTBNDRPG" on page 147.

8. If your converted source member still has compilation problems, these are most likely caused because your primary source member contains /COPY compiler directives. You have two choices to correct this situation:

   a. Reconvert your source member specifying EXPCPY(*YES) to expand copy members into your converted source member.

   b. Manually correct any remaining errors using the compiler listing as a guide.

   Refer to "Resolving Conversion Problems" on page 129 for further information.

9. After your converted source member has compiled successfully, retest the program before putting it back into production.

The CVTRPGSRC Command

To convert your RPG III or RPG/400 source to the new RPG IV format, you use the CVTRPGSRC command to start the Conversion Aid. Table 38 shows the parameters of the command based on their function.

Table 38 (Page 1 of 2). CVTRPGSRC Parameters and Their Default Values Grouped by Function	
Program Identification	
FROMFILE	Identifies library and file name of RPG source to be converted
FROMMBR	Identifies which source members are to be converted
TOFILE(*LIBL/QRPGLESRC)	Identifies library and file name of converted output
TOMBR(*FROMMBR)	Identifies file member names of converted source
Conversion Processing	
TOMBR	If *NONE is specified, then no file members are saved

Table 38 (Page 2 of 2). CVTRPGSRC Parameters and Their Default Values Grouped by Function	
EXPCPY(*NO)	Determines if /COPY statements are included in converted output
INSRTPL(*NO)	Indicates if specification templates are to be included in converted output
Conversion Feedback	
CVTRPT(*YES)	Determines whether to produce conversion report
SECLVL(*NO)	Determines whether to include second-level message text
LOGFILE(*LIBL/QRNCVTLG)	Identifies log file for audit report
LOGMBR(*FIRST)	Identifies which member of the log file to use for audit report

The syntax for the CVTRPGSRC command is shown below.

Job: B,I Pgm: B,I REXX: B,I Exec

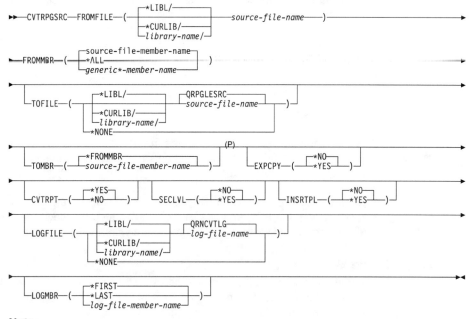

Note:
P All parameters preceding this point can be specified by position.

If you need prompting, type CVTRPGSRC and press F4. The CVTRPGSRC screen appears, lists the parameters, and supplies default values. For a description of a parameter on the display, place your cursor on the parameter and press F1. Extended help for all of the parameters is available by pressing F1 on any parameter and then pressing F2.

Converting a Member Using the Defaults

You can take advantage of the default values supplied on the CVTRPGSRC command. Simply enter:

```
CVTRPGSRC FROMFILE(file name) FROMMBR(member name)
```

This will result in the conversion of the specified source member. The output will be placed in the file QRPGLESRC in whichever library in the library list contains this file. The /COPY members will not be expanded, no specification templates will be inserted, and the conversion report will be produced. The log file QRNCVTLG will be updated.

Note: The files QRPGLESRC and QRNCVTLG must already exist.

Converting All Members in a File

You can convert all of the members in a source physical file by specifying FROMMBR(*ALL) and TOMBR(*FROMMBR) on the CVTRPGSRC command. The Conversion Aid will attempt to convert all members in the file specified. If one member fails to convert, the conversion process will still continue.

For example, if you want to convert all source members in the file QRPGSRC to the file QRPGLESRC, you would enter:

```
CVTRPGSRC  FROMFILE(OLDRPG/QRPGSRC)
           FROMMBR(*ALL)
           TOFILE(NEWRPG/QRPGLESRC)
           TOMBR(*FROMMBR)
```

This command converts all of the source members in library OLDRPG in the source physical file QRPGSRC. The new members are created in library NEWRPG in the source physical file QRPGLESRC.

If you prefer to keep all source (DDS source, RPG source, etc.) in the same file, you can still convert the RPG source members in one step by specifying FROMMBR(*ALL). The Conversion Aid will only convert members with a valid RPG type.

Converting Some Members in a File

If you need to convert only some members that are in a source physical file and these members share a common prefix in the member name, then you can convert them by specifying the prefix followed by an * (asterisk).

For example, if you want to convert all members with a prefix of PAY, you would enter:

```
CVTRPGSRC  FROMFILE(OLDRPG/QRPGSRC)
           FROMMBR(PAY*)
           TOFILE(NEWRPG/QRPGLESRC)
           TOMBR(*FROMMBR)
```

This command converts all of the source members in library OLDRPG in the source physical file QRPGSRC. The new members are created in library NEWRPG in the source physical file QRPGLESRC.

Performing a Trial Conversion

You can do a trial run for any source member that you suspect you may have problems converting. You will then get a conversion report for the converted source member that may identify certain conversion errors.

For example, to perform a trial conversion on the source member PAYROLL, type:

```
CVTRPGSRC  FROMFILE(OLDRPG/QRPGSRC)
           FROMMBR(PAYROLL)
           TOFILE(*NONE)
```

The TOMBR parameter should be specified as *FROMMBR. However, because this is the default, you do not need to specify it unless the default value has been changed.

The CVTRPT parameter should be specified as *YES — this is also the default. If it is not, then the conversion will stop immediately.

Using the TOFILE(*NONE) parameter stops the Conversion Aid from generating a converted member, but still allows it to produce a conversion report. For more information on the conversion report, see "Analyzing Your Conversion" on page 126.

Obtaining Conversion Reports

The Conversion Aid normally produces a conversion report each time you issue the command. The name of the spooled file corresponds to the file name specified in the TOFILE parameter. If you try to convert a member that already exists or has an unsupported member type, then a message is printed in the job log indicating that these members have not been converted. The log file, if requested, is also updated to reflect that no conversion has occurred. However, no information regarding these members is placed in the report.

The conversion report includes the following information:

- CVTRPGSRC command options
- Source section that includes:
    - conversion errors or warnings
    - CALL operations
    - /COPY directives
- Message summary
- Final summary

The conversion error messages provide you with suggestions on how to correct the error. In addition, any CALL operations and /COPY directives in the unconverted source are flagged to help you in identifying the various parts of the application you are converting. In general, you should convert all RPG components of an application at the same time.

If you do not want a conversion report, then specify CVTRPT(*NO).

Converting Auto Report Source Members

When an auto report source member (type RPT or RPT38) is detected in an RPG III or OPM RPG/400 source program, the Conversion Aid calls the CRTRPTPGM command to expand the source member and then converts it. (This is because auto report is not supported by ILE RPG.)

The auto report program produces a spooled file each time it is called by the Conversion Aid. You may want to check this file to see if any errors occurred on the auto report expansion, because these errors will not be in the conversion report.

In particular, you may want to check the auto report spooled file for an error message indicating that /COPY members were not found. The Conversion Aid will not know if these files are missing. However, without these files, it may not be able to successfully convert your source.

Note: If the source member type of the member to be converted is not RPT or RPT38 and the member *is* an auto report source member, you should assign the correct source member type (RPT or RPT38) to the member before converting it; otherwise, conversion errors may occur.

Converting Source Members with Embedded SQL

When converting code that contains embedded SQL and the SQL code is continued over multiple lines, the following will occur:

- If there are continuation lines but column 74 is blank, the line is simply copied to the ILE member.

  Note: This could be a problem if column 74 happens to be a blank character inside a character string.

- If column 74 is not blank, all of the SQL code from that line to the /END-EXEC will be concatenated and copied to the ILE member filling up all 80 columns. If this occurs:

  - Any comments in column 75 on will be ignored.

  - Any embedded comment lines (C*) will be copied to the ILE member before the concatenated code is copied.

  - Problems could arise if DBCS literals are split.

  If you do not want this concatenation and reformatting to occur, ensure that column 74 is blank.

Inserting Specification Templates

Because the source specifications for RPG IV are new, you may want to have specification templates inserted into the converted source. To have templates inserted, specify INSRTPL(*YES) on the CVTRPGSRC command. The default is INSRTPL(*NO).

Converting Source from a Data File

The Conversion Aid will convert source from a data file. Because data files generally do not have sequence numbers, the minimum record length of the file for placing the converted output is 80 characters. The recommended record length is 100 characters for a data file.

Note: If your data file has sequence numbers, you should remove them prior to running the Conversion Aid.

Example of Source Conversion

The example shows a sample RPG III source member that is to be converted to RPG IV. Figure 39 on page 123 shows the source of the RPG III version.

```
H                                               TSTPGM
FFILE1   IF  E                  DISK            COMM1
FQSYSPRT O   F     132     OF   LPRINTER
LQSYSPRT  60FL 560L
E                   ARR1    3   3  1               COMM2
E                   ARR2    3   3  1
IFORMAT1
I           OLDNAME                    NAME
I* DATA STRUCTURE COMMENT
IDS1      DS
I                             1   3 FIELD1
I* NAMED CONSTANT COMMENT
I           'XYZ'            C         CONST1     COMM3
I                            4   6 ARR1
C         ARR1,3   DSPLY
C                  READ FORMAT1               01
C         NAME     DSPLY
C                  SETON                 LR
C                  EXCPTOUTPUT
OQSYSPRT E   01        OUTPUT
O                      ARR2,3    10
**
123
**
456
```

Figure 39. RPG III Source for TEST1

To convert this source, enter:

```
CVTRPGSRC  FROMFILE(MYLIB/QRPGSRC) FROMMBR(TEST1)
           TOFILE(MYLIB/QRPGLESRC) INSRTPL(*YES)
```

The converted source is shown in Figure 40 on page 124.

```
1  .....H*unctions+++++++++++++++++++++++++++++++++++++++++++++++++++++++++++++++Comments+++++++++
2     H DFTNAME(TSTPGM)
3  .....F*ilename++IPEASFRlen+LKlen+AIDevice+.Functions+++++++++++++++++++++++++++Comments+++++++++
4     FFILE1     IF   E                  DISK                                        COMM1
5     FQSYSPRT   O    F  132             PRINTER OFLIND(*INOF)
6     F                                          FORMLEN(60)
7     F                                          FORMOFL(56)
8  .....D*ame+++++++++++ETDsFrom+++To/L+++IDc.Functions+++++++++++++++++++++++++++Comments+++++++++
9     D ARR2          S              1   DIM(3) CTDATA PERRCD(3)
10    D* DATA STRUCTURE COMMENT
11    D DS1            DS
12    D  FIELD1               1      3
13    D  ARR1                 4      6
14    D                                  DIM(3) CTDATA PERRCD(3)                    COMM2
15    D* NAMED CONSTANT COMMENT
16    D CONST1         C                  CONST('XYZ')                              COMM3
17 .....I*ilename++SqNORiPos1+NCCPos2+NCCPos3+NCC................................Comments+++++++++
18 .....I*.............Ext_field+Fmt+SPFrom+To+++DcField+++++++++L1M1FrP1MnZr......Comments+++++++++
19    IFORMAT1
20    I              OLDNAME                       NAME
21 .....C*0N01Factor1+++++++Opcode(E)+Factor2+++++++Result++++++++Len++D+HiLoEq....Comments+++++++++
22    C     ARR1(3)      DSPLY
23    C                  READ      FORMAT1                                    01
24    C     NAME         DSPLY
25    C                  SETON                                           LR
26    C                  EXCEPT    OUTPUT
27    OQSYSPRT   E        OUTPUT          01
28    O                   ARR2(3)              10
29 **CTDATA ARR1
30 123
31 **CTDATA ARR2
32 456
```

Figure 40. Converted (RPG IV) Source for TEST1

Note the following about the converted source:

- The new specification types are H (control), F (file), D (definition), I (input), C (calculation), and O (output); they must be entered in this order.

  The converted source contains specification templates for the new types, because INSRTPL(*YES) was specified on CVTRPGSRC.

- The control, file, and definition specifications are keyword oriented. See lines 2, 4-7, and 9-16.

- The Integrated Language Environment member has a new specification type, definition. It is used to define stand-alone fields, arrays, and named constants as well as data structures.

  In this example:

  - ARR2 is defined as a stand-alone array (Line 9)

  - Data structure DS1 is defined as a data structure with two subfields, FIELD1 and ARR1 (Lines 11 - 14)

  - Constant CONST1 is defined as a constant (Line 16)

The input (I) specifications are now used only to define records and fields of a file. See Lines 19 - 20.

- The extension (E) specifications have been eliminated. Arrays and tables are now defined using definition specifications.

- Record address file (RAF) entries on extension specifications have been replaced by the keyword RAFDATA on the File Description specification.

- The line counter specifications have been eliminated. They have been replaced by the keywords FORMLEN and FORMOFL on the file description specification. See Lines 6 and 7.

- All specification types have been expanded to allow for 10-character names for fields and files.

- In RPG IV, data structures (which are defined using definition specifications) must precede the input specifications.

  Note that in the converted source, the data structure DS1 (Line 11) has been moved to precede the specification containing the FORMAT1 information (Line 19).

- In RPG III, named constants can appear in the middle of a data structure. This is not allowed in RPG IV.

  In the converted source, CONST1 (Line 16) has been moved to follow data structure DS1 (Line 11).

- If a specification is moved, any comment that precedes it is also moved.

  In the converted source, the comments above CONST1 and DS1 were moved with the following specifications.

- In RPG III, to define an array as a data structure subfield, you define both the array and a data structure subfield with the same name. This double definition is not allowed in RPG IV. Instead, you specify the array attributes when you define the subfields using the new keyword syntax.

  In this example, ARR1 is defined twice in the OPM version, but has been merged into a single definition in converted source. See Lines 13 and 14.

  The merging of RPG III array specifications may result in the reordering of the array definitions. If the reordered arrays are compile-time arrays, then the loading of array data may be affected. To overcome this problem, RPG IV provides a keyword format for the ** records. Following **, you enter one of the keywords FTRANS, ALTSEQ, or CTDATA. If the keyword is CTDATA, you enter the array or table name in positions 10-19.

  In this example, the array ARR2 now precedes array ARR1 due to the merging of the two RPG III specifications for ARR2. The Conversion Aid has inserted the keywords and array names in the converted ** records, which ensures the correct loading of the compile-time data. See Lines 29 and 31.

- Note that array syntax has changed. The notation ARR1,3 in RPG III is ARR1(3) in RPG IV. See line 28.

Analyzing Your Conversion

The Conversion Aid provides you with two ways to analyze your conversion results. They are:

- The conversion error report
- The log file

Using the Conversion Report

The Conversion Aid generates a conversion report if you specify the CVTRPT(*YES) parameter on the CVTRPGSRC command. The spooled file name is the same as the file name specified on the TOFILE parameter.

The conversion report consists of four parts:

1. CVTRPGSRC command options
2. source section
3. message summary
4. final summary

The first part of the listing includes a summary of the command options used by CVTRPGSRC. Figure 41 shows the command summary for a sample conversion.

```
5769RG1 V4R2M0  980228RN        IBM ILE RPG                        AS400S01    12/30/97 20:41:35      Page      1

   Command  . . . . . . . . . . . . :   CVTRPGSRC
     Issued by  . . . . . . . . . . :     DAVE

   From file  . . . . . . . . . . . :   QRPGSRC
     Library  . . . . . . . . . . . :     MYLIB
   From member  . . . . . . . . . . :   REPORT

   To file. . . . . . . . . . . . . :   QRPGLESRC
     Library  . . . . . . . . . . . :     MYLIB
   To member  . . . . . . . . . . . :   *FROMMBR

   Log file . . . . . . . . . . . . :   *NONE
     Library  . . . . . . . . . . . :
   Log member . . . . . . . . . . . :   *FIRST

   Expand copy members. . . . . . . :   *NO
   Print conversion report  . . . . :   *YES
   Include second level text. . . . :   *YES
   Insert specification template. . :   *YES
```

Figure 41. Command Summary of Sample Conversion Report

The source section includes lines that have informational, warning, or error messages associated with them. These lines have an asterisk (*) in column 1 for ease of browsing in SEU. The message summary contains all three message types.

Two informational messages that may be of particular interest are:

- RNM0508 — flags /COPY statements
- RNM0511 — flags CALL operations

All /COPY members in a program must be converted for the corresponding ILE RPG program to compile without errors. Similarly, you may want to convert all members related by CALL at the same time. Use this part of the report to assist you in identifying these members. Figure 42 on page 127 shows the source section for the sample conversion.

```
5769RG1 V4R2M0  980228RN        IBM ILE RPG                        AS400S01   12/30/97 20:41:35    Page     2

   From file . . . . . . . . . . . :   MYLIB/QRPGSRC(REPORT)
   To file. . . . . . . . . . . . :    MYLIB/QRPGLESRC(REPORT)
   Log file . . . . . . . . . . . :    *NONE

                    C o n v e r s i o n    R e p o r t

 Sequence <---------------------- Source Specifications ---------------------------><-------------- Comments --------------> Page
 Number    ....1....+....2....+....3....+....4....+....5....+....6....+....7....+....8....+....9....+...10....+...11....+...12 Line

   000002 C                CALL       PROG1
 *RNM0511 00 CALL operation code found.

   000003 C/COPY COPYCODE
 *RNM0508 00 /COPY compiler directive found.

   000004 C                FREE       PROG2
 *RNM0506 30 FREE operation code is not supported in RPG IV.

      * * * * *  E N D   O F   S O U R C E  * * * * *
```

Figure 42. Sample Source Section of Conversion Report

The message summary of the listing shows you the different messages that were issued. If you specify SECLVL(*YES), second-level messages will appear in the message summary. Figure 43 on page 128 shows the messages section for the sample conversion, including second-level messages.

```
5769RG1 V4R2M0  980228RN       IBM ILE RPG                    AS400S01   12/30/97 20:41:35    Page    2
                    M e s s a g e   S u m m a r y

  Msg id  Sv Number Message text

 *RNM0508 00     1 /COPY compiler directive found.
                   Cause . . . . . :   In order for this RPG IV source to
                     compile correctly, ensure that all /COPY source members
                     included in this source member have also been converted to
                     RPG IV.
                   Recovery  . . . :   Ensure that all /COPY source
                     members are converted prior to compiling in RPG IV. In some
                     cases, problems may result when attempting to convert and
                     compile source members that make use of the /COPY compiler
                     directive.  If this situation results, specify *YES for the
                     EXPCPY parameter on the CVTRPGSRC command to expand the
                     /COPY member(s) into the converted source.  For further
                     information see the ILE RPG for AS/400 Programmers Guide.

 *RNM0511 00     1 CALL operation code found.
                   Cause . . . . . :   RPG specifications that contain CALL
                     operation codes have been identified because the user may
                     wish to:
                       -- change the CALL operation code to CALLB to take
                     advantage of static binding
                       -- convert all programs in an application to RPG IV.
                   Recovery  . . . :   Convert the CALL
                     operation code to a CALLB if you wish to take advantage of
                     static binding or convert the called program to RPG IV if
                     you wish to convert all programs in an application.

 *RNM0506 30     1 FREE operation code is not supported in RPG IV.
                   Cause . . . . . :   The RPG III or RPG/400 program contains
                     the FREE operation code which is not supported in RPG IV.
                   Recovery  . . . :   Remove the FREE operation and replace
                     it with alternative code so that the programming logic is
                     not affected prior to compiling the converted source.

        * * * * *   E N D   O F   M E S S A G E   S U M M A R Y   * * * * *
```

Figure 43. Sample Message Summary of Conversion Report

The final summary of the listing provides message and record statistics. A final status message is also placed in the job log. Figure 44 shows the messages section for the sample conversion.

```
                   F i n a l   S u m m a r y
  Message Totals:
    Information  (00) . . . . . . . :      2
    Warning      (10) . . . . . . . :      0
    Severe Error (30+) . . . . . . :      1
  -------------------------------- -------
    Total . . . . . . . . . . . . :      3

  Source Totals:
    Original Records Read . . . . . . :      3
    Converted Records Written . . . . :      4
    Highest Severity Message Issued . :     30

        * * * * *   E N D   O F   F I N A L   S U M M A R Y   * * * * *

        * * * * *   E N D   O F   C O N V E R S I O N   * * * * *
```

Figure 44. Sample Final Summary of Conversion Report

Using the Log File

By browsing the log file, you can see the results of your conversions. The log file is updated after each conversion operation. It tracks:

- Source members and their library names
- Converted source file names and their library names
- Highest severity error found

For example, if no errors are found, the conversion status is set to 0. If severe errors are found, the status is set to 30.

If you try to convert a member with an unsupported member type or a member that already exists, then the conversion will not take place as this is a severe error (severity 40 or higher). A record will be added to the log file with the conversion status set to 40. The TOFILE, TOMBR, and TO LIBRARY will be set to blank to indicate that a TOMBR was not generated (as the conversion did not take place).

The log file is an externally described, physical database file. A model of this file is provided in library QRPGLE in file QARNCVTLG. It has one record format called QRNCVTLG. All field names are six characters in length and follow the naming convention LGxxxx, where xxxx describes the fields.

Use the following CRTDUPOBJ command to create a copy of this model in your own library, referred to here as MYLIB. You may want to name your log file QRNCVTLG, as this is the default log file name for the Conversion Aid.

```
CPYF FROMFILE(QRPGLE/QARNCVTLG) TOFILE(MYLIB/QRNCVTLG)
     CRTFILE(*YES)
```

Resolving Conversion Problems

Conversion problems may arise for one or more of the following reasons:

- The RPG III source has compilation errors
- Certain features of the RPG III language are not supported by RPG IV
- One or more /COPY compiler directives exist in the RPG III source
- Use of externally described data structures
- Behavioral differences between the OPM and ILE run time

Each of these areas is discussed in the sections that follow.

Compilation Errors in Existing RPG III Code

The Conversion Aid assumes that you are attempting to convert a valid RPG III program, that is, a program with no compilation errors. If this is not the case, then unpredictable results may occur during conversion. If you believe your program contains compilation errors, compile it first using the RPG III compiler and correct any errors before performing the conversion.

Unsupported RPG III Features

A few features of the RPG III language are *not* supported in RPG IV. The most notable of these are:

- The auto report function
- The FREE operation code
- The DEBUG operation code

Because the auto report function is not supported, the Conversion Aid will automatically expand these programs (that is, call auto report) prior to performing the conversion if the type is RPT or RPT38.

You must replace the FREE or DEBUG operation code with equivalent logic either before or after conversion.

If you specify the CVTRPT(*YES) option on the CVTRPGSRC command, you will receive a conversion report that identifies most of these types of problems.

For further information on converting auto report members, see "Converting Auto Report Source Members" on page 121. For further information on differences between RPG III and RPG IV, see Stage 16, "Behavioral Differences Between OPM RPG/400 and ILE RPG for AS/400" on page 137.

Use of the /COPY Compiler Directive

In some cases, errors will not be found until you actually compile the converted RPG IV source. Conversion errors of this type are usually related to the use of the /COPY compiler directive. These errors fall into two categories: merging problems and context-sensitive problems. Following is a discussion of why these problems occur and how you might resolve them.

Merging Problems

Because of differences between the RPG III and RPG IV languages, the Conversion Aid must reorder certain source statements. An example of this reordering is shown in "Example of Source Conversion" on page 122 for the RPG III source member TEST1. If you compare the placement of the data structure DS1 in Figure 39 on page 123 and in Figure 40 on page 124, you can see that the data structure DS1 was moved so that it precedes the record format FORMAT1.

Now suppose that the RPG III member TEST1 was split into two members, TEST2 and COPYDS1, where the data structure DS1 and the named constant CONST1 are in a copy member COPYDS1. This copy member is included in source TEST2. Figure 45 on page 131 and Figure 46 on page 131 show the source for TEST2 and COPYDS1, respectively.

```
H                                                 TSTPGM
FFILE1   IF  E                    DISK            COMM1
FQSYSPRT O   F    132     OF    LPRINTER
LQSYSPRT  60FL 560L
E                      ARR1   3   3  1            COMM2
E                      ARR2   3   3  1
IFORMAT1
I            OLDNAME                       NAME
 /COPY COPYDS1
C          ARR1,3    DSPLY
C                    READ FORMAT1                 01
C          NAME      DSPLY
C                    SETON                    LR
C                    EXCPTOUTPUT
OQSYSPRT E   01         OUTPUT
O                       ARR2,3    10
**
123
**
456
```

Figure 45. RPG III Source for TEST2

```
I* DATA STRUCTURE COMMENT
IDS1        DS
I                                1   3 FIELD1
I* NAMED CONSTANT COMMENT
I            'XYZ'          C        CONST1       COMM3
I                                4   6 ARR1
```

Figure 46. RPG III Source for COPYDS1

In this situation, the Conversion Aid would convert both member TEST2 and the copy member COPYDS1 correctly. However, when the copy member is included at compile time, it will be inserted below FORMAT1, because this is where the /COPY directive is located. As a result, all source lines in the copy member COPYDS1 will get a "source record is out of sequence" error. In RPG IV, definition specifications must precede input specifications.

Note: The Conversion Aid could not move the /COPY directive above FORMAT1 because the contents of /COPY member are unknown.

There are two methods of correcting this type of problem:

1. Use the EXPCPY(*YES) option of the CVTRPGSRC command to include all /COPY members in the converted RPG IV source member.

   This approach is easy and will work most of the time. However, including the /COPY members in each source member reduces the maintainability of your application.

2. Manually correct the code after conversion using the information in the ILE RPG compiler listing and the *ILE RPG for AS/400 Reference*.

Other examples of this type of problem include:

- Line specifications and Record Address Files

  In RPG III the line counter specification and the Record Address File of the extension specification are changed to keywords (RAFDATA, FORMLEN, and FORMOFL) on the file description specification. If the content of a /COPY member contains only the line counter specification or the Record Address File of the extension specification but not the corresponding file description specification, the Conversion Aid does not know where to insert the keywords.

- Extension specification arrays and data structure subfields

  As mentioned in "Example of Source Conversion" on page 122, you are not allowed to define a stand-alone array and a data structure subfield with the same name in RPG IV. Therefore, as shown in the example TEST1 (Figure 40 on page 124), the Conversion Aid must merge these two definitions. However, if the array and the data structure subfield are not in the same source member (that is, one or both is in a /COPY member), this merging cannot take place and a compile-time error will result.

- Merged compile-time array and compile-time data (**) records

  As shown in the example TEST1 (Figure 40 on page 124), if compile-time arrays are merged with data structure subfield definitions, the loading of array data may be affected. To overcome this problem, compile-time array data are changed to the new **CTDATA format if at least one compile-time array is merged. However, if the arrays and the data do not reside in the same source file (that is, one or both are in a COPY member) the naming of compile-time data records using the **CTDATA format cannot proceed properly.

Context-Sensitive Problems

In RPG III, there are occasions when it is impossible to determine the type of specifications in a /COPY member without the context of the surrounding specifications of the primary source member. There are two instances of this problem:

- In data structure subfields or program-described file fields

```
I* If the RPG III source member contains only the source
I* statements describing fields FIELD1 and FIELD2 below, the
I* Conversion Aid is unsure how to convert them.  These
I* statements may be data structure fields (which are converted
I* to definition specifications) or program-described file
I* fields (which are converted to input specifications).
I                                      1   3 FIELD1
I                                      4   6 FIELD2
```

Figure 47. RPG III /COPY File with Input Fields Only

- In renaming an externally described data structure field or an externally described file field

```
I* If the RPG III source member contains only the source
I* statement describing field CHAR below, the Conversion
I* Aid is unsure how to convert it.  This statement may be
I* a rename of an externally described data structure field
I* which is converted to a definition specification) or
I* a rename of an externally described file field)
I* (which is converted to an input specification).
I               CHARACTER                       CHAR
```

Figure 48. RPG III Source with a Renamed Field

In the above two instances, a data structure is assumed and definition specifications
are produced. A block of comments containing the input specification code is also
produced. For example, the Conversion Aid will convert the source in Figure 47 on
page 132 to the code shown in Figure 49. If Input specification code is required, delete
the definition specifications and blank out the asterisks from the corresponding Input
specifications.

```
D* If the RPG III source member contains only the source
D* statements describing fields FIELD1 and FIELD2 below, the
D* Conversion Aid is unsure how to convert them.  These
D* statements may be data structure fields (which are converted
D* to definition specifications) or program-described file
D* fields (which are converted to input specifications).
D FIELD1                  1       3
D FIELD2                  4       6
I*                                1   3  FIELD1
I*                                4   6  FIELD2
```

Figure 49. RPG IV Source After Converting Source with Input Fields Only

Remember that you have two ways of correcting these types of problems. Either use
the EXPCPY(*YES) option of the CVTRPGSRC command or manually correct the code
after conversion.

Use of Externally Described Data Structures

There are two problems that you may have to fix manually even though you specify the
EXPCPY(*YES) option on the CVTRPGSRC command.

- The merging of an array with an externally described DS subfield

- The renaming and initializing of an externally described DS subfield

These problems are related to the use of externally described data structures.

Because these problems will generate compile-time errors, you can use the information
in the ILE RPG compiler listing and the *ILE RPG for AS/400 Reference* to correct them.

Merging an Array with an Externally Described DS Subfield

As mentioned earlier, you are not allowed to define a stand-alone array and a data
structure subfield with the same name in RPG IV. In general, the Conversion Aid will

merge these two definitions. However, if the subfield is in an externally described data structure, this merging is not handled and you will be required to manually correct the converted source member.

For example, the field ARRAY in Figure 50 is included twice in Figure 51. It is included once as a stand-alone array and once in the externally described data structure EXTREC. When converted, the RPG IV source generated is shown in Figure 52. This code will not compile because ARRAY is defined twice. To correct this problem, delete the stand-alone array and add a subfield with the keywords to data structure DSONE as shown in Figure 53.

```
A              R RECORD
A                CHARACTER     10
A                ARRAY         10
```

Figure 50. DDS for External Data Structure

```
E                      ARRAY     10 1
IDSONE      E DSEXTREC
C           CHAR      DSPLY
C                     SETON                        LR
```

Figure 51. RPG III Source Using External Data Structure with Array

```
D ARRAY           S             1    DIM(10)
D DSONE           E DS               EXTNAME(EXTREC)
C     CHAR          DSPLY
C                   SETON                          LR
```

Figure 52. RPG IV Source with Two Definitions for the Array

```
D DSONE         E DS              EXTNAME(EXTREC)
D   ARRAY       E                 DIM(10)
C     CHAR        DSPLY
C                 SETON                            LR
```

Figure 53. Corrected RPG IV Source with a Single Definition for the Array

Renaming and Initializing an Externally Described DS Subfield

In RPG III, when both renaming and initializing a field in an externally described data structure, you had to use two source lines, as shown for the field CHAR in Figure 54 on page 135. The converted source also contains two source lines, as shown in Figure 55 on page 135. This use of two source lines for a field will result in a compile-time error, because the field CHAR is defined twice. To correct this code, you must combine the keywords of the field CHAR into a single line as shown in Figure 56 on page 135, where the key fields INZ and EXTFLD have been combined and only one instance on the field CHAR is shown.

```
IDSONE       E DSEXTREC
I                 CHARACTER                          CHAR
I I               'XYZ'                              CHAR
C              CHAR       DSPLY
C                         SETON                                    LR
```

Figure 54. RPG III Source with Renamed and Initialized External Subfield

```
D DSONE       E DS                EXTNAME(EXTREC)
D  CHAR       E                   EXTFLD(CHARACTER)
D  CHAR       E                   INZ('XYZ')
C      CHAR         DSPLY
C                   SETON                                          LR
```

Figure 55. RPG IV Source with Two Definitions for Renamed Subfield

```
D DSONE       E DS                EXTNAME(EXTREC)
D  CHAR       E                   EXTFLD(CHARACTER)  INZ('XYZ')
C      CHAR         DSPLY
C                   SETON                                          LR
```

Figure 56. Corrected RPG IV Source with a Single Definition

Run-time Differences

If you have prerun-time arrays that overlap in data structures, the order of loading these arrays at run time may be different in RPG III and in RPG IV. This difference in order can cause the data in the overlapping section to differ. The order in which the arrays are loaded is the order in which they are encountered in the source. This order may have changed when the arrays were being merged with the subfields during conversion.

In general, you should avoid situations where an application consists of OPM and ILE programs that are split across the OPM default activation group and a named activation group. When spilt across these two activation groups, you are mixing OPM behavior with ILE behavior and your results may be hard to predict. Refer to *ILE RPG for AS/400 Programming Guide* or *ILE Concepts* for further information.

Stage 16. Behavioral Differences Between OPM RPG/400 and ILE RPG for AS/400

The following lists note differences in the behavior of the OPM RPG/400 compiler and ILE RPG.

Compiling

1. If you specify CVTOPT(*NONE) in OPM RPG, all externally described fields that are of a type or with attributes not supported by RPG will be ignored. If you specify CVTOPT(*NONE) in ILE RPG, all externally described fields will be brought into the program with the same type as specified in the external description.

2. In RPG IV, there is no dependency between DATEDIT and DECEDIT in the control specification.

3. Regarding the ILE RPG create commands (CRTBNDRPG and CRTRPGMOD):

   - The IGNDECERR parameter on the CRTRPGPGM command has been replaced by the FIXNBR parameter on the ILE RPG create commands. IGNDECDTA ignores any decimal data errors and continues with the next machine instruction. In some cases, this can cause fields to be updated with incorrect and sometimes unpredictable values. FIXNBR corrects the data in a predictable manner before it is used.

   - There is a new parameter, TRUNCNBR, for controlling whether numeric over-flow is allowed.

   - There are no auto report features or commands in RPG IV.

   - You cannot request an MI listing from the compiler.

4. In a compiler listing, line numbers start at 1 and increment by one for each line of source or generated specifications. Source IDs are numeric that is, there are no more AA000100 line numbers for /COPY members or expanded DDS.

5. RPG IV requires that all compiler directives appear *before* compile-time data, including /TITLE. When RPG IV encounters a /TITLE directive, it will treat it as data. (RPG III treats /TITLE specifications as compiler directives anywhere in the source.)

   The Conversion Aid will remove any /TITLE specifications it encounters in compile-time data.

6. ILE RPG is more rigorous in detecting field overlap in data structures. For some calculation operations involving overlapping operands, ILE RPG issues a message, while the OPM compiler does not.

7. In ILE RPG, the word NOT cannot be used as a variable name. NOT is a special word that is used as an operator in expressions.

8. At compile time, the source is read using the CCSID of the main source file, while for OPM RPG, the source is read using the CCSID of the job.

Running

1. The FREE operation is not supported by RPG IV.

2. Certain MCH messages may appear in the job log that do not appear under OPM (for example, MCH1202). The appearance of these messages does not indicate a change in the behavior of the program.

3. If you use the nonbindable API QMHSNDPM to send messages from your program, you may need to add 1 to the stack offset parameter to allow for the presence of the program-entry procedure in the stack. This will only be the case if the ILE procedure is the user-entry procedure and if you used the special value of '*' for the call message queue and a value of greater than 0 for the stack offset.

4. ILE RPG does not interpret return codes that are not 0 or 1 for calls to non-RPG programs or procedures that end without an exception.

5. When recursion is detected, OPM RPG/400 displays inquiry message RPG8888. ILE RPG signals escape message RNX8888; no inquiry message is displayed for this condition. Note that this only applies to main procedures. Recursion is allowed for subprocedures.

6. If decimal-data errors occur during the initialization of a zoned-decimal or packed-decimal subfield, then the reset values (those values use to restore the subfield with the RESET operation) may not be valid. For example, it may be that the sub-field was not initialized or that it was overlaid on another initialized subfield of a different type. If a RESET operation is attempted for that subfield, then in OPM RPG/400 a decimal-data error would occur. However, a RESET to the same sub-field in ILE RPG will complete successfully; after the RESET, the subfield has the same invalid value. As a result, attempts to use the value will get a decimal data error.

Debugging and Exception Handling

1. The DEBUG operation is not supported in RPG IV.

2. You cannot use RPG tags, subroutine names, or points in the cycle, such as *GETIN and *DETC for setting breakpoints when using the ILE source debugger.

3. Function checks are normally left in the job log by both OPM RPG and ILE RPG. However, in ILE RPG, if you have coded an error indicator, 'E' extender, or *PSSR error routine, then the function check will not appear.

   You should remove any code that deletes function checks, because the presence of the indicator, 'E' extender, or *PSSR will prevent function checks from occurring.

4. Call performance for LR-on will be greatly improved by having no PSDS or a PSDS no longer than 80 bytes, because some of the information that fills the PSDS after 80 bytes is costly to obtain. If the PSDS is not coded or is too short to contain the date and time the program started, these two values will not be available in a for-matted dump. All other PSDS values will be available, no matter how long the PSDS is.

5. The prefix for ILE RPG inquiry messages is RNQ. If you use the default reply list, you must add RNQ entries similar to your existing RPG entries.

6. In OPM, if a CL program calls your RPG program followed by a MONMSG and the RPG program receives a notify or status message, the CL MONMSG will not handle the notify or status message. If you are calling ILE RPG from ILE CL and both are in the same activation group, the ILE CL MONMSG will handle the notify or status message and the RPG procedure will halt immediately without an RPG error message.

7. When displaying a variable using the ILE source debugger, you will get unreliable results if:

   • the ILE RPG program uses an externally described file *and*

   • the variable is defined in the data base file, but not referenced in the ILE RPG program.

I/O

1. In ILE RPG, you can read a record in a file opened for update, and created or overridden with SHARE(*YES), and then update this locked record in another program that has opened the same file for update.

2. You cannot modify the MR indicator using the MOVE or SETON operations (RPG III only prevents using SETON with MR).

3. The File Type entry on the File specification no longer dictates the type of I/O operations that must be present in the calculation specifications.

   For example, in RPG III, if you define a file as an update file, then you must have an UPDAT operation later in the program. This is no longer true in RPG IV. However, your file definition still must be consistent with the I/O operations present in the program. So if you have an UPDATE operation in your source, the file must be defined as an update file.

4. ILE RPG will allow record blocking even if the COMMIT keyword is specified on the file description specification.

5. In RPG IV, a file opened for update will also be opened as delete capable. You do not need any DELETE operations to make it delete capable.

6. In RPG IV, you do not have to code an actual number for the number of devices that will be used by a multiple-device file. If you specify MAXDEV(*FILE) on a file description specification, then the number of save areas created for SAVEDS and SAVEIND is based on the number of devices that your file can handle. (The SAVEDS, SAVEIND, and MAXDEV keywords on an RPG IV file description specification correspond to the SAVDS, IND, and NUM options on an RPG III file description specification continuation line, respectively.)

   In ILE RPG, the total number of program devices that can be acquired by the program cannot be different from the maximum number of devices defined in the device file. OPM RPG/400 allows this through the NUM option.

7. In ILE RPG, the ACQ and REL operation codes can be used with single device files.

8. In ILE RPG, the relative record number and key fields in the database-specific feedback section of the INFDS are updated on each input operation when doing blocked reads.

9. When a referential constraint error occurs in OPM RPG/400, the status code is set to "01299" (I/O error). In ILE RPG, the status code is set to "01022", "01222", or "01299", depending on the type of referential constraint error that occurs:

   - If data management is not able to allocate a record due to a referential constraint error, a CPF502E notify message is issued. ILE RPG will set the status code to "01222" and OPM RPG/400 will set the status code to "01299".

     If you have no error indicator, 'E' extender, or INFSR error subroutine, ILE RPG will issue the RNQ1222 inquiry message and OPM RPG/400 will issue the RPG1299 inquiry message. The main difference between these two messages is that RNQ1222 allows you to retry the operation.

   - If data management detects a referential constraint error that has caused it to issue either a CPF503A, CPF502D, or CPF502F notify message, ILE RPG will set the status code to "01022" and OPM RPG/400 will set the status code to "01299".

     If you have no error indicator, 'E' extender, or INFSR error subroutine, ILE RPG will issue the RNQ1022 inquiry message and OPM RPG will issue the RPG1299 inquiry message.

   - All referential constraint errors detected by data management that cause data management to issue an escape message will cause both OPM and ILE RPG to set the status code to "01299".

10. In ILE RPG, the database-specific feedback section of the INFDS is updated regardless of the outcome of the I/O operation. In OPM RPG/400, this feedback section is not updated if the record-not-found condition is encountered.

11. ILE RPG relies more on data-management error handling than does OPM RPG/400. This means that in some cases you will find certain error messages in the job log of an ILE RPG program, but not of an OPM RPG/400 program. Some differences you will notice in error handling are:

    - When doing an UPDATE on a record in a database file that has not been locked by a previous input operation, both ILE RPG and OPM RPG/400 set the status code to "01211". ILE RPG detects this situation when data management issues a CPF501B notify message and places it in the job log.

    - When handling WORKSTN files and trying to do I/O to a device that has not been acquired or defined, both ILE and OPM RPG will set the status to "01281". ILE RPG detects this situation when data management issues a CPF5068 escape message and places it in the job log.

12. When doing READE, REDPE (READPE in ILE), or SETLL on a database file, or when doing sequential-within-limits processing by a record-address-file, OPM RPG/400 does key comparisons using the *HEX collating sequence. This may give

different results than expected when DDS features are used that cause more than one search argument to match a given key in the file. For example, if ABSVAL is used on a numeric key, both -1 and 1 would succeed as search arguments for a key in the file with a value of 1. Using the hexadecimal collating sequence, a search argument of -1 will not succeed for an actual key of 1.

ILE RPG does key comparisons using *HEX collating sequence only for pre-V3R1 DDM files.

13. ILE RPG allows the To File and the From File specified for prerun-time arrays and tables to be different. In OPM RPG, both file names must be the same; if they are different, the diagnostic message QRG3038 is issued.

14. When translation of a RAF-Controlled file is specified, the results using ILE RPG may differ from OPM RPG/400, depending on the translation table. This is due to the different sequence of operations. In OPM RPG/400, the sequence is: retrieve record, translate and compare; in ILE RPG, the sequence is: translate, compare and retrieve record.

DBCS Data in Character Fields

1. In OPM RPG/400, position 57 (Transparency Check) of the control specification allows you to specify whether the RPG/400 compiler should scan character literals and constants for DBCS characters. If you specify that the compiler should scan for transparent literals and if a character literal that starts with an apostrophe followed by a shift-out fails the transparency check, the literal is reparsed as a literal that is not transparent.

In ILE RPG, there is no option on the control specification to specify whether the compiler should perform transparency check on character literals. If a character literal contains a shift-out control character, regardless of the position of the shift-out character within the character literal, the shift-out character signifies the beginning of DBCS data. The compiler will check for the following:

- A matching shift-in for each shift-out (that is, the shift-out and shift-in control characters should be balanced)

- An even number (minimally two) between the shift-in and the shift-out

- The absence of an embedded shift-out in the DBCS data

If the above conditions are not met, the compiler will issue a diagnostic message, and the literal will not be reparsed. As a result, if there are character literals in your OPM RPG programs that fail the transparency check performed by the OPM RPG compiler, such programs will get compilation errors in ILE RPG.

2. In OPM RPG/400, if there are two consecutive apostrophes enclosed within shift-out and shift-in control characters inside a character literal, the two consecutive apostrophes are considered as a single apostrophe if the character literal is not a transparent literal. The character literal will not be a transparent literal if:

- The character literal does not start with an apostrophe followed by a shift-out

- The character literal fails the transparency check performed by the compiler

- The user has not specified that a transparency check should be performed by the compiler

In ILE RPG, if there are two consecutive apostrophes enclosed within shift-out and shift-in control characters inside a character literal, the apostrophes will not be considered as a single apostrophe. A pair of apostrophes inside a character literal will only be considered as a single apostrophe if they are not enclosed within shift-out and shift-in control characters.

3. In ILE RPG, if you want to avoid the checking of literals for shift-out characters (that is, you do not want a shift-out character to be interpreted as such), then you should specify the entire literal as a hexadecimal literal. For example, if you have a literal 'AoB' where 'o' represents a shift-out control character, you should code this literal as X'C10EC2'.

Stage 17. RPG Programming in Integrated Language Environment

ILE provides RPG users with improvements or enhancements in the following areas of application development:

- Program creation
- Program management
- Program call
- Source debugging
- Bindable application program interfaces (APIs)
- Multithreaded applications

Each of the above areas is explained briefly in the following paragraphs and discussed further in the following chapters.

Program Creation

In ILE, program creation consists of:

1. Compiling source code into modules
2. Binding (combining) one or more modules into a program object

You can create a program object much like you do in the OPM framework, with a one-step process using the Create Bound RPG Program (CRTBNDRPG) command. This command creates a temporary module, which is then bound into a program object. It also allows you to bind other objects through the use of a binding directory.

Alternatively, you may create a program using separate commands for compilation and binding. This two-step process allows you to reuse a module or update one module without recompiling the other modules in a program. In addition, because you can combine modules from any ILE language, you can create and maintain mixed-language programs.

In the two-step process, you create a module object using the Create RPG Module (CRTRPGMOD) command. This command compiles the source statements into a module object. A module is a nonrunnable object; it must be bound into a program object to be run. To bind one or more modules together, use the Create Program (CRTPGM) command.

Service programs are a means of packaging the procedures in one or more modules into a separately bound object. Other Integrated Language Environment programs can access the procedures in the service program, although there is only one copy of the service program on the system. The use of service programs facilitates modularity and maintainability. You can use off-the-shelf service programs developed by third parties or, conversely, package your own service programs for third-party use. A service program is created using the Create Service Program (CRTSRVPGM) command.

You can create a binding directory to contain the names of modules and service programs that your program or service program may need. A list of binding directories can be specified when you create a program on the CRTBNDRPG, CRTSRVPGM, and CRTPGM commands. They can also be specified on the CRTRPGMOD command; however, the search for a binding directory is done when the module is bound at CRTPGM or CRTSRVPGM time. A binding directory can reduce program size, because modules or service programs listed in a binding directory are used only if they are needed.

Figure 57 shows the two approaches to program creation.

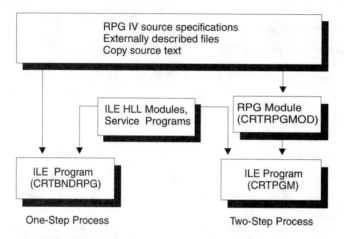

Figure 57. Program Creation in Integrated Language Environment

After a program is created, you can update the program using the Update Program (UPDPGM) or Update Service Program (UPDSRVPGM) commands. This is useful, because it means you only need to have the new or changed module objects available to update the program.

For more information on the one-step process, see "Creating a Program Using CRTBNDRPG" on page 147. For more information on the two-step process, see "Creating a Program with the CRTRPGMOD and CRTPGM Commands" on page 154.

Program Management

Integrated Language Environment provides a common basis for:

- Managing program flow
- Sharing resources
- Using application program interfaces (APIs)
- Handling exceptions during a program's run time

It gives RPG users much better control over resources than was previously possible.

Integrated Language Environment programs and service programs are activated into activation groups, which are specified at program-creation time. The process of getting a program or service program ready to run is known as activation. Activation allocates resources within a job so that one or more programs can run in that space. If the specified activation group for a program does not exist when the program is called, then it is created within the job to hold the program's activation.

An activation group is the key element governing an Integrated Language Environment application's resources and behavior. For example, you can scope commitment-control operations to the activation group level. You can also scope file overrides and shared open data paths to the activation group of the running application. Finally, the behavior of a program upon termination is also affected by the activation group in which the program runs.

You can dynamically allocate storage for a run-time array using the bindable APIs provided for all ILE programming languages. These APIs allow single- and mixed-language applications to access a central set of storage management functions and offer a storage model to languages that do not now provide one. RPG offers some storage management capabilities using operation codes.

Program Call

In ILE, you can write applications in which ILE RPG programs and OPM RPG/400 programs continue to interrelate through the traditional use of dynamic program calls. When using such calls, the calling program specifies the name of the called program on a call statement. The called program's name is resolved to an address at run time, just before the calling program passes control to the called program.

You can also write Integrated Language Environment applications that can interrelate with faster static calls. Static calls involve calls between procedures. A procedure is a self-contained set of code that performs a task and then returns to the caller. An ILE RPG module consists of an optional main procedure followed by zero or more subprocedures. Because the procedure names are resolved at bind time (that is, when you create the program), static calls are faster than dynamic calls.

Static calls also allow

- Operational descriptors
- Omitted parameters
- The passing of parameters by value
- The use of return values
- A greater number of parameters to be passed

Operational descriptors and omitted parameters can be useful when calling bindable APIs or procedures written in other Integrated Language Environment languages.

Source Debugging

In Integrated Language Environment, you can perform source-level debugging on any single- or mixed-language Integrated Language Environment application. The ILE source debugger also supports OPM programs. You can control the flow of a program by using debug commands while the program is running. You can set conditional and unconditional job or thread breakpoints prior to running the program.

After you call the program, you can then step through a specified number of statements and display or change variables. When a program stops because of a breakpoint, a step command, or a run-time error, the pertinent module is shown on the display at the point where the program stopped. At that point, you can enter more debug commands.

Bindable APIs

ILE offers a number of bindable APIs that can be used to supplement the function currently offered by ILE RPG. The bindable APIs provide program calling and activation capability, condition and storage management, math functions, and dynamic screen management.

Some APIs that you may want to consider using in an ILE RPG application include:

- CEETREC – Signal the termination-imminent condition
- CEE4ABN – Abnormal end
- CEECRHP – Create your own heap
- CEEDSHP – Discard your own heap
- CEEFRST – Free storage in your own heap
- CEEGTST – Get heap storage in your own heap
- CEECZST – Reallocate storage in your own heap
- CEEDOD – Decompose operational descriptor

Note: You cannot use these or any other Integrated Language Environment bindable APIs from a program created with DFTACTGRP(*YES). This is because bound calls are not allowed in this type of program.

For more information on these Integrated Language Environment bindable APIs, see *ILE RPG for AS/400 Programming Guide* and the *System API Reference*.

Multithreaded Applications

The AS/400 now supports multithreading. However, this support is not yet available ILE RPG procedures. If you want to call an ILE RPG procedure in a multithreaded application, you must ensure that only one thread is calling any ILE RPG procedure at a time. You should also be aware that some functions in ILE RPG are not thread-safe.

Stage 18. Creating an ILE Program

This chapter shows how to create an ILE program from RPG IV source with:

- the Create Bound RPG Program (CRTBNDRPG) command
- the Create RPG Module (CRTRPGMOD) command and Create Program (CRTPGM) command

Creating a Program Using CRTBNDRPG

With the Create Bound RPG Program (CRTBNDRPG) command, you can create one of two types of Integrated Language Environment programs:

1. OPM-compatible programs with no static binding

2. Single-module Integrated Language Environment programs with static binding

Whether you obtain a program of the first type or the second type depends on whether the DFTACTGRP parameter of CRTBNDRPG is set to *YES or *NO, respectively.

Creating a program of the first type produces a program that behaves like an OPM program in the areas of open scoping, override scoping, and RCLRSC. This high degree of compatibility is due in part to its running in the same activation group as OPM programs, namely, in the default activation group.

However, with this high compatibility comes the inability to have static binding. Static binding refers to the ability to call procedures (in other modules or service programs) and to use procedure pointers. The inability to have static binding means that you cannot:

- Use the CALLB operation in your source
- Call a prototyped procedure
- Bind to other modules during program creation

Creating a program of the second type produces a program with Integrated Language Environment characteristics such as static binding. You can specify at program-creation time the activation group the program is to run in and any modules for static binding. In addition, you can call procedures from your source.

Using the CRTBNDRPG Command

The Create Bound RPG (CRTBNDRPG) command creates a program object from RPG IV source in one step. It also allows you to bind other modules or service programs using a binding directory.

The command starts the ILE RPG compiler and creates a temporary module object in the library QTEMP. It then binds it into a program object of type *PGM. After the program object is created, the temporary module used to create the program is deleted.

The CRTBNDRPG command is useful when you want to create a program object from stand-alone source code (code that does not require modules to be bound together), because it combines the steps of creating and binding. Furthermore, it allows you to create an OPM-compatible program.

Note: If you want to keep the module object bind it with other modules into a program object, you must create the module using the CRTRPGMOD command. For more information, see "Creating a Program with the CRTRPGMOD and CRTPGM Commands" on page 154.

You can use the CRTBNDRPG command interactively, in batch, or from a Command Language (CL) program. If you are using the command interactively and require prompting, type CRTBNDRPG and press F4 (Prompt). If you need help, type CRTBNDRPG and press F1 (Help).

Table 39 summarizes the parameters of the CRTBNDRPG command and shows their default values.

Table 39 (Page 1 of 2). CRTBNDRPG Parameters and Their Default Values Grouped by Function	
Program Identification	
PGM(*CURLIB/*CTLSPEC)	Determines created program name and library
SRCFILE(*LIBL/QRPGLESRC)	Identifies source file and library
SRCMBR(*PGM)	Identifies file member containing source specifications
TEXT(*SRCMBRTXT)	Provides brief description of program
Program Creation	
GENLVL(10)	Conditions program creation to error severity (0-20)
OPTION(*GEN)	*GEN/*NOGEN; determines if program is created
DBGVIEW(*STMT)	Specifies type of debug view, if any, to be included in program
OPTIMIZE(*NONE)	Determines level of optimization, if any
REPLACE(*YES)	Determines if program should replace existing program
BNDDIR(*NONE)	Specifies the binding directory to be used for symbol resolution
USRPRF(*USER)	Specifies the user profile that will run program
AUT(*LIBCRTAUT)	Specifies type of authority for created program
TGTRLS(*CURRENT)	Specifies the release level the object is to be run on
ENBPFRCOL(*PEP)	Specifies whether performance collection is enabled
DEFINE(*NONE)	Specifies condition names that are defined before the compilation begins
PRFDTA(*NOCOL)	Specifies the program profiling data attribute
Compiler Listing	
OUTPUT(*PRINT)	Determines if there is a compiler listing
INDENT(*NONE)	Determines if indentation should show in listing and identifies character for marking it

Table 39 (Page 2 of 2). CRTBNDRPG Parameters and Their Default Values Grouped by Function	
OPTION(*XREF *NOSECLVL *SHOWCPY *NOSHOWSKP *EXPDDS *EXT)	Specifies the contents of compiler listing
Data Conversion Options	
CVTOPT(*NONE)	Specifies how various data types from externally described files are handled
ALWNULL(*NO)	Determines if the program will accept values from null-capable fields
FIXNBR(*NONE)	Determines which decimal data that is not valid is to be fixed by the compiler
Run-Time Considerations	
DFTACTGRP(*YES)	Identifies whether this program always runs in the OPM default activation group
ACTGRP(QILE)	Identifies the activation group in which the program should run
SRTSEQ(*HEX)	Specifies the sort sequence table to be used
LANGID(*JOBRUN)	Used with SRTSEQ to specify the language identifier for sort sequence
TRUNCNBR(*YES)	Specifies the action to take when numeric overflow occurs for packed-decimal, zoned-decimal, and binary fields in fixed-format operations

The entire syntax diagram for the CRTBNDRPG command is shown below.

Job: B,I Pgm: B,I REXX: B,I Exec

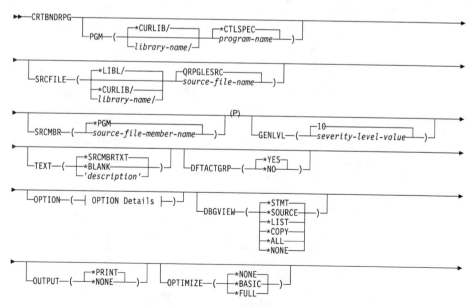

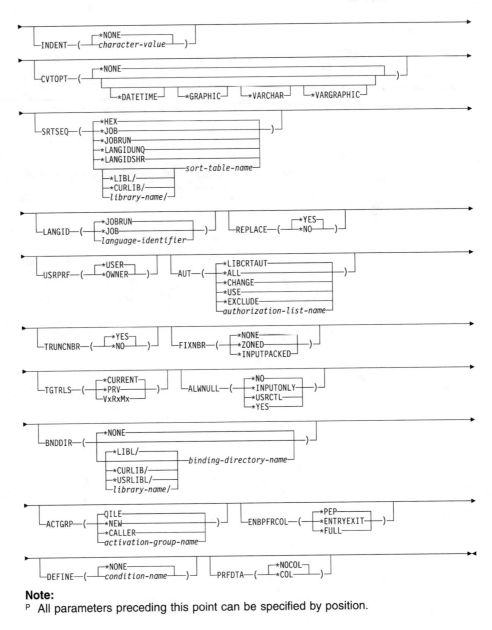

Note:

P All parameters preceding this point can be specified by position.

OPTION Details:

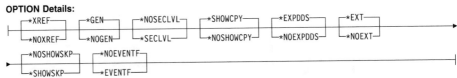

For information on any of the parameters for CRTBNDRPG, enter the command name on a command line, press PF4 (Prompt), and then press PF1 (Help) for any parameter for which you want information.

Creating an OPM-Compatible Program Object

In this example, you use the CRTBNDRPG command to create an OPM-compatible program object from the source for the payroll program shown in Figure 58 on page 152.

1. To create the object, type:

```
CRTBNDRPG PGM(MYLIB/PAYROLL)
          SRCFILE(MYLIB/QRPGLESRC)
          TEXT('ILE RPG program')  DFTACTGRP(*YES)
```

The CRTBNDRPG command creates the program PAYROLL in MYLIB, which will run in the default activation group. By default, a compiler listing is produced.

Note: The setting of DFTACTGRP(*YES) is what provides the OPM compatibility. This setting also prevents you from entering a value for the ACTGRP and BNDDIR parameters. Furthermore, if the source contains any bound procedure calls, an error is issued and the compilation ends.

2. Type one of the following CL commands to see the listing that is created:

- DSPJOB and then select option 4 (*Display spooled files*)
- WRKJOB
- WRKOUTQ *queue-name*
- WRKSPLF

```
*-------------------------------------------------------------------*
* DESCRIPTION:  This program creates a printed output of employee's pay  *
*               for the week.                                            *
*-------------------------------------------------------------------*

H DATEDIT(*DMY/)

*-------------------------------------------------------------------*
* File Definitions                                                   *
*-------------------------------------------------------------------*
FTRANSACT  IP   E           K DISK
FEMPLOYEE  IF   E           K DISK
FQSYSPRT   O    F    80       PRINTER

*-------------------------------------------------------------------*
* Variable Declarations                                              *
*-------------------------------------------------------------------*
D Pay            S              8P 2

*-------------------------------------------------------------------*
* Constant Declarations                                              *
*-------------------------------------------------------------------*
D Heading1       C               'NUMBER  NAME              RATE  H-
D                                 OURS  BONUS    PAY       '
D Heading2       C               '_____ _____, _____ _-
D                                  ___  _____  _____'

*-------------------------------------------------------------------*
* For each record in the transaction file (TRANSACT), if the employee  *
* is found, compute the employees pay and print the details.           *
*-------------------------------------------------------------------*
C     TRN_NUMBER    CHAIN     EMP_REC                              99
C                   IF        NOT *IN99
C                   EVAL (H)  Pay = EMP_RATE * TRN_HOURS + TRN_BONUS
C                   ENDIF
```

Figure 58 (Part 1 of 2). A Sample Payroll Calculation Program

```
*---------------------------------------------------------------*
* Report Layout                                                 *
* -- print the heading lines if 1P is on                        *
* -- if the record is found (indicator 99 is off) print the payroll *
*    details otherwise print an exception record                *
* -- print 'END OF LISTING' when LR is on                       *
*---------------------------------------------------------------*
OQSYSPRT   H    1P                        2  3
O                                                35 'PAYROLL REGISTER'
O                        *DATE        Y    60
O          H    1P                    2
O                                         60 Heading1
O          H    1P                    2
O                                         60 Heading2
O          D    N1PN99                2
O                   TRN_NUMBER              5
O                   EMP_NAME               24
O                   EMP_RATE      L        33
O                   TRN_HOURS     L        40
O                   TRN_BONUS     L        49
O                   Pay                    60 '$   0. '
O          D    N1P 99                2
O                   TRN_NUMBER              5
O                                         35 '** NOT ON EMPLOYEE FILE **'
O          T    LR
O                                         33 'END OF LISTING'
```

Figure 58 (Part 2 of 2). A Sample Payroll Calculation Program

Creating a Program with Static Binding

In this example, you create a program COMPUTE using CRTBNDRPG, to which you bind a service program at program-creation time.

Assume that you want to bind the program COMPUTE to services that you have purchased to perform advanced mathematical computations. The binding directory to which you must bind your source is called MATH. This directory contains the name of a service program that contains the various procedures that make up the services.

To create the object, type:

```
CRTBNDRPG PGM(MYLIB/COMPUTE)
          DFTACTGRP(*NO) ACTGRP(GRP1) BNDDIR(MATH)
```

The source will be bound to the service program specified in the binding directory MATH at program-creation time. This means that calls to the procedures in the service program will take less time than if they were dynamic calls.

When the program is called, it will run in the named activation group GRP1. The default value ACTGRP parameter on CRTBNDRPG is QILE. However, it is recommended that you run your application as a unique group to ensure that the associated resources are fully protected.

Note: DFTACTGRP must be set to *NO for you to enter a value for the ACTGRP and BNDDIR parameters.

Creating a Program with the CRTRPGMOD and CRTPGM Commands

The two-step process of program creation consists of compiling source into modules using CRTRPGMOD and then binding one or more module objects into a program using CRTPGM. With this process, you can create permanent modules. This in turn allows you to modularize an application without recompiling the whole application. It also allows you to reuse the same module in different applications.

Creating a Module Object

A **module** is a nonrunnable object (type *MODULE) that is the output of an Integrated Language Environment compiler. It is the basic building block of an Integrated Language Environment program.

An ILE RPG module consists of one or more procedures, and the file control blocks and static storage used by all the procedures in the module. The procedures that can make up an ILE RPG module are:

- An optional **main procedure**, which consists of the set of H, F, D, I, C, and O specifications that begin the source. The main procedure has its own LR semantics and logic cycle, neither of which is affected by those of other ILE RPG modules in the program.

- Zero or more **subprocedures**, which are coded on P, D, and C specifications. Subprocedures do not use the RPG cycle. A subprocedure may have local storage that is available for use only by the subprocedure itself.

The main procedure (if coded) can always be called by other modules in the program. Subprocedures may be local to the module or exported. If they are local, they can only be called by other procedures in the module; if they are exported from the module, they can be called by any procedure in the program.

Module creation consists of compiling a source member, and, if that is successful, creating a *MODULE object. The *MODULE object includes a list of imports and exports referenced within the module. It also includes debug data if you request this at compile time.

A module cannot be run by itself. You must bind one or more modules together to create a program object (type *PGM), which can then be run. You can also bind one or more modules together to create a service program object (type *SRVPGM). You then access the procedures within the bound modules through static procedure calls.

This ability to combine modules allows you to:

- Reuse pieces of code. This generally results in smaller programs. Smaller programs give you better performance and easier debugging capabilities.

- Maintain shared code with little chance of introducing errors to other parts of the overall program.

- Manage large programs more effectively. Modules allow you to divide your old program into parts that can be managed separately. If that needs to be enhanced, you only need to recompile those modules, which have been changed.

- Create mixed-language programs where you bind together modules written in the best language for the task.

For more information about the concept of modules, refer to *ILE Concepts* .

Using the CRTRPGMOD Command

You create a module using the Create RPG Module (CRTRPGMOD) command. You can use the command interactively, as part of a batch input stream, or from a Command Language (CL) program.

The parameters of the CRTRPGMOD command are the same as those of the CRTBNDRPG command, except that CRTRPGMOD does not have:

- DFTACTGRP

- ACTGRP

- USRPRF

If you are using the command interactively and need prompting, type CRTRPGMOD and press F4 (Prompt). If you need help, type CRTRPGMOD and press F1 (Help).

Creating a NOMAIN Module: In this example, you create an NOMAIN module object TRANSSVC using the CRTRPGMOD command and its default settings. TRANSSVC contains prototyped procedures that perform transaction services for procedures in other modules. The source for TRANSSVC shown in Figure 59 on page 156. The prototypes for the procedures in TRANSSVC are stored in a /COPY member, as shown in Figure 60 on page 158.

1. To create a module object, type:

```
CRTRPGMOD MODULE(MYLIB/TRANSSVC)  SRCFILE(MYLIB/QRPGLESRC)
```

The module will be created in the library MYLIB with the name specified in the command, TRANSSVC. The source for the module is the source member TRANSSVC in file QRPGLESRC in the library MYLIB.

You bind a module containing NOMAIN to another module using one of the following commands:

a. CRTPGM command

b. CRTSRVPGM command

c. CRTBNDRPG command where the NOMAIN module is included in a binding directory.

2. After it is bound, this module object can be debugged using a statement view. A compiler listing for the module is also produced.

3. Type one of the following CL commands to see the compiler listing:

- DSPJOB and then select option 4 (*Display spooled files*)
- WRKJOB
- WRKOUTQ *queue-name*
- WRKSPLF

```
*====================================================================*
* MODULE NAME:    TRANSSVC (Transaction Services)
* RELATED FILES:  N/A
* RELATED SOURCE: TRANSRPT
* EXPORTED PROCEDURES:  Trans_Inc  -- calculates the income
*     for the transaction using the data in the fields in the
*     parameter list.  It returns to the caller after all
*     the calculations are done.
*
*     Prod_Name --  retrieves the product name based on the
*     input parameter with the product number.
*====================================================================*
* This module contains only subprocedures; it is a NOMAIN module.
H  NOMAIN
*--------------------------------------------------------------------
* Pull in the prototypes from the /COPY member
*--------------------------------------------------------------------
/COPY TRANSP
```

Figure 59 (Part 1 of 3). Source for TRANSSVC Member

```
     *---------------------------------------------------------------------
     * Subprocedure Trans_Inc
     *---------------------------------------------------------------------
P Trans_Inc       B                         EXPORT
D Trans_Inc       PI           11P 2
D   ProdNum                    10P 0   VALUE
D   Quantity                    5P 0   VALUE
D   Discount                    2P 2   VALUE

D Factor          S             5P 0
     *
C                 SELECT
C                 WHEN      ProdNum = 1
C                 EVAL      Factor = 1500
C                 WHEN      ProdNum = 2
C                 EVAL      Factor = 3500
C                 WHEN      ProdNum = 5
C                 EVAL      Factor = 20000
C                 WHEN      ProdNum = 8
C                 EVAL      Factor = 32000
C                 WHEN      ProdNum = 12
C                 EVAL      Factor = 64000
C                 OTHER
C                 EVAL      Factor = 0
C                 ENDSL

C                 RETURN    Factor * Quantity * (1 - Discount)

P Trans_Inc       E
```

Figure 59 (Part 2 of 3). Source for TRANSSVC Member

```
      *-------------------------------------------------------------------
      * Subprocedure Prod_Name
      *-------------------------------------------------------------------
     P Prod_Name       B                        EXPORT
     D Prod_Name       PI            40A
     D   ProdNum                     10P 0    VALUE
      *
     C                 SELECT
     C                 WHEN      ProdNum = 1
     C                 RETURN    'Large'
     C                 WHEN      ProdNum = 2
     C                 RETURN    'Super'
     C                 WHEN      ProdNum = 5
     C                 RETURN    'Super Large'
     C                 WHEN      ProdNum = 8
     C                 RETURN    'Super Jumbo'
     C                 WHEN      ProdNum = 12
     C                 RETURN    'Incredibly Large Super Jumbo'
     C                 OTHER
     C                 RETURN    '***Unknown***'
     C                 ENDSL

     P  Prod_Name      E
```

Figure 59 (Part 3 of 3). Source for TRANSSVC Member

```
      * Prototype for Trans_Inc
     D Trans_Inc       PR            11P 2
     D   Prod                        10P 0    VALUE
     D   Quantity                     5P 0    VALUE
     D   Discount                     2P 2    VALUE

      * Prototype for Prod_Name
     D Prod_Name       PR            40A
     D   Prod                        10P 0    VALUE
```

Figure 60. Source for TRANSP /COPY Member

Creating a Module for Source Debugging

In this example, you create an ILE RPG module object that you can debug using the source debugger. The module TRANSRPT contains a main procedure that drives the report processing. It calls the procedures in TRANSSVC to perform certain required tasks. The source for this module is shown in Figure 61 on page 159.

To create a module object, type:

```
CRTRPGMOD MODULE(MYLIB/TRANSRPT)  SRCFILE(MYLIB/QRPGLESRC)
          DBGVIEW(*SOURCE)
```

The module is created in the library MYLIB with the same name as the source file on which it is based, TRANSRPT. This module object can be debugged using a source view.

A compiler listing for the TRANSRPT module will be produced.

```
*===================================================================*
* MODULE NAME:     TRANSRPT
* RELATED FILES:   TRNSDTA   (PF)
* RELATED SOURCE:  TRANSSVC (Transaction services)
* EXPORTED PROCEDURE:  TRANSRPT
*       The procedure TRANSRPT reads every transasction record
*       stored in the physical file TRNSDTA. It calls the
*       subprocedure Trans_Inc which performs calculations and
*       returns a value back.  Then it calls Prod_Name to
*       to determine the product name.  TRANSRPT then prints
*       the transaction record out.
*===================================================================*
FTRNSDTA  IP  E               DISK
FQSYSPRT  O   F   80          PRINTER       OFLIND(*INOF)


 /COPY QRPGLE,TRANSP

 * Define the readable version of the product name like the
 * return value of the procedure 'Prod_Name'
D    ProdName    S           30A

D    Income      S           10P 2
D    Total       S           +5      LIKE(Income)
 *
ITRNSREC        01

 * Calculate the income using subprocedure Trans_Inc
C                 EVAL      Income = Trans_Inc(PROD : QTY : DISC)
C                 EVAL      Total = Total + Income
 * Find the name of the product
C                 EVAL      ProdName = Prod_Name(PROD)

OQSYSPRT  H   1P                      1
O         OR  OF
O                                          12 'Product name'
O                                          40 'Quantity'
O                                          54 'Income'
OQSYSPRT  H   1P                      1
O         OR  OF
O                                          30 '----------+
                                              ----------+
                                              ----------'
O                                          40 '--------'
O                                          60 '------------'
OQSYSPRT  D   01                      1
O                     ProdName             30
O                     QTY          1       40
O                     Income       1       60
OQSYSPRT  T   LR                      1
O                                             'Total: '
O                     Total        1
```

Figure 61. Source for TRANSRPT Module

The DDS for the file TRNSDTA is shown in Figure 62 on page 160. The /COPY member is shown in Figure 60 on page 158.

```
A******************************************************************
A* RELATED FILES:  TRNSRPT                                        *
A* DESCRIPTION:    This is the physical file TRNSDTA. It has      *
A*                 one record format called TRNSREC.              *
A******************************************************************
A* PARTS TRANSACTION FILE -- TRNSDTA
A          R TRNSREC
A            PROD          10S 0       TEXT('Product')
A            QTY            5S 0       TEXT('Quantity')
A            DISCOUNT       2S 2       TEXT('Discount')
```

Figure 62. DDS for TRNSDTA

Behavior of Bound ILE RPG Modules

In ILE RPG, the *main procedure* is the boundary for the scope of LR semantics and the RPG cycle. The *module* is the boundary for the scope of open files.

In any ILE program, there may be several RPG cycles active; there is one RPG cycle for each RPG module that has a main procedure. The cycles are independent: setting on LR in one main procedure has no effect on the cycle in another.

Binding Modules into a Program

Binding is the process of creating a runnable Integrated Language Environment program by combining one or more modules and optional service programs, and resolving symbols passed between them. The system code that does this combining and resolving is called a **binder** on the AS/400 system.

As part of the binding process, a procedure must be identified as the startup procedure, or **program entry procedure**. When a program is called, the program entry procedure receives the parameters from the command line and is given initial control for the program. The user's code associated with the program entry procedure is the user entry procedure.

If an ILE RPG module contains a main procedure, it implicitly also contains a program entry procedure. Therefore, any ILE RPG module may be specified as the entry module as long as it is not a NOMAIN module.

Figure 63 on page 161 gives an idea of the internal structure of a program object. It shows the program object TRPT, which was created by binding the two modules TRANSRPT and TRANSSVC. TRANSRPT is the entry module.

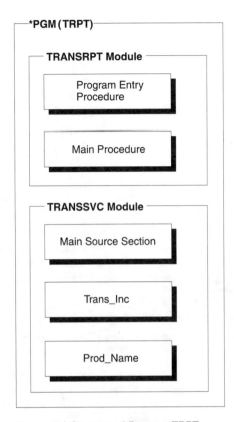

Figure 63. Structure of Program TRPT

Within a bound object, procedures can interrelate using static procedure calls. These bound calls are faster than external calls. Therefore, an application consisting of a single bound program with many bound calls should perform faster than a similar application consisting of separate programs with many external, interapplication calls.

In addition to binding modules together, you can also bind them to service programs (type *SRVPGM). Service programs allow you to code and maintain modules separately from the program modules. Common routines can be created as service programs, and if the routine changes, the change can be incorporated by binding the service program again. The programs that use these common routines do not have to be recreated.

For information on the binding process and the binder, refer to the *ILE Concepts*.

Using the CRTPGM Command

The Create Program (CRTPGM) command creates a program object from one or more previously created modules and, if required, one or more service programs. You can bind modules created by any of the ILE Create Module commands: CRTRPGMOD, CRTCMOD, CRTCBLMOD, or CRTCLMOD.

Note: The modules and/or service programs required must have been created prior to using the CRTPGM command.

Before you create a program object using the CRTPGM command, you should:

1. Establish a program name

2. Identify the module or modules and, if required, service programs you want to bind into a program object

3. Identify the entry module

   You indicate which module contains the program entry procedure through the ENTMOD parameter of CRTPGM. The default is ENTMOD(*FIRST), meaning that the module containing the first program entry procedure found in the list for the MODULE parameter is the entry module.

   Assuming you have only one module with a main procedure, that is, all modules but one have NOMAIN specified, you can accept the default (*FIRST). Alternatively, you can specify (*ONLY); this will provide a check that in fact only one module has a main procedure. For example, in both of the following situations you could specify ENTMOD(*ONLY).

   - You bind an RPG module to a C module without a main() function

   - You bind two RPG modules, where one has NOMAIN on the control specification

   Note: If you are binding more than one ILE RPG module with a main procedure, then you should specify the name of the module that you want to receive control when the program is called. You can also specify *FIRST if the module with a main procedure precedes any other modules with main procedures on the list specified for the MODULE parameter.

4. Identify the activation group that the program is to use

   Specify the named activation group QILE if your program has no special requirements or if you are not sure which group to use. In general, it is a good idea to run an application in its own activation group. Therefore, you may want to name the activation group after the application.

   Note that the default activation group for CRTPGM is *NEW. This means that your program will run in its own activation group and the activation group will terminate when the program does. Whether or not you set LR on, your program will have a fresh copy of its data the next time you call it.

To create a program object using the CRTPGM command, perform the following steps:

1. Enter the CRTPGM command

2. Enter the appropriate values for the command parameter

Table 40 on page 163 lists the CRTPGM command parameters and their default values. For a full description of the CRTPGM command and its parameters, refer to the *CL Reference*.

Table 40. Parameters for CRTPGM Command and Their Default Values

Parameter Group	Parameter(Default Value)
Identification	PGM(*library name/program name*) MODULE(*PGM)
Program access	ENTMOD(*FIRST)
Binding	BNDSRVPGM(*NONE) BNDDIR(*NONE)
Run time	ACTGRP(*NEW)
Miscellaneous	OPTION(*GEN *NODUPPROC *NODUPVAR *WARN *RSLVREF) DETAIL(*NONE) ALWUPD(*YES) ALWRINZ(*NO) REPLACE(*YES) AUT(*LIBCRTAUT) TEXT(*ENTMODTXT) TGTRLS(*CURRENT) USRPRF(*USER)

After you have entered the CRTPGM command, the system performs the following actions:

1. Copies listed modules into what will become the program object, and links any service programs to the program object

2. Identifies the module containing the program entry procedure, and locates the first import in this module

3. Checks the modules in the order in which they are listed, and matches the first import with a module export

4. Returns to the first module, and locates the next import

5. Resolves all imports in the first module

6. Continues to the next module, and resolves all imports

7. Resolves all imports in each subsequent module until all of the imports have been resolved

8. If any imports cannot be resolved with an export, the binding process terminates without creating a program object

9. After all the imports have been resolved, the binding process completes and the program object is created

Note: If you have specified that a variable or procedure is to be exported (using the EXPORT keyword), it is possible that the variable or procedure name will be identical to a variable or procedure in another procedure within the bound program object. In this case, the results may not be as expected. See *ILE Concepts* for information on how to handle this situation.

Binding Multiple Modules: This example shows you how to use the CRTPGM command to bind two ILE RPG modules into a program TRPT. In this program, the following occurs:

- The module TRANSRPT reads each transaction record from a file, TRNSDTA
- It then calls procedure Trans_Inc and Proc_Name in module TRANSSVC using bound calls within expressions
- Trans_Inc calculates the income pertaining to each transaction and returns the value to the caller
- Proc_Name determines the product name and returns it
- TRANSRPT then prints the transaction record

Source for TRANSRPT, TRANSSVC, and TRNSDTA is shown in Figure 61 on page 159, Figure 59 on page 156, and Figure 62 on page 160, respectively.

1. First create the module TRANSRPT. Type:

   ```
   CRTRPGMOD MODULE(MYLIB/TRANSRPT)
   ```

2. Then create module TRANSSVC by typing:

   ```
   CRTRPGMOD MODULE(MYLIB/TRANSSVC)
   ```

3. To create the program object, type:

   ```
   CRTPGM PGM(MYLIB/TRPT) MODULE(TRANSRPT TRANSSVC)
          ENTMOD(*FIRST) ACTGRP(TRPT)
   ```

The CRTPGM command creates a program object, TRPT, in the library MYLIB.

Note that TRANSRPT is listed first in the MODULE parameter. ENTMOD(*FIRST) will find the first module with a program entry procedure. Because only one of the two modules has a program entry procedure, the modules can be entered in either order.

The program TRPT will run in the named activation group TRPT. The program runs in a named group to ensure that no other programs can affect its resources.

Figure 64 shows an output file created when TRPT is run.

```
Product name                     Quantity    Income
------------------------------   --------    ------------
Large                                 245    330,750.00
Super                                  15     52,500.00
Super Large                             0           .00
Super Jumbo                           123  2,952,000.00
Incredibly Large Super Jumbo           15    912,000.00
***Unknown***                          12           .00
Total:        4,247,250.00
```

Figure 64. File QSYSPRT for TRPT

Stage 19. New Operation Codes and Built-In Functions

This chapter provides reference information on the new RPG IV opcodes and built-in functions. It is based on information in the *ILE RPG for AS/400 Reference* .

New Operation Codes

RPG IV has the following new opcode extenders:

(D)	Pass operational descriptors on bound call
(D)	Date field
(E)	Error handling
(M)	Default precision rules
(N)	Set pointer to *NULL after successful DEALLOC
(R)	No intermediate value will have fewer decimal positions than the result
(T)	Time field
(Z)	Timestamp field

As well, RPG IV still has the following opcode extenders:

(H)	Half-adjust the result
(N)	Do not lock record on input if file is update
(P)	Pad the result with blanks

RPG IV has the following new opcodes:

ADDDUR (E)	Add a duration
ALLOC (E)	Allocate storage
CALLB (D E)	Call a bound procedure
CALLP (E M/R)	Call a prototyped procedure or program
DEALLOC (E/N)	Free storage
DOU (M/R)	Do until
DOW (M/R)	Do while
EVAL (H M/R)	Evaluation an expression
EXTRCT (E)	Extract date, time, and timestamp fields
IF (M/R)	If (an expression)
REALLOC (E)	Reallocate storage with new length
SUBDUR (E)	Subtract or calculate a duration
TEST (E)	Test the validity of date, time, and timestamp fields
WHEN (M/R)	When (an expression)

Each of the new operation codes is described below.

ADDDUR (Add Duration)

Code	Factor 1	Factor 2	Result Field	Indicators		
ADDDUR (E)	Date/Time	Duration:Duration Code	Date/Time	_	ER	_

The ADDDUR operation adds the duration specified in factor 2 to a date or time and places the resulting Date, Time, or Timestamp in the result field.

Factor 1 is optional and may contain a Date, Time, or Timestamp field, subfield, array, array element, literal, or constant. If factor 1 contains a field name, array, or array element, then its data type must be the same data type as the field specified in the result field. If factor 1 is not specified, the duration is added to the field specified in the result field.

Factor 2 is required and contains two subfactors. The first is a duration and may be a numeric field, array element, or constant with zero decimal positions. If the duration is negative, then it is subtracted from the date. The second subfactor must be a valid duration code indicating the type of duration. The duration code must be consistent with the result field data type. You can add a year, month, or day duration, but not a minute duration to a date field.

The result field must be a date, time, or timestamp data type field, array, or array element. If factor 1 is blank, the duration is added to the value in the result field. If the result field is an array, the value in factor 2 is added to each element of the array. If the result field is a time field, the result will always be a valid Time. For example, adding 59 minutes to 23:59:59 would give 24:58:59. Because this time is not valid, the compiler adjusts it to 00:58:59.

When adding a duration in months to a date, the general rule is that the month portion is increased by the number of months in the duration and the day portion is unchanged. The exception to this is when the resulting day portion would exceed the actual number of days in the resulting month. In this case, the resulting day portion is adjusted to the actual month end date. The following examples (which assume a *YMD format) illustrate this point.

- '98/05/30' ADDDUR 1:*MONTH results in '98/06/30'

  The resulting month portion has been increased by one; the day portion is unchanged.

- '98/05/31' ADDDUR 1:*MONTH results in '98/06/30'

  The resulting month portion has been increased by one; the resulting day portion has been adjusted, because June has only 30 days.

Similar results occur when adding a year duration. For example, adding one year to '92/02/29' results in '93/02/28', an adjusted value, because the resulting year is not a leap year.

An error situation arises when one of the following occurs:

- The value of the Date, Time, or Timestamp field in factor 1 is invalid
- Factor 1 is blank and the value of the result field before the operation is invalid
- Overflow or underflow occurred (that is, the resulting value is greater than *HIVAL or less than *LOVAL)

In an error situation:

- An error (status code 112 or 113) is signalled
- The error indicator (columns 73-74) — if specified — is set on, or the %ERROR built-in function — if the 'E' extender is specified — is set to return '1'
- The value of the result field remains unchanged

To handle exceptions with program status codes 112 or 113, either the operation code extender 'E' or an error indicator ER can be specified, but not both.

Note: The system places a 15-digit limit on durations. Adding a duration with more than 15 significant digits will cause errors or truncation. These problems can be avoided by limiting the first subfactor in Factor 2 to 15 digits.

```
*...1....+....2....+....3....+....4....+....5....+....6....+....7...+....
HKeywords++++++++++++++++++++++++++++++++++++++++++++++++++++++++++++++++
H TIMFMT(*USA) DATFMT(*MDY&)
DName++++++++++ETDsFrom+++To/L+++IDc.Keywords+++++++++++++++++++++++++++++
 *
DDateconst      C                      CONST(D'12 31 92')
 *
 * Define a Date field and initialize
 *
DLoandate       S              D   DATFMT(*EUR) INZ(D'12 31 92')
DDuedate        S              D   DATFMT(*ISO)
Dtimestamp      S              Z
Danswer         S              T
CL0N01Factor1+++++++Opcode(E)+Factor2+++++++Result++++++++Len++D+HiLoEq....
 * Determine a DUEDATE which is xx years, yy months, zz days later
 * than LOANDATE.
C     LOANDATE    ADDDUR    XX:*YEARS      DUEDATE
C                 ADDDUR    YY:*MONTHS     DUEDATE
C                 ADDDUR    ZZ:*DAYS       DUEDATE
 * Determine the date 23 days later
 *
C                 ADDDUR    23:*D          DUEDATE

 * Add a 1234 microseconds to a timestamp
 *
C                 ADDDUR    1234:*MS       timestamp

 * Add 12 HRS and 16 minutes to midnight
 *
C     T'00:00 am' ADDDUR    12:*Hours      answer
C                 ADDDUR    16:*Minutes    answer

 * Subtract 30 days from a loan due date
 *
C                 ADDDUR    -30:*D         LOANDUE
```

Figure 65. ADDDUR Operations

ALLOC (Allocate Storage)

Code	Factor 1	Factor 2	Result Field	Indicators		
ALLOC (E)		Length	Pointer	_	ER	_

The ALLOC operation allocates storage in the default heap of the length specified in factor 2. The result field pointer is set to point to the new heap storage. The storage is uninitialized.

Factor 2 must be a numeric with zero decimal positions. It can be a literal, constant, stand-alone field, subfield, table name, or array element. The value must be between 1 and 16776704. If the value is out of range at run time, an error will occur with status 425. If the storage could not be allocated, an error will occur with status 426. If these errors occur, the result field pointer remains unchanged.

The result field must be a basing pointer scalar variable (a standalone field, data structure subfield, table name, or array element).

To handle exceptions with program status codes 425 or 426, either the operation code extender 'E' or an error indicator ER can be specified, but not both.

```
D Ptr1             S            *
D Ptr2             S            *
C                  ALLOC    7             Ptr1
 * Now Ptr1 points to 7 bytes of storage
 *
C                  ALLOC (E) 12345678     Ptr2
 * This is a large amount of storage, and sometimes it may
 * be unavailable.  If the storage could not be allocated,
 * %ERROR will return '1', the status is set to 00426, and
 * %STATUS will return 00426.
```

Figure 66. ALLOC Operations

CALLB (Call a Bound Procedure)

Code	Factor 1	Factor 2	Result Field	Indicators	
CALLB (D E)		Procedure name or procedure pointer	Plist name	_ ER	LR

The CALLB operation is used to call bound procedures written in any of the ILE languages.

The operation extender D may be used to include operational descriptors. This is similar to calling a prototyped procedure with CALLP when its parameters have been defined with keyword OPDESC. (Operational descriptors provide the programmer with run-time resolution of the exact attributes of character or graphic strings passed (that is, length and type of string).

Factor 2 is required and must be a literal or constant containing the name of the procedure to be called, or a procedure pointer containing the address of the procedure to be called. All references must be able to be resolved at bind time. The procedure name provided is case sensitive and may contain more than 10 characters, but no more than 255. If the name is longer than 255, it will be truncated to 255. The result field is optional and may contain a PLIST name.

To handle CALLB exceptions (program status codes 202, 211, or 231), either the operation code extender 'E' or an error indicator ER can be specified, but not both.

An indicator specified in positions 75-76 will be set on when the call ends with LR set on.

```
DName++++++++++ETDsFrom+++To/L+++IDc.Keywords++++++++++++++++++++++++++++++++
 * Define a procedure pointer
D
D ProcPtr         S              *    PROCPTR INZ(%PADDR('Create_Space'))
D Extern          S              10
D
CL0N01Factor1+++++++Opcode(E)+Factor2+++++++Result++++++++Len++D+HiLoEq....
 * The following call linkage would be STATIC
C                   CALLB     'BOUNDPROC'
 * The following call linkage would be DYNAMIC
C                   CALL      Extern
 * The following call linkage would be STATIC, using a procedure pointer
C                   CALLB     ProcPtr
```

Figure 67. CALLB Operation

CALLP (Call a Prototyped Procedure or Program)

Code	Factor 1	Extended Factor 2
CALLP (E M/R)		NAME{ (Parm1 {:Parm2...}) }

The CALLP operation is used to call prototyped procedures or programs.

Unlike the other call operations, CALLP uses a free-form syntax. You use the extended-factor 2 entry to specify the name of the prototype of the called program or procedure, as well as any parameters to be passed. (This is similar to calling a built-in function.) A maximum of 255 parameters is allowed for a program call, and a maximum of 399 for a procedure call.

The compiler then uses the prototype name to obtain an external name, if required, for the call. If the keyword EXTPGM is specified on the prototype, the call will be a dynamic external call; otherwise, it will be a bound procedure call.

A prototype for the program or procedure being called must be included in the definition specifications preceding the CALLP.

Note that if CALLP is used to call a procedure that returns a value, that value will not be available to the caller. If the value is required, call the prototyped procedure from within an expression.

To handle CALLP exceptions (program status codes 202, 211, and 231), the operation code extender 'E' can be specified.

Note: The E extender is only active during the final call for CALLP. If an error occurs on a call that is done as part of the parameter processing, control will not pass to the next operation. For example, if FileRecs is a procedure returning a numeric value and an error occurs when FileRecs is called in the following statement, the E extender would have no effect.

```
CALLP (E) PROGNAME(FileRecs(Fld) + 1)
```

```
    *-----------------------------------------------------------
    *  This prototype for QCMDEXC defines two parameters:
    *  1- a character field that may be shorter in length
    *      than expected
    *  2- any numeric field
    *-----------------------------------------------------------
D qcmdexc         PR                    EXTPGM('QCMDEXC')
D   cmd                      200A       OPTIONS(*VARSIZE)  CONST
D   cmdlen                    15P 5 CONST
    ...
C                 CALLP       QCMDEXC('WRKSPLF' :
                                 %size ('WRKSPLF'))
```

Figure 68. Calling a Prototyped Program Using CALLP

The following example of CALLP is from the service program example in *ILE RPG for AS/400 Programming Guide*. CvtToHex is a procedure in a service program created to hold conversion routines. CvtToHex converts an input string to its hexadecimal form. The prototyped calls are to the ILE CEE API, CEEDOD (Retrieve Operational Descriptor). It is used to determine the length of the input string.

```
 *=================================================================*
 * CvtToHex - convert input string to hex output string
 *=================================================================*
D/COPY MYLIB/QRPGLESRC,CVTHEXPR


 *-----------------------------------------------------------------*
 * Main entry parameters
 * 1. Input:   string                      character(n)
 * 2. Output:  hex string                  character(2 * n)
 *-----------------------------------------------------------------*
D CvtToHex        PI                        OPDESC
D   InString                     16383      CONST OPTIONS(*VARSIZE)
D   HexString                    32766      OPTIONS(*VARSIZE)


 *-----------------------------------------------------------------*
 * Prototype for CEEDOD (Retrieve operational descriptor)
 *-----------------------------------------------------------------*
D CEEDOD          PR
D                              10I 0 CONST
D                              10I 0
D                              10I 0
D                              10I 0
D                              10I 0
D                              10I 0
D                              12A    OPTIONS(*OMIT)

 * Parameters passed to CEEDOD
D ParmNum         S            10I 0
D DescType        S            10I 0
D DataType        S            10I 0
D DescInfo1       S            10I 0
D DescInfo2       S            10I 0
D InLen           S            10I 0
D HexLen          S            10I 0


 *-----------------------------------------------------------------*
 * Other fields used by the program
 *-----------------------------------------------------------------*
D HexDigits       C                   CONST('0123456789ABCDEF')
D IntDs           DS
D   IntNum                      5I 0 INZ(0)
D   IntChar                     1     OVERLAY(IntNum:2)
D HexDs           DS
D   HexC1                       1
D   HexC2                       1
D InChar          S             1
D Pos             S             5P 0
D HexPos          S             5P 0
```

Figure 69 (Part 1 of 2). Calling a Prototyped Procedure Using CALLP

```
         *----------------------------------------------------------------*
         * Use the operational descriptors to determine the lengths of    *
         * the parameters that were passed.                               *
         *----------------------------------------------------------------*
C                       CALLP     CEEDOD(1       : DescType : DataType :
C                                      DescInfo1 : DescInfo2: Inlen    :
C                                      *OMIT)
C                       CALLP     CEEDOD(2       : DescType : DataType :
C                                      DescInfo1 : DescInfo2: HexLen   :
C                                      *OMIT)


         *----------------------------------------------------------------*
         * Determine the length to handle (minimum of the input length    *
         * and half of the hex length)                                    *
         *----------------------------------------------------------------*
C                       IF        InLen > HexLen / 2
C                       EVAL      InLen = HexLen / 2
C                       ENDIF


         *----------------------------------------------------------------*
         * For each character in the input string, convert to a 2-byte    *
         * hexadecimal representation (for example, '5' --> 'F5')         *
         *----------------------------------------------------------------*
C                       EVAL      HexPos = 1
C                       DO        InLen         Pos
C                       EVAL      InChar = %SUBST(InString : Pos :1)
C                       EXSR      GetHex
C                       EVAL      %SUBST(HexString : HexPos : 2) = HexDs
C                       EVAL      HexPos = HexPos + 2
C                       ENDDO


         *----------------------------------------------------------------*
         * Done; return to caller.                                        *
         *----------------------------------------------------------------*
C                       RETURN


         *================================================================*
         * GetHex - subroutine to convert 'InChar' to 'HexDs'             *
         *                                                                *
         * Use division by 16 to separate the two hexadecimal digits.     *
         * The quotient is the first digit, the remainder is the second.  *
         *================================================================*
C     GetHex            BEGSR
C                       EVAL      IntChar = InChar
C     IntNum            DIV       16            X1                5 0
C                       MVR                     X2                5 0
         *----------------------------------------------------------------*
         * Use the hexadecimal digit (plus 1) to substring the list of    *
         * hexadecimal characters '012...CDEF'.                           *
         *----------------------------------------------------------------*
C                       EVAL      HexC1 = %SUBST(HexDigits:X1+1:1)
C                       EVAL      HexC2 = %SUBST(HexDigits:X2+1:1)
C                       ENDSR
```

Figure 69 (Part 2 of 2). Calling a Prototyped Procedure Using CALLP

DEALLOC (Free Storage)

Code	Factor 1	Factor 2	Result Field	Indicators		
DEALLOC (E/N)			Pointer	_	ER	_

The DEALLOC operation frees one previous allocation of heap storage. The result field of DEALLOC is a pointer that must contain the value previously set by a heap-storage allocation operation (either an ALLOC operation in RPG or some other heap-storage allocation mechanism). It is not sufficient to simply point to heap storage; the pointer must be set to the beginning of an allocation.

The storage pointed to by the pointer is freed for subsequent allocation by this program or any other in the activation group.

If operation code extender N is specified, the pointer is set to *NULL after a successful deallocation.

To handle DEALLOC exceptions (program status code 426), either the operation code extender 'E' or an error indicator ER can be specified, but not both. The result field pointer will not be changed if an error occurs, even if 'N' is specified.

The result field must be a basing pointer scalar variable (a stand-alone field, data structure subfield, table name, or array element).

No error is given at run time if the pointer is already *NULL.

```
*...1....+....2....+....3....+....4....+....5....+....6....+....7...+....
DName++++++++++ETDsFrom+++To/L+++IDc.Keywords+++++++++++++++++++++++++++++
*
D Ptr1             S             *
D Fld1             S             1A
D BasedFld         S             7A  BASED(Ptr1)
CL0N01Factor1+++++++Opcode(E)+Factor2+++++++Result++++++++Len++D+HiLoEq....
*
* 7 bytes of storage are allocated from the heap and
* Ptr1 is set to point to it
C                  ALLOC     7             Ptr1
*
* The DEALLOC frees the storage.  This storage is now available
* for allocation by this program or any other program in the
* activation group.  (Note that the next allocation may or
* may not get the same storage back).
C                  DEALLOC                 Ptr1
*
* Ptr1 still points at the deallocated storage, but this pointer
* should not be used with its current value.  Any attempt to
* access BasedFld which is based on Ptr1 is invalid.
C                  EVAL      Ptr1 = %addr(Fld1)
*
* The DEALLOC is not valid because the pointer is set to the
* address of program storage.  %ERROR is set to return '1',
* the program status is set to 00426 (%STATUS returns 00426),
* and the pointer is not changed.
C                  DEALLOC(E)              Ptr1
*
* Allocate and deallocate storage again.  Since operational
* extender N is specified, Ptr1 has the value *NULL after the
* DEALLOC.
C                  ALLOC     7             Ptr1
C                  DEALLOC(N)              Ptr1
```

Figure 70. DEALLOC Operations

DOU (Do Until)

Code	Factor 1	Extended Factor 2
DOU (M/R)		Expression

The DOU operation code precedes a group of operations that you want to execute at least once and possibly more than once. Its function is similar to that of the DOUxx operation code. An associated ENDDO statement marks the end of the group. It differs in that the logical condition is expressed by an indicator valued expression in the extended factor 2 entry. The operations controlled by the DOU operation are performed until the expression in the extended factor 2 field is true.

Level and conditioning indicators are valid. Factor 1 must be blank. Extended factor 2 contains the expression to be evaluated.

```
CL0N01Factor1+++++++Opcode(E)+Extended-factor2+++++++++++++++++++++++++++..
C                              Extended-factor2-continuation+++++++++++++++
 * In this example, the do loop will be repeated until the F3
 * is pressed.
C                   DOU       *INKC
C                   :
C                   :
C                   ENDDO
C
 * The following do loop will be repeated until *In01 is on
 * or until FIELD2 is greater than FIELD3
C
C                   DOU       *IN01 OR (Field2 > Field3)
C                   :
C                   :
C                   ENDDO
 * The following loop will be repeated until X is greater than the number
 * of elements in Array
C
C                   DOU       X > %elem(Array)
C                   EVAL      Total = Total + Array(x)
C                   EVAL      X = X + 1
C                   ENDDO
C
 *
```

Figure 71. DOU Operation

DOW (Do While)

Code	Factor 1	Extended Factor 2
DOW (M/R)		Expression

The DOW operation code precedes a group of operations that you want to process when a given condition exists. Its function is similar to that of the DOWxx operation code. An associated ENDDO statement marks the end of the group. It differs in that the logical condition is expressed by an indicator valued expression in the extended-factor 2 entry. The operations controlled by the DOW operation are performed while the expression in the extended factor 2 field is true.

Level and conditioning indicators are valid. Factor 1 must be blank. Factor 2 contains the expression to be evaluated.

```
CL0N01Factor1+++++++Opcode(E)+Extended-factor2+++++++++++++++++++++++++++++..
C                              Extended-factor2-continuation+++++++++++++++++
 * In this example, the do loop will be repeated until the condition
 * is false. That is when A > 5 and/or B+C are not equal to zero.
C
C                   DOW       A <= 5 AND B+C = 0
C                   :
C                   :
C                   ENDDO
C
```

Figure 72. DOW Operation

EXTRCT (Extract Date/Time/Timestamp)

Code	Factor 1	Factor 2	Result Field	Indicators		
EXTRCT (E)		Date/Time: Duration Code	Target	_	ER	_

The EXTRCT operation code will return one of:

- The year, month, or day part of a date or timestamp field
- The hours, minutes, or seconds part of a time or timestamp field
- The microseconds part of the timestamp field

to the field specified in the result field.

The Date, Time, or Timestamp from which the information is required is specified in factor 2, followed by the duration code. The entry specified in factor 2 can be a field, subfield, table element, or array element. The duration code must be consistent with the data type of factor 2.

Factor 1 must be blank.

The result field can be any numeric or character field, subfield, or array/table element. The result field is cleared before the extracted data is assigned. For a character result field, the data is put left adjusted into the result field.

Note: When using the EXTRCT operation with a Julian Date (format *JUL), specifying a duration code of *D will return the day of the month; specifying *M will return the month of the year. If you require the day and month to be in the three-digit format, you can use a basing pointer to obtain it.

To handle EXTRCT exceptions (program status code 112), either the operation code extender 'E' or an error indicator ER can be specified, but not both.

```
D LOGONDATE      S           D
D DATE_STR       S          15
D MONTHS         S           8  DIM(12) CTDATA
C*0N01Factor1+++++++Opcode(E)+Factor2+++++++Result++++++++Len++D+HiLoEq....
```

```
 * Move the job date to LOGONDATE.  By default, LOGONDATE has an *ISO
 * date format, which contains a 4-digit year.  *DATE also contains a
 * 4-digit year, but in a different format, *USA.
```

```
C       *USA        MOVE      *DATE          LOGONDATE
```

```
 *
 * Extract the month from a date field to a 2-digit field
 * that is used as an index into a character array containing
 * the names of the months.  Then extract the day from the
 * timestamp to a 2-byte character field which can be used in
 * an EVAL concatenation expression to form a string.
 * For example, if LOGONDATE is March 17, 1996, LOGMONTH will
 * contain 03, LOGDAY will contain 17, and DATE_STR will contain
 * 'March 17'.
```

```
C                   EXTRCT    LOGONDATE:*M  LOGMONTH        2 0
C                   EXTRCT    LOGONDATE:*D  LOGDAY          2
C                   EVAL      DATE_STR = %TRIMR(MONTHS(LOGMONTH))
C                                        + ' ' + LOGDAY
C                   SETON                                       LR
** CTDATA MONTHS
January
February
March
April
May
June
July
August
September
October
November
December
```

Figure 73. EXTRCT Operations

IF (If)

Code	Factor 1	Extended Factor 2
IF (M/R)	Blank	Expression

The IF operation code allows a series of operation codes to be processed if a condition is met. Its function is similar to that of the IFxx operation code. It differs in that the logical condition is expressed by an indicator-valued expression in the extended factor 2 entry. The operations controlled by the IF operation are performed when the expression in the extended factor 2 field is true.

```
CLON01Factor1+++++++Opcode(E)+Extended-factor2++++++++++++++++++++++++++++..
C                              Extended-factor2-continuation+++++++++++++++
 * The operations controlled by the IF operation are performed
 * when the expression is true.  That is A is greater than 10 and
 * indicator 20 is on.
C
C                   IF        A>10 AND *IN(20)
C                   :
C                   ENDIF
 *
 * The operations controlled by the IF operation are performed
 * when Date1 represents a later date then Date2
C
C                   IF        Date1 > Date2
C                   :
C                   ENDIF
 *
```

Figure 74. IF Operations

REALLOC (Reallocate Storage with New Length)

Code	Factor 1	Factor 2	Result Field	Indicators		
REALLOC (E)		Length	Pointer	_	ER	_

The REALLOC operation changes the length of the heap storage pointed to by the result-field pointer to the length specified in factor 2. The result field of REALLOC contains a basing pointer variable. The result field pointer must contain the value previously set by a heap-storage allocation operation (either an ALLOC or REALLOC operation in RPG or some other heap-storage function, such as CEEGTST). It is not sufficient to simply point to heap storage; the pointer must be set to the beginning of an allocation.

New storage is allocated of the specified size and the value of the old storage is copied to the new storage. Then, the old storage is deallocated. If the new length is shorter, the value is truncated on the right. If the new length is longer, the new storage to the right of the copied data is uninitialized.

The result field pointer is set to point to the new storage.

If the operation does not succeed, an error condition occurs, but the result field pointer will not be changed. If the original pointer was valid and the operation failed because there was insufficient new storage available (status 425), the original storage is not deallocated, so the result field pointer is still valid with its original value.

If the pointer is valid but it does not point to storage that can be deallocated, then status 426 (error in storage management operation) will be set.

To handle exceptions with program status codes 425 or 426, either the operation code extender 'E' or an error indicator ER can be specified, but not both.

Factor 2 contains a numeric variable or constant that indicates the new size of the storage (in bytes) to be allocated. Factor 2 must be numeric with zero decimal positions. The value must be between 1 and 16776704.

```
D Ptr1            S                 *
D Fld             S          32767A      BASED(Ptr1)
 * The ALLOC operation allocates 7 bytes to the pointer Ptr1.
 * After the ALLOC operation, only the first 7 bytes of variable
 * Fld can be used.
C                    ALLOC     7                   Ptr1
C                    EVAL      %SUBST(Fld : 1 : 7) = '1234567'
C                    REALLOC   10                  Ptr1
 * Now 10 bytes of Fld can be used.
C                    EVAL      %SUBST(Fld : 1 : 10) = '123456789A'
```

Figure 75. REALLOC Operation

SUBDUR (Subtract Duration)

Code	Factor 1	Factor 2	Result Field	Indicators		
SUBDUR (E) (duration)	Date/Time/ Timestamp	Date/Time/ Timestamp	Duration: Duration code	–	ER	–
SUBDUR (E) (new date)	Date/Time/ Timestamp	Duration:Duration Code	Date/Time/ Timestamp	–	ER	–

The SUBDUR operation has been provided to:

- Subtract a duration to establish a new Date, Time, or Timestamp

- Calculate a duration

Subtract a Duration

The SUBDUR operation can be used to subtract a duration specified in factor 2 from a field or constant specified in factor 1 and place the resulting Date, Time, or Timestamp in the field specified in the result field.

Factor 1 is optional and may contain a Date, Time or Timestamp field, array, array element, literal, or constant. If factor 1 contains a field name, array, or array element then its data type must be the same type as the field specified in the result field. If factor 1 is not specified, then the duration is subtracted from the field specified in the result field.

Factor 2 is required and contains two subfactors. The first is a numeric field, array, or constant with zero decimal positions. If the field is negative, then the duration is added to the field. The second subfactor must be a valid duration code indicating the type of duration. The duration code must be consistent with the result field data type. For example, you can subtract a year, month, or day duration, but not a minute duration from a date field.

The result field must be a date, time, or timestamp data type field, array, or array element. If factor 1 is blank, the duration is subtracted from the value in the result field. If the result field is an array, the value in factor 2 is subtracted from each element in the array. If the result field is a time field, the result will always be a valid Time. For example, subtracting 59 minutes from 00:58:59 would give -00:00:01. Because this time is not valid, the compiler adjusts it to 23:59:59.

When subtracting a duration in months from a date, the general rule is that the month portion is decreased by the number of months in the duration, and the day portion is unchanged. The exception to this is when the resulting day portion would exceed the actual number of days in the resulting month. In this case, the resulting day portion is adjusted to the actual month-end date. The following examples (which assume a *YMD format) illustrate this point.

- '95/05/30' SUBDUR 1:*MONTH results in '95/04/30'

The resulting month portion has been decreased by one; the day portion is unchanged.

- '95/05/31' SUBDUR 1:*MONTH results in '95/04/30'

The resulting month portion has been decreased by one; the resulting day portion has been adjusted because April has only 30 days.

Similar results occur when subtracting a year duration. For example, subtracting one year from '92/02/29' results in '91/02/28', an adjusted value because the resulting year is not a leap year.

Note: The system places a 15 digit limit on durations. Subtracting a duration with more than 15 significant digits will cause errors or truncation. These problems can be avoided by limiting the first subfactor in factor 2 to 15 digits.

Calculate a Duration

The SUBDUR operation can also be used to calculate a duration between:

1. Two dates

2. A date and a timestamp

3. Two times

4. A time and a timestamp

5. Two timestamps

The data types in factor 1 and factor 2 must be compatible types, as specified above.

Factor 1 is required and must contain a Date, Time, or Timestamp field, subfield, array, array element, constant, or literal.

Factor 2 is required and must also contain a Date, Time, or Timestamp field, array, array element, literal, or constant. The duration code must be consistent with one of the following:

- Factor 1 and factor 2
- *Years(*Y), *Months(*M), and *Days(*D), if factor 1 or factor 2 is a Date
- Timestamp, *Hours(*H), *Minutes(*MN), and *Seconds(*S), when factor 1 or factor 2 is a Time or Timestamp.

The result of the calculation is a complete unit; any rounding is downwards. The calculation of durations includes microseconds.

For example, if the actual duration is 384 days and the result is requested in years, the result will be one complete year, because there are 1.05 years in 384 days. A duration of 59 minutes requested in hours will result in 0 hours.

The result field consists of two subfactors. The first is the name of a zero decimal numeric field, array, or array element in which the result of the operation will be placed.

The second subfactor contains a duration code denoting the type of duration. The result field will be negative if the date in factor 1 is earlier than the date in factor 2.

Note: Calculating a microsecond duration (*mseconds) can exceed the 15 digit system limit for durations and cause errors or truncation. This situation will occur when there is more than a 32 year and nine month difference between the factor 1 and factor 2 entries.

Possible Error Situations

1. For subtracting durations:
   - If the value of the Date, Time, or Timestamp field in factor 1 is invalid
   - If factor 1 is blank and the value of the result field before the operation is invalid
   - If the result of the operation is greater than *HIVAL or less than *LOVAL

2. For calculating durations:
   - If the value of the Date, Time, or Timestamp field in factor 1 or factor 2 is invalid
   - If the result field is not large enough to hold the resulting duration

In each of these cases, an error will be signalled.

If an error is detected, an error will be generated with one of the following program status codes:

- 00103: Result field not large enough to hold result
- 00112: Date, Time, or Timestamp value not valid
- 00113: A Date overflow or underflow occurred (that is, the resulting Date is greater than *HIVAL or less than *LOVAL)

The value of the result field remains unchanged. To handle exceptions with program status codes 103, 112 or 113, either the operation code extender 'E' or an error indicator ER can be specified, but not both.

SUBDUR Examples

```
CLON01Factor1+++++++Opcode(E)+Factor2+++++++Result++++++++Len++D+HiLoEq....
 * Determine a LOANDATE which is xx years, yy months, zz days prior to
 * the DUEDATE.

C     DUEDATE        SUBDUR    XX:*YEARS      LOANDATE
C                    SUBDUR    YY:*MONTHS     LOANDATE
C                    SUBDUR    ZZ:*DAYS       LOANDATE

 * Add 30 days to a loan due date
 *
C                    SUBDUR    -30:*D         LOANDUE

 * Calculate the number or days between a LOANDATE and a DUEDATE.

C     LOANDATE       SUBDUR    DUEDATE        NUM_DAYS:*D      5 0

 * Determine the number of seconds between LOANDATE and DUEDATE.

C     LOANDATE       SUBDUR    DUEDATE        NUM_SECS:*S      5 0
```

Figure 76. SUBDUR Operations

TEST (Test Date/Time/Timestamp)

Code	Factor 1	Factor 2	Result Field	Indicators		
TEST (E)			Date/Time orTimestamp Field	–	ER	–
TEST (D E)	Date Format		Character or Numeric field	–	ER	–
TEST (E T)	Time Format		Character or Numeric field	–	ER	–
TEST (E Z)	Timestamp Format		Character or Numeric field	–	ER	–

The TEST operation code allows users to test the validity of date, time, or timestamp fields prior to using them.

- If the result field contains fields declared as Date, Time, or Timestamp:
  - Factor 1 must be blank
  - Operation code extenders 'D', 'T', and 'Z' are not allowed
- If the result field contains fields declared as character or numeric, then one of the operation code extenders 'D', 'T', or 'Z' must be specified.

  Note: If the result field is a character field with no separators, factor 1 must contain the date, time, or timestamp format followed by a zero.

  - If the operation code extender includes 'D' (test Date):
    - Factor 1 is optional and may contain any of the valid Date formats.
    - If factor 1 is blank, the format specified on the control specification with the DATFMT keyword is assumed. If this keyword is not specified, *ISO is assumed.
  - If the operation code extender includes 'T' (test Time):
    - Factor 1 is optional and may contain any of the valid Time formats.
    - If factor 1 is blank, the format specified on the control specification with the TIMFMT keyword is assumed. If this keyword is not specified, *ISO is assumed.

      Note: The *USA date format is not allowed with the operation code extender (T). The *USA date format has an AM/PM restriction that cannot be converted to numeric when a numeric result field is used.
  - If the operation code extender includes 'Z' (test Timestamp),
    - Factor 1 is optional and may contain *ISO or *ISO0.

Numeric fields and character fields without separators are tested for valid digit portions of a Date, Time, or Timestamp value. Character fields are tested for both valid digits and separators.

For the test operation, either the operation code extender 'E' or an error indicator ER must be specified, but not both. If the content of the result field is not valid, program status code 112 is signaled. Then, the error indicator is set on or the %ERROR built-in function is set to return '1' depending on the error handling method specified.

```
*...1....+....2....+....3....+....4....+....5....+....6....+....7...+....
DName++++++++++ETDsFrom+++To/L+++IDc.Keywords+++++++++++++++++++++++++++++
D
D Datefield      S             D   DATFMT(*JIS)
D Num_Date       S            6P 0 INZ(910921)
D Char_Time      S             8   INZ('13:05 PM')
D Char_Date      S             6   INZ('041596')
D Char_Tstmp     S            20   INZ('19960723140856834000')
D Char_Date2   . S            9A   INZ('402/10/66')
D Char_Date3     S            8A   INZ('2120/115')
D
CL0N01Factor1+++++++Opcode(E)+Factor2+++++++Result++++++++Len++D+HiLoEq....
 *
 * Indicator 18 will not be set on, since the character field is a
 * valid *ISO timestamp field, without separators.
C    *ISO0      TEST (Z)           Char_Tstmp           18
 * Indicator 19 will not be set on, since the character field is a
 * valid *MDY date, without separators.
C    *MDY0      TEST (D)           Char_Date            19
 *
 * %ERROR will return '1', since Num_Date is not *DMY.
 *
C    *DMY       TEST (DE)          Num_Date
 *
 * No Factor 1 since result is a D data type field
 * %ERROR will return '0', since the field
 * contains a valid date
C
C               TEST (E)           Datefield
C
 * In the following test, %ERROR will return '1' since the
 * Timefield does not contain a valid USA time.
C
C    *USA       TEST (ET)          Char_Time
C
 * In the following test, indicator 20 will be set on since the
 * character field is a valid *CMDY, but there are separators.C
C    *CMDY0     TEST (D)           char_date2           20
C
 * In the following test, %ERROR will return '0' since
 * the character field is a valid *LONGJUL date.C
C    *LONGJUL   TEST (DE)          char_date3
```

Figure 77. TEST (E D/T/Z) Example

WHEN (When True Then Select)

Code	Factor 1	Extended Factor 2
WHEN (M/R)		Indicator Expression

The WHEN operation code is similar to the WHENxx operation code in that it controls the processing of lines in a SELECT operation. It differs in that the condition is specified by a logical expression in the extended factor 2 entry. The operations controlled by the WHEN operation are performed when the expression in the extended factor 2 field is true.

```
CL0N01Factor1+++++++Opcode(E)+Extended-factor2+++++++++++++++++++++++++++..
 *
C                   SELECT
C                   WHEN    *INKA
C                   :
C                   :
C                   :
C                   WHEN    NOT(*IN01) AND (DAY = 'FRIDAY')
C                   :
C                   :
C                   :
C                   WHEN    %SUBST(A:(X+4):3) = 'ABC'
C                   :
C                   :
C                   :
C                   OTHER
C                   :
C                   :
C                   :
C                   ENDSL
```

Figure 78. WHEN Operations

New Built-In Functions

RPG IV has the following BIFs:

- arithmetic
    - "%ABS (Absolute Value of Expression)" on page 191
- data conversion
    - "%CHAR (Convert to Character Data)" on page 194
    - "%DEC (Convert to Packed Decimal Format)" on page 195
    - "%DECH (Convert to Packed Decimal Format with Half Adjust)" on page 195
    - "%EDITC (Edit Value Using an Editcode)" on page 197
    - "%EDITFLT (Convert to Float External Representation)" on page 200
    - "%EDITW (Edit Value Using an Editword)" on page 201
    - "%FLOAT (Convert to Floating Format)" on page 208
    - "%INT (Convert to Integer Format)" on page 212
    - "%INTH (Convert to Integer Format with Half Adjust)" on page 212
- data information
    - "%DECPOS (Get Number of Decimal Positions)" on page 196
    - "%ELEM (Get Number of Elements)" on page 202
    - "%LEN (Get or Set Length)" on page 213
    - "%SIZE (Get Size in Bytes)" on page 224
- editing
    - "%EDITC (Edit Value Using an Editcode)" on page 197
    - "%EDITFLT (Convert to Float External Representation)" on page 200
    - "%EDITW (Edit Value Using an Editword)" on page 201
- exception/error handling
    - "%ERROR (Return Error Condition)" on page 207
    - "%STATUS (Return File or Program Status)" on page 226
- feedback
    - "%EOF (Return End or Beginning of File Condition)" on page 203
    - "%EQUAL (Return Exact Match Condition)" on page 205
    - "%ERROR (Return Error Condition)" on page 207
    - "%FOUND (Return Found Condition)" on page 209
    - "%NULLIND (Query or Set Null Indicator)" on page 216
    - "%OPEN (Return File Open Condition)" on page 217

%ABS (Absolute Value of Expression)

```
%ABS(numeric expression)
```

%ABS returns the absolute value of the numeric expression specified as the parameter. If the value of the numeric expression is nonnegative, the value is returned unchanged. If the value is negative, the value returned is the value of the expression, but with the negative sign removed.

%ABS may be used either in expressions or as parameters to keywords. When used with keywords, the operand must be a numeric literal, a constant name representing a numeric value, or a built-in function with a numeric value known at compile time.

```
DName++++++++++ETDsFrom+++To/L+++IDc.Keywords++++++++++++++++++++++++++++
D f8              s              8f   inz (-1)
D i10             s             10i 0 inz (-123)
D p7              s              7p 3 inz (-1234.567)


CL0N01Factor1+++++++Opcode&ExtExtended-factor2++++++++++++++++++++++++++++
C                 eval      f8  = %abs (f8)
C                 eval      i10 = %abs (i10 - 321)
C                 eval      p7  = %abs (p7)
 * The value of "f8" is now 1.
 * The value of "i10" is now 444.
 * The value of "p7" is now 1234.567.
```

Figure 79. %ABS Example

%ADDR (Get Address of Variable)

```
%ADDR(variable)
%ADDR(variable(index))
%ADDR(variable(expression))
```

%ADDR returns a value of type basing pointer. The value is the address of the specified variable. It may only be compared with and assigned to items of type basing pointer.

If %ADDR with an array index parameter is specified as parameter for definition specification keywords INZ or CONST, the array index must be known at compile time. The index must be either a numeric literal or a numeric constant.

In an EVAL operation where the result of the assignment is an array with no index, %ADDR on the right hand side of the assignment operator has a different meaning depending on the argument for the %ADDR. If the argument for %ADDR is an array name without an index and the result is an array name, each element of the result array will contain the address of the beginning of the argument array. If the argument for %ADDR is an array name with an index of (*), then each element of the result array will contain the address of the corresponding element in the argument array. This is illustrated in Figure 80 on page 193.

If the variable specified as parameter is a table, multiple occurrence data structure, or subfield of a multiple occurrence data structure, the address will be the address of the current table index or occurrence number.

If the variable is based, %ADDR returns the value of the basing pointer for the variable. If the variable is a subfield of a based data structure, the value of %ADDR is the value of the basing pointer plus the offset of the subfield.

If the variable is specified as a PARM of the *ENTRY PLIST, %ADDR returns the address passed to the program by the caller.

```
DName++++++++++ETDsFrom+++To/L+++IDc.Keywords+++++++++++++++++++++++++++++
 *
 * The following set of definitions is valid since the array
 * index has a compile-time value
 *
D  ARRAY          S               20A  DIM (100)
 * Set the pointer to the address of the seventh element of the array.
D  PTR            S                *   INZ (%ADDR(ARRAY(SEVEN)))
D  SEVEN          C                    CONST (7)
 *
D DS1             DS                   OCCURS (100)
D                                20A
D  SUBF                          10A
D                                30A
D CHAR10          S               10A  BASED (P)
D PARRAY          S                *   DIM(100)

CLON01Factor1+++++++Opcode(E)+Factor2+++++++Result++++++++Len++D+HiLoEq..
CLON01Factor1+++++++Opcode(E)+Extended-factor2+++++++++++++++++++++++++++
 *
C     23          OCCUR     DS1
C                 EVAL      SUBF = *ALL'abcd'
C                 EVAL      P = %ADDR (SUBF)
C                 IF        CHAR10 = SUBF
 *                     This condition is true
C                 ENDIF
C                 IF        %ADDR (CHAR10) = %ADDR (SUBF)
 *                     This condition is also true
C                 ENDIF
 * The following statement also changes the value of SUBF
C                 EVAL      CHAR10 = *ALL'efgh'
C                 IF        CHAR10 = SUBF
 *                     This condition is still true
C                 ENDIF
 *-----------------------------------------------------------------
C     24          OCCUR     DS1
C                 IF        CHAR10 = SUBF
 *                     This condition is no longer true
C                 ENDIF
 *-----------------------------------------------------------------
 * The address of an array element is taken using an expression
 * as the array index
 *
C                 EVAL      P = %ADDR (ARRAY (X + 10))
 *-----------------------------------------------------------------
 * Each element of the array PARRAY contains the address of the
 * first element of the array ARRAY.
C                 EVAL      PARRAY = %ADDR(ARRAY)
 * Each element of the array PARRAY contains the address of the
 * corresponding element of the array ARRAY
C                 EVAL      PARRAY = %ADDR(ARRAY(*))
```

Figure 80. %ADDR Example

%CHAR (Convert to Character Data)

%CHAR(expression)

%CHAR converts the value of the expression from graphic, date, time, or timestamp data to type character. The converted value remains unchanged, but is returned in a format that is compatible with character data.

For graphic data, the value returned includes the shift-in and shift-out characters. For example, if a five character graphic field is converted, the returned value is 12 characters (10 bytes of graphic data plus the two shift characters). If the value of the expression has a variable length, the value returned is in varying format.

For date, time, or timestamp data, the returned value includes any separator characters.

```
DName+++++++++++ETDsFrom+++To/L+++IDc.Keywords+++++++++++++++++++++++++++++
D ChineseName      S                20G  VARYING INZ(G'oXXYYZZi')
D date             S                 D   INZ(D'1997/02/03')
D time             S                 T   INZ(T'12:23:34')
D result           S                100A VARYING

CLON01Factor1+++++++Opcode(E)+Factor2+++++++Result++++++++Len++D+HiLoEq..
CLON01Factor1+++++++Opcode(E)+Extended-factor2++++++++++++++++++++++++++++
C                   EVAL      result = 'It is ' + %CHAR(time)
C                             + ' on ' + %CHAR(date)
 * result = 'It is 12:23:34 on 1997/02/03'
 *
C                   EVAL      result = 'The time is now '
C                             + %SUBST(%CHAR(time):1:5) + '.'
 * result = 'The time is now 12:23.'
 *
C                   EVAL      result = 'The customer''s name is '
C                             + %CHAR(ChineseName) + '.'
 * result = 'The customer's name is oXXYYZZi.'
```

Figure 81. %CHAR Example

%DEC (Convert to Packed Decimal Format)

`%DEC(numeric expression{:precision:decimal places})`

%DEC converts the value of the `numeric expression` to decimal (packed) format with `precision` digits and `decimal places` decimal positions. The precision and decimal places must be numeric literals, named constants that represent numeric literals, or built-in functions with a numeric value known at compile-time.

Parameters precision and decimal places may be omitted if the type of numeric expression is not float. If these parameters are omitted, the precision and decimal places are taken from the attributes of numeric expression.

%DECH (Convert to Packed Decimal Format with Half Adjust)

`%DECH(numeric expression :precision:decimal places )`

%DECH is the same as %DEC, except that if numeric expression is a decimal or float value, half adjust is applied to the value of numeric expression when converting to the desired precision. No message is issued if half adjust cannot be performed.

Unlike, %DEC, all three parameters are required.

```
DName++++++++++ETDsFrom+++To/L+++IDc.Keywords++++++++++++++++++++++++++++++
D p7              s               7p 3 inz (1234.567)
D s9              s               9s 5 inz (73.73442)
D f8              s               8f   inz (123.456789)
D result1         s              15p 5
D result2         s              15p 5
D result3         s              15p 5

CL0N01Factor1+++++++Opcode&ExtExtended-factor2++++++++++++++++++++++++++++++
C                 eval       result1 = %dec (p7) + 0.011
C                 eval       result2 = %dec (s9 : 5: 0)
C                 eval       result3 = %dech (f8: 5: 2)
 * The value of "result1" is now 1234.57800.
 * The value of "result2" is now   73.00000
 * The value of "result3" is now  123.46000.
```

Figure 82. %DEC and %DECH Example

%DECPOS (Get Number of Decimal Positions)

%DECPOS(numeric expression)

%DECPOS returns the number of decimal positions of the numeric variable or expression. The value returned is a constant, and so may participate in constant folding.

The numeric expression must not be a float variable or expression.

```
DName+++++++++++ETDsFrom+++To/L+++IDc.Keywords+++++++++++++++++++++++++++++
D p7              s               7p 3 inz (8236.567)
D s9              s               9s 5 inz (23.73442)
D result1         s               5i 0
D result2         s               5i 0
D result3         s               5i 0

CL0N01Factor1+++++++Opcode&ExtExtended-factor2+++++++++++++++++++++++++++++
C                   eval      result1 = %decpos (p7)
C                   eval      result2 = %decpos (s9)
C                   eval      result3 = %decpos (p7 * s9)
 * The value of "result1" is now  3.
 * The value of "result2" is now  5.
 * The value of "result3" is now  8.
```

Figure 83. %DECPOS Example

See Figure 99 on page 215 for an example of %DECPOS with %LEN.

%EDITC (Edit Value Using an Editcode)

```
%EDITC(numeric : editcode {: *ASTFILL | *CURSYM | currency-symbol})
```

This function returns a character result representing the numeric value edited according to the edit code. In general, the rules for the numeric value and edit code are identical to those for editing numeric values in output specifications. The third parameter is optional and, if specified, must be one of:

*ASTFILL   Indicates that asterisk protection is to be used. This means that leading zeros are replaced with asterisks in the returned value. For example, %EDITC(0012.5 : 'K' : *ASTFILL) returns '***12.5-'.

*CURSYM   Indicates that a floating currency symbol is to be used. The actual symbol will be the one specified on the control specification in the CURSYM keyword, or the default, '$'. When *CURSYM is specified, the currency symbol is placed in the the result just before the first significant digit. For example, %EDITC(0012.5 : 'K' : *CURSYM) returns ' $12.5-'.

currency-symbol

    Indicates that floating currency is to be used with the provided currency symbol. It must be a one-byte character constant (literal, named constant, or expression that can be evaluated at compile time).

Float expressions are not allowed in the first parameter (you can use %DEC to convert a float to an editable format). In the second parameter, the edit code is specified as a character constant; supported edit codes are: 'A' - 'D', 'J' - 'Q', 'X' - 'Z', and '1' - '9'. The constant can be a literal, named constant, or an expression whose value can be determined at compile time.

```
DName++++++++++ETDsFrom+++To/L+++IDc.Keywords+++++++++++++++++++++++++++++
D msg             S             100A
D salary          S               9P 2

 * If the value of salary is 2451.53, then the value of salary * 12
 * is 29418.36. The edited version of salary * 12 using the A edit
 * code with floating currency is ' $29,418.36 '.
 * The value of msg is 'The annual salary is $29,418.36'

CL0N01Factor1+++++++Opcode&ExtExtended-factor2++++++++++++++++++++++++++++++
C                   EVAL      msg = 'The annual salary is '
C                               + %trim(%editc(salary * 12
C                                          :'A': *CURSYM))

 * If the value of salary is 2451.53, then the value of salary * 12
 * is 29418.36. The edited version of salary * 12 using the A edit
 * code with floating currency is ' $29,418.36 '.
 * The value of msg is 'The annual salary is $29,418.36'
C                   EVAL      msg = 'The annual salary is '
C                               + %trim(%editc(salary * 12
C                                          :'A': '&'))

 * In the next example, the value of msg is 'Salary is $***29,418.36'
 * Note that the '$' comes from the text, not from the edit code.
C                   EVAL      msg = 'Salary is $'
C                               + %trim(%editc(salary * 12
C                                          :'B': *ASTFILL))

 * In the next example, the value of msg is 'The date is 1996/06/27'
C                   EVAL      msg = 'The date is '
C                               + %trim(%editc(*date : 'Y'))
```

Figure 84. %EDITC Example 1

A common requirement is to edit a field as follows:

- Leading zeros are suppressed
- Parentheses are placed around the value if it is negative

The following accomplishes this using an %EDITC in a subprocedure:

```
DName++++++++++ETDsFrom+++To/L+++IDc.Keywords++++++++++++++++++++++++++++++++
D neg             S              5P 2      inz(-12.3)
D pos             S              5P 2      inz(54.32)
D editparens      PR            50A
D   val                         30P 2      value
D editedVal       S             10A
CL0N01Factor1+++++++Opcode&ExtExtended-factor2++++++++++++++++++++++++++++++++
C                     EVAL      editedVal = editparens(neg)
 * Now editedVal has the value '(12.30)   '
C                     EVAL      editedVal = editparens(pos)
 * Now editedVal has the value ' 54.32    '


 *----------------------------------------------------------------
 * Subprocedure EDITPARENS
 *----------------------------------------------------------------
P editparens      B
D editparens      PI            50A
D   val                         30P 2      value
D lparen          S             1A         inz(' ')
D rparen          S             1A         inz(' ')
D res             S             50A

 * Use parentheses if the value is negative
C                     IF        val < 0
C                     EVAL      lparen = '('
C                     EVAL      rparen = ')'
C                     ENDIF

 * Return the edited value
 * Note that the '1' edit code does not include a sign so we
 * don't have to calculate the absolute value.
C                     RETURN    lparen            +
C                               %editc(val : '1') +
C                               rparen

P editparens      E
```

Figure 85. %EDITC Example 2

%EDITFLT (Convert to Float External Representation)

```
%EDITFLT(numeric expression)
```

%EDITFLT converts the value of the numeric expression to the character external display representation of float. The result is either 14 or 23 characters. If the argument is a four-byte float field, the result is 14 characters. Otherwise, it is 23 characters.

If specified as a parameter to a definition specification keyword, the parameter must be a numeric literal, float literal, numeric-valued constant name, or built-in function. When specified in an expression, constant folding is applied if the numeric expression has a constant value.

```
DName+++++++++++ETDsFrom+++To/L+++IDc.Keywords++++++++++++++++++++++++++++
D f8              s             8f   inz (50000)
D string          s            40a

CL0N01Factor1+++++++Opcode&ExtExtended-factor2+++++++++++++++++++++++++++++
C                   eval      string = 'Float value is '
C                             + %editflt (f8 - 4e4) + '.'

* Value of "string" is 'Float value is +1.000000000000000E+004. '
```

Figure 86. %EDITFLT Example

%EDITW (Edit Value Using an Editword)

`%EDITW(numeric : editword)`

This function returns a character result representing the numeric value edited according to the edit word. The rules for the numeric value and edit word are identical to those for editing numeric values in output specifications.

Float expressions are not allowed in the first parameter. Use %DEC to convert a float to an editable format.

The edit word must be a character constant.

```
DName++++++++++ETDsFrom+++To/L+++IDc.Keywords++++++++++++++++++++++++++++
D amount          S              30A
D salary          S               9P 2
D editwd          C                        '$ ,    , **Dollars& &Cents'

 * If the value of salary is 2451.53, then the edited version of
 * (salary * 12) is '$***29,418*Dollars 36 Cents'. The value of
 * amount is 'The annual salary is $***29,418*Dollars 36 Cents'.
CL0N01Factor1+++++++Opcode&ExtExtended-factor2++++++++++++++++++++++++++++
C                   EVAL      amount = 'The annual salary is '
C                               + %editw(salary * 12 : editwd)
```

Figure 87. %EDITW Example

%ELEM (Get Number of Elements)

```
%ELEM(table_name)
%ELEM(array_name)
%ELEM(multiple_occurrence_data_structure_name)
```

%ELEM returns the number of elements in the specified array, table, or multiple-occurrence data structure. The value returned is in unsigned integer format (type U). It may be specified anywhere a numeric constant is allowed in the definition specification or in an expression in the extended factor 2 field.

The parameter must be the name of an array, table, or multiple occurrence data structure.

```
DName++++++++++ETDsFrom+++To/L+++IDc.Keywords+++++++++++++++++++++++++++
D arr1d            S               20    DIM(10)
D table            S               10    DIM(20) ctdata
D mds              DS              20    occurs(30)
D num              S                5P

 * like_array will be defined with a dimension of 10.
 * array_dims will be defined with a value of 10.

D like_array       S                     like(arr1d) dim(%elem(arr1d))
D array_dims       C                     const (%elem (arr1d))
C*L0N01Factor1+++++++Opcode(E)+Extended-factor2+++++++++++++++++++++++++
 *
 * In the following examples num will be equal to 10, 20, and 30.
 *
C                   EVAL      num = %elem (arr1d)
C                   EVAL      num = %elem (table)
C                   EVAL      num = %elem (mds)
```

Figure 88. %ELEM Example

%EOF (Return End or Beginning of File Condition)

%EOF{(file_name)}

%EOF returns '1' if the most recent read operation or write to a subfile ended in an end-of-file or beginning-of-file condition; otherwise, it returns '0'.

The operations that set %EOF are:

- READ
- READC
- READE
- READP
- READPE
- WRITE (subfile only).

When a full-procedural file is specified, this function returns '1' if the previous operation in the list above, for the specified file, resulted in an end-of-file or beginning-of-file condition. For primary and secondary files, %EOF is available only if the file name is specified. It is set to '1' if the most recent input operation during *GETIN processing resulted in an end-of-file or beginning-of-file condition. Otherwise, it returns '0'.

This function is allowed for input, update, and record-address files, and for display files allowing WRITE to subfile records.

```
*...1....+....2....+....3....+....4....+....5....+....6....+....7...+....
FFilename++IPEASFRlen+LKlen+AIDevice+.Keywords++++++++++++++++++++++++++++
 * File INFILE has record format INREC
FINFILE    IF  E             DISK
CL0N01Factor1+++++++Opcode(E)+Factor2+++++++Result++++++++Len++D+HiLoEq....
 * Read a record
C                    READ    INREC
 * If end-of-file was reached ...
C                    IF      %EOF
C ...
C                    ENDIF
```

Figure 89. %EOF without a Filename Parameter

```
*...1....+....2....+....3....+....4....+....5....+....6....+....7...+....
FFilename++IPEASFRlen+LKlen+AIDevice+.Keywords+++++++++++++++++++++++++++++
 * This program is comparing two files
 *
FFILE1     IF   E              DISK
FFILE2     IF   E              DISK
F
CL0N01Factor1++++++Opcode(E)+Factor2++++++Result++++++++Len++D+HiLoEq....
 * Loop until either FILE1 or FILE2 has reached end-of-file
C                   DOU       %EOF(FILE1) OR %EOF(FILE2)
 * Read a record from each file and compare the records
 *
C                   READ      REC1
C                   READ      REC2

C                   SELECT

C                   WHEN      %EOF(FILE1) AND %EOF(FILE2)
 * Both files have reached end-of-file
C                   EXSR      EndCompare

C                   WHEN      %EOF(FILE1)
 * FILE1 is shorter than FILE2
C                   EXSR      F1Short

C                   WHEN      %EOF(FILE2)
 * FILE2 is shorter than FILE1
C                   EXSR      F2Short
C                   OTHER
 * Both files still have records to be compared
C                   EXSR      CompareRecs
C                   ENDSL

C                   ENDDO

 ...
```

Figure 90. %EOF with a Filename Parameter

%EQUAL (Return Exact Match Condition)

%EQUAL{(file_name)}

%EQUAL returns '1' if the most recent relevant operation found an exact match; otherwise, it returns '0'.

The operations that set %EQUAL are:

- SETLL
- LOOKUP

If %EQUAL is used without the optional file_name parameter, then it returns the value set for the most recent relevant operation.

For the SETLL operation, this function returns '1' if a record is present whose key or relative record number is equal to the search argument.

For the LOOKUP operation with the EQ indicator specified, this function returns '1' if an element is found that exactly matches the search argument.

If a file name is specified, this function applies to the most recent SETLL operation for the specified file. This function is allowed only for files that allow the SETLL operation code.

```
 *...1....+....2....+....3....+....4....+....5....+....6....+....7...+....
FFilename++IPEASFRlen+LKlen+AIDevice+.Keywords++++++++++++++++++++++++++++
 * File CUSTS has record format CUSTREC
FCUSTS     IF   E          K DISK
CL0N01Factor1+++++++Opcode(E)+Factor2+++++++Result++++++++Len++D+HiLoEq....
 * Check if the file contains a record with a key matching Cust
C     Cust          SETLL     CUSTREC
C                   IF        %EQUAL
C ... an exact match was found in the file
C                   ENDIF
```

Figure 91. %EQUAL with SETLL Example

```
DName+++++++++++ETDsFrom+++To/L+++IDc.Keywords++++++++++++++++++++++++++++++
D TabNames         S              10A  DIM(5) CTDATA ASCEND
D SearchName       S              10A
 * Position the table at or near SearchName
 * Here are the results of this program for different values
 * of SearchName:
 *   SearchName    |  DSPLY
 *   -------------+-----------------------------
 *   'Catherine ' |  'Next greater    Martha'
 *   'Andrea    ' |  'Exact           Andrea'
 *   'Thomas    ' |  'Not found       Thomas'

   CL0N01Factor1+++++++Opcode(E)+Factor2+++++++Result++++++++Len++D+HiLoEq....
C     SearchName    LOOKUP    TabNames                              10  10
C                   SELECT

C                   WHEN      %EQUAL
 * An exact match was found
C     'Exact     'DSPLY                     TabNames

C                   WHEN      %FOUND
 * A name was found greater than SearchName
C     'Next greater'DSPLY                   TabNames

C                   OTHER
 * Not found.  SearchName is greater than all the names in the table
C     'Not found 'DSPLY                     SearchName

C                   ENDSL

C                   RETURN
**CTDATA TabNames
Alexander
Andrea
Bohdan
Martha
Samuel
```

Figure 92. %EQUAL and %FOUND with LOOKUP Example

%ERROR (Return Error Condition)

%ERROR returns '1' if the most recent operation with extender 'E' specified resulted in an error condition. This is the same as the error indicator being set on for the operation. Before an operation with extender 'E' specified begins, %ERROR is set to return '0' and remains unchanged following the operation if no error occurs. All operations that allow an error indicator can also set the %ERROR built-in function. The CALLP operation can also set %ERROR.

For examples of the %ERROR built-in function, see Figure 107 on page 227 and Figure 108 on page 228.

%FLOAT (Convert to Floating Format)

%FLOAT(numeric expression)

%FLOAT converts the value of the numeric expression to float format. This built-in function may only be used in expressions.

```
DName+++++++++++ETDsFrom+++To/L+++IDc.Keywords++++++++++++++++++++++++++++
D p1              s              15p 0 inz (1)
D p2              s              25p13 inz (3)
D result1         s              15p 5
D result2         s              15p 5
D result3         s              15p 5


CL0N01Factor1+++++++Opcode&ExtExtended-factor2+++++++++++++++++++++++++++
C                 eval          result1 = p1 / p2
C                 eval          result2 = %float (p1) / p2
C                 eval          result3 = %float (p1 / p2)
 * The value of "result1" is now  0.33000.
 * The value of "result2" is now  0.33333.
 * The value of "result3" is now  0.33333.
```

Figure 93. %FLOAT Example

%FOUND (Return Found Condition)

`%FOUND{(file_name)}`

%FOUND returns '1' if the most recent relevant file operation found a record, a string operation found a match, or a search operation found an element. Otherwise, this function returns '0'.

The operations that set %FOUND are:

- File operations:
  - CHAIN
  - DELETE
  - SETGT
  - SETLL
- String operations:
  - CHECK
  - CHECKR
  - SCAN

    Note: Built-in function %SCAN does not change the value of %FOUND.

- Search operations:
  - LOOKUP

If %FOUND is used without the optional file_name parameter, then it returns the value set for the most recent relevant operation. When a file_name is specified, then it applies to the most recent relevant operation on that file.

For file operations, %FOUND is opposite in function to the "no record found NR" indicator.

For string operations, %FOUND is the same in function as the "found FD" indicator.

For the LOOKUP operation, %FOUND returns '1' if the operation found an element satisfying the search conditions. For an example of %FOUND with LOOKUP, see Figure 92.

```
*...1....+....2....+....3....+....4....+....5....+....6....+....7...+....
FFilename++IPEASFRlen+LKlen+AIDevice+.Keywords+++++++++++++++++++++++++++++
 * File CUSTS has record format CUSTREC
FCUSTS     IF   E           K DISK
CL0N01Factor1+++++++Opcode(E)+Factor2+++++++Result++++++++Len++D+HiLoEq....
 * Check if the customer is in the file
C     Cust          CHAIN     CUSTREC
C                    IF        %FOUND
C ...
C                    ENDIF
```

Figure 94. %FOUND Used to Test a File Operation without a Parameter

```
*...1....+....2....+....3....+....4....+....5....+....6....+....7...+....
FFilename++IPEASFRlen+LKlen+AIDevice+.Keywords+++++++++++++++++++++++++++++
 * File MASTER has all the customers
 * File GOLD has only the "privileged" customers
FMASTER    IF   E           K DISK
FGOLD      IF   E           K DISK
CL0N01Factor1+++++++Opcode(E)+Factor2+++++++Result++++++++Len++D+HiLoEq....
 * Check if the customer exists, but is not a privileged customer
C     Cust          CHAIN     MASTREC
C     Cust          CHAIN     GOLDREC
 * Note that the file name is used for %FOUND, not the record name
C                    IF        %FOUND(MASTER) AND NOT %FOUND(GOLD)
C ...
C                    ENDIF
```

Figure 95. %FOUND Used to Test a File Operation with a Parameter

```
 *...1....+....2....+....3....+....4....+....5....+....6....+....7...+....
DName++++++++++ETDsFrom+++To/L+++IDc.Keywords+++++++++++++++++++++++++++++++
D Numbers        C                   '0123456789'
D Position       S              5I 0
CL0N01Factor1+++++++Opcode(E)+Factor2+++++++Result++++++++Len++D+HiLoEq....
 * If the actual position of the name is not required, just use
 * %FOUND to test the results of the SCAN operation.
 * If Name has the value 'Barbara' and Line has the value
 * 'in the city of Toronto.     ', then %FOUND will return '0'.
 * If Line has the value 'the city of Toronto where Barbara lives, '
 * then %FOUND will return '1'.
C     Name         SCAN      Line
C                  IF        %FOUND
C                  EXSR      PutLine
C                  ENDIF
 * If Value contains the value '12345.67', Position would be set
 * to 6 and %FOUND would return the value '1'.
 * If Value contains the value '10203040', Position would be set
 * to 0 and %FOUND would return the value '0'.
C     Numbers      CHECK     Value          Position
C                  IF        %FOUND
C                  EXSR      HandleNonNum
C                  ENDIF
```

Figure 96. %FOUND Used to Test a String Operation

%INT (Convert to Integer Format)

%INT(numeric expression)

%INT converts the value of the numeric expression to integer. Any decimal digits are truncated. This built-in function may only be used in expressions. %INT can be used to truncate the decimal positions from a float or decimal value, allowing it to be used as an array index.

%INTH (Convert to Integer Format with Half Adjust)

%INTH(numeric expression)

%INTH is the same as %INT, except that if the numeric expression is a decimal or float value, half adjust is applied to the value of the numeric expression when converting to integer type. No message is issued if half adjust cannot be performed.

```
DName++++++++++++ETDsFrom+++To/L+++IDc.Keywords++++++++++++++++++++++++++++++
D p7              s                 7p 3 inz (1234.567)
D s9              s                 9s 5 inz (73.73442)
D f8              s                 8f  inz (123.789)
D result1         s                15p 5
D result2         s                15p 5
D result3         s                15p 5
D array           s                 1a   dim (200)
D a               s                 1a


CL0N01Factor1+++++++Opcode&ExtExtended-factor2++++++++++++++++++++++++++++++
C                   eval      result1 = %int (p7) + 0.011
C                   eval      result2 = %int (s9)
C                   eval      result3 = %inth (f8)
 * The value of "result1" is now 1234.01100.
 * The value of "result2" is now   73.00000
 * The value of "result3" is now  124.00000.

C                   eval      a = array (%inth (f8))
 * %INT and %INTH can be used as array indexes
```

Figure 97. %INT and %INTH Example

%LEN (Get or Set Length)

%LEN(expression)

%LEN can be used to get the length of a variable expression or to set the current length of a variable-length field.

The parameter must not be a figurative constant.

%LEN Used for Its Value

When used on the right-hand side of an expression, this function returns the number of digits or characters of the variable expression.

For numeric expressions, the value returned represents the precision of the expression and not necessarily the actual number of significant digits. For a float variable or expression, the value returned is either 4 or 8. When the parameter is a numeric literal, the length returned is the number of digits of the literal.

For character or graphic expressions, the value returned is the number of characters in the value of the expression. For variable-length values, such as the value returned from a built-in function or a variable-length field, the value returned by %LEN is the actual length of the character or graphic value.

Note that if the parameter is a built-in function or expression that has a value computable at compile time, the length returned is the actual number of digits of the constant value rather than the maximum possible value that could be returned by the expression.

For all other data types, the value returned is the number of bytes of the value.

```
DName++++++++++ETDsFrom+++To/L+++IDc.Keywords+++++++++++++++++++++++++++++
D num1            S              7P 2
D num2            S              5S 1
D num3            S              5I 0 inz(2)
D chr1            S             10A  inz('Toronto   ')
D chr2            S             10A  inz('Munich    ')
D ptr             S               *

CL0N01Factor1+++++++Opcode(E)+Factor2++++++Result++++++++Len++D+HiLoEq..
CL0N01Factor1+++++++Opcode(E)+Extended-factor2++++++++++++++++++++++++++++
 * Numeric expressions:
C                   eval      num1 = %len(num1)           <=== 7
C                   eval      num1 = %decpos(num2)        <=== 1
C                   eval      num1 = %len(num1*num2)      <=== 12
C                   eval      num1 = %decpos(num1*num2)   <=== 3

 * Character expressions:
C                   eval      num1 = %len(chr1)           <=== 10
C                   eval      num1 = %len(chr1+chr2)      <=== 20
C                   eval      num1 = %len(%trim(chr1))    <=== 7
C                   eval      num1 = %len(%subst(chr1:1:num3)
C                             + ' ' + %trim(chr2))        <=== 9

 * %len and %decpos can be useful with other built-in functions:

 * Although this division is performed in float, the result is
 * converted to the same precision as the result of the eval:
C                   eval      num1 = 27 + %dec (%float(num1)/num3
C                             : %len(num1)
C                             : %decpos(num1))

 * Allocate sufficient space to hold the result of the catenation
 * (plus an extra byte for a trailing null character):
C                   eval      num3 = %len(chr1+chr2)+1
C                   alloc     num3      ptr
C                   eval      %str(ptr : num3) = chr1 + chr2
```

Figure 98. %DECPOS and %LEN Example

%LEN Used to Set the Length of Variable-Length Fields

When used on the left-hand side of an expression, this function sets the current length of a variable-length field. If the set length is greater than the current length, the characters in the field between the old length and the new length are set to blanks.

Note: %LEN can only be used on the left-hand-side of an expression when the parameter is variable length.

```
DName++++++++++ETDsFrom+++To/L+++IDc.Keywords+++++++++++++++++++++++++++++
 *
D city           S               40A   VARYING INZ('North York')
D n1             S                5i 0

CL0N01Factor1+++++++Opcode(E)+Factor2+++++++Result++++++++Len++D+HiLoEq..
CL0N01Factor1+++++++Opcode(E)+Extended-factor2+++++++++++++++++++++++++++
 * %LEN used to get the current length of a variable-length field:
C                    EVAL      n1 = %LEN(city)
 * Current length, n1 = 10
 *
 * %LEN used to set the current length of a variable-length field:
C                    EVAL      %LEN(city) = 5
 * city = 'North' (length is 5)
 *
C                    EVAL      %LEN(city) = 15
 * city = 'North            '  (length is 15)
```

Figure 99. %LEN with Variable-Length Field Example

%NULLIND (Query or Set Null Indicator)

%NULLIND(fieldname)

The %NULLIND built-in function can be used to query or set the null indicator for null-capable fields. This built-in function can only be used if the ALWNULL(*USRCTL) keyword is specified on a control specification or as a command parameter. The fieldname can be a null-capable array element, data structure, stand-alone field, sub-field, or multiple occurrence data structure.

%NULLIND can only be used in expressions in extended factor 2.

When used on the right-hand side of an expression, this function returns the setting of the null indicator for the null-capable field. The setting can be *ON or *OFF.

When used on the left-hand side of an expression, this function can be used to set the null indicator for null-capable fields to *ON or *OFF. The content of a null-capable field remains unchanged.

```
CL0N01Factor1+++++++Opcode(E)+Extended-factor2++++++++++++++++++++++++++
 *
 * Test the null indicator for a null-capable field.
 *
C                   IF        %NULLIND(fieldname1)
C                   :
C                   ENDIF
 *
 * Set the null indicator for a null-capable field.
 *
C                   EVAL      %NULLIND(fieldname1) = *ON
C                   EVAL      %NULLIND(fieldname2) = *OFF
```

Figure 100. %NULLIND Example

%OPEN (Return File Open Condition)

%OPEN(file_name)

%OPEN returns '1' if the specified file is open. A file is considered open if it has been opened by the RPG program during initialization or by an OPEN operation and has not subsequently been closed. If the file is conditioned by an external indicator and the external indicator was off at program initialization, the file is considered closed, and %OPEN returns '0'.

```
*...1....+....2....+....3....+....4....+....5....+....6....+....7...+....
FFilename++IPEASFRlen+LKlen+AIDevice+.Keywords+++++++++++++++++++++++++++++
 * The printer file is opened in the calculation specifications
FQSYSPRT   O   F 132        PRINTER USROPN
CL0N01Factor1+++++++Opcode(E)+Factor2+++++++Result++++++++Len++D+HiLoEq....
 * Open the file if it is not already open
C                   IF        NOT %OPEN(QSYSPRT)
C                   OPEN      QSYSPRT
C                   ENDIF
...
```

Figure 101. %OPEN Example

%PADDR (Get Procedure Address)

%PADDR(string)

%PADDR returns a value of type procedure pointer. The value is the address of the entry point specified as the argument.

%PADDR may be compared with and assigned only to items of type procedure pointer.

The parameter to %PADDR must be a character or hexadecimal literal, or a constant name that represents a character or hexadecimal literal. The entry point name specified by the character string must be found at program bind time and must be in the correct case.

```
DName+++++++++++ETDsFrom+++To/L+++IDc.Keywords+++++++++++++++++++++++++++++
D
D PROC            S                    *    PROCPTR
D                                           INZ (%PADDR ('FIRSTPROG'))
D PROC1           S                    *    PROCPTR
CL0N01Factor1+++++++Opcode(E)+Factor2+++++++Result++++++++Len++D+HiLoEq..
CL0N01Factor1+++++++Opcode(E)+Extended-factor2+++++++++++++++++++++++++++++
 *
 *   The following statement calls procedure 'FIRSTPROG'.
 *
C                   CALLB     PROC
 *-------------------------------------------------------------------
 * The following statements call procedure 'NextProg'.
 * This a C procedure and is in mixed case.  Note that
 * the procedure name is case sensitive.
 *
C                   EVAL      PROC1 = %PADDR ('NextProg')
C                   CALLB     PROC1
```

Figure 102. %PADDR Example

%PARMS (Return Number of Parameters)

%PARMS returns the number of parameters that were passed to the procedure in which %PARMS is used. For the main procedure, %PARMS is the same as *PARMS.

The value returned by %PARMS is not available if the program or procedure that calls %PARMS does not pass a minimal operational descriptor. The ILE RPG compiler always passes one, but other languages do not. So if the caller is written in another ILE language, it will need to pass an operational descriptor on the call. If the operational descriptor is not passed, the value returned by %PARMS cannot be trusted.

```
DName+++++++++++ETDsFrom+++To/L+++IDc.Keywords++++++++++++++++++++++++++++
 * Prototype for procedure MaxInt which calculates the maximum
 * value of its parameters (at least 2 parameters must be passed)
D MaxInt          PR              10I 0
D  p1                             10I 0 VALUE
D  p2                             10I 0 VALUE
D  p3                             10I 0 VALUE OPTIONS(*NOPASS)
D  p4                             10I 0 VALUE OPTIONS(*NOPASS)
D  p5                             10I 0 VALUE OPTIONS(*NOPASS)

D Fld1            S               10A   DIM(40)
D Fld2            S               20A
D Fld3            S              100A
CL0N01Factor1+++++++Opcode(E)+Factor2+++++++Result++++++++Len++D+HiLoEq..
CL0N01Factor1+++++++Opcode(E)+Extended-factor2++++++++++++++++++++++++++++
C     *ENTRY      PLIST
C                 PARM                      MaxSize           10 0

 * Make sure the main procedure was passed a parameter
C                 IF        %PARMS < 1
C     'No parms'  DSPLY
C                 RETURN
C                 ENDIF

 * Determine the maximum size of Fld1, Fld2 and Fld3
C                 EVAL      MaxSize = MaxInt(%size(Fld1:*ALL) :
C                                            %size(Fld2) :
C                                            %size(Fld3))

C     'MaxSize is' DSPLY                    MaxSize
C                 RETURN
```

Figure 103 (Part 1 of 2). %PARMS Example

```
DName++++++++++ETDsFrom+++To/L+++IDc.Keywords++++++++++++++++++++++++++++
 *----------------------------------------------------------------
 * MaxInt - return the maximum value of the passed parameters
 *----------------------------------------------------------------
P MaxInt           B
D MaxInt           PI            10I 0
D  p1                            10I 0 VALUE
D  p2                            10I 0 VALUE
D  p3                            10I 0 VALUE OPTIONS(*NOPASS)
D  p4                            10I 0 VALUE OPTIONS(*NOPASS)
D  p5                            10I 0 VALUE OPTIONS(*NOPASS)
D Max               S            10I 0 INZ(*LOVAL)

CL0N01Factor1+++++++Opcode(E)+Factor2+++++++Result++++++++Len++D+HiLoEq..
CL0N01Factor1+++++++Opcode(E)+Extended-factor2++++++++++++++++++++++++++++
 * Branch to the point in the calculations where we will never
 * access unpassed parameters.
C                   SELECT
C                   WHEN      %PARMS = 2
C                   GOTO      PARMS2
C                   WHEN      %PARMS = 3
C                   GOTO      PARMS3
C                   WHEN      %PARMS = 4
C                   GOTO      PARMS4
C                   WHEN      %PARMS = 5
C                   GOTO      PARMS5
C                   ENDSL

 * Determine the maximum value.  Max was initialized to *LOVAL.
C     PARMS5        TAG
C                   IF        p5 > Max
C                   EVAL      Max = p5
C                   ENDIF
 *
C     PARMS4        TAG
C                   IF        p4 > Max
C                   EVAL      Max = p4
C                   ENDIF
 *
C     PARMS3        TAG
C                   IF        p3 > Max
C                   EVAL      Max = p3
C                   ENDIF
 *
C     PARMS2        TAG
C                   IF        p2 > Max
C                   EVAL      Max = p2
C                   ENDIF
C                   IF        p1 > Max
C                   EVAL      Max = p1
C                   ENDIF

C                   RETURN    Max
P MaxInt           E
```

Figure 103 (Part 2 of 2). %PARMS Example

%REPLACE (Replace Character String)

```
%REPLACE(replacement string: source string{:start position {:source
length to replace}})
```

%REPLACE returns the character string produced by inserting a replacement string into the source string, starting at the start position and replacing the specified number of characters.

The first and second parameters must be of type character or graphic and can be in either fixed- or variable-length format. The second parameter must be the same type as the first.

The third parameter represents the starting position, measured in characters, for the replacement string. If it is not specified, the starting position is at the beginning of the source string. The value may range from one to the current length of the source string plus one.

The fourth parameter represents the number of characters in the source string to be replaced. If zero is specified, then the replacement string is inserted before the specified starting position. If the parameter is not specified, the number of characters replaced is the same as the length of the replacement string. The value must be greater than or equal to zero, and less than or equal to the current length of the source string.

The starting position and length may be any numeric value or numeric expression with no decimal positions.

The returned value is varying length if the source string or replacement string are varying length, or if the start position or source length to replace are variables. Otherwise, the result is fixed length.

```
DName++++++++++ETDsFrom+++To/L+++IDc.Keywords+++++++++++++++++++++++++++++++
D var1            S             30A    INZ('Windsor') VARYING
D var2            S             30A    INZ('Ontario') VARYING
D var3            S             30A    INZ('Canada') VARYING
D fixed1          S             15A    INZ('California')
D date            S              D     INZ(D'1997-02-03')
D result          S            100A    VARYING
CL0N01Factor1+++++++Opcode(E)+Factor2+++++++Result++++++++Len++D+HiLoEq..
CL0N01Factor1+++++++Opcode(E)+Extended-factor2+++++++++++++++++++++++++++++
C
C                       EVAL      result = var1 + ', ' + 'ON'
 * result = 'Windsor, ON'
 *
 * %REPLACE with 2 parameters to replace text at begining of string:
C                       EVAL      result = %REPLACE('Toronto': result)
 * result = 'Toronto, ON'
 *
 * %REPLACE with 3 parameters to replace text at specified position:
C                       EVAL      result = %REPLACE(var3: result:
C                                            %SCAN(',': result)+2)
 * result = 'Toronto, Canada'
 *
 * %REPLACE with 4 parameters to insert text:
C                       EVAL      result = %REPLACE(', '+var2: result:
C                                            %SCAN(',': result): 0)
 * result = 'Toronto, Ontario, Canada'
 *
 * %REPLACE with 4 parameters to replace strings with different lengths:
C                       EVAL      result = %REPLACE('Scarborough': result:
C                                            1: %SCAN(',': result)-1)
 * result = 'Scarborough, Ontario, Canada'
 *
 * %REPLACE with 4 parameters to delete text:
C                       EVAL      result = %REPLACE('': result: 1:
C                                            %SCAN(',': result)+1)
 * result = 'Ontario, Canada'
 *
 * %REPLACE with 4 parameters to add text to the end of the string:
C                       EVAL      result = %REPLACE(', ' + %CHAR(date):
C                                            result:
C                                            %LEN(result)+1: 0)
 * result = 'Ontario, Canada, 1997-02-03'
 *
 * %REPLACE with 3 parameters to replace fixed-length text at
 * specified position:  (fixed1 has fixed-length of 15 chars)
C                       EVAL      result = %REPLACE(fixed1: result:
C                                            %SCAN(',': result)+2)
 * result = 'Ontario, California     -03'
 *
 * %REPLACE with 4 parameters to prefix text at beginning:
C                       EVAL      result = %REPLACE('Somewhere else: ':
C                                            result: 1: 0)
 * result = 'Somewhere else: Ontario, California     -03'
```

Figure 104. %REPLACE Example

%SCAN (Scan for Characters)

```
%SCAN(search argument : source string {: start})
```

%SCAN returns the first position of the search argument in the source string, or 0 if it was not found. If the start position is specified, the search begins at the starting position. The result is always the position in the source string even if the starting position is specified. The starting position defaults to 1.

The first parameter must be of type character or graphic. The second parameter must be the same type as the first parameter. The third parameter, if specified, must be numeric with zero decimal positions.

When any parameter is variable in length, the values of the other parameters are checked against the current length, not the maximum length.

The type of the return value is unsigned integer. This built-in function can be used anywhere that an unsigned integer expression is valid.

Note: Unlike the SCAN operation code, %SCAN cannot return an array containing all occurrences of the search string and its results cannot be tested using the %FOUND built-in function.

```
DName+++++++++++ETDsFrom+++To/L+++IDc.Keywords+++++++++++++++++++++++++++
D source          S              15A  inz('Dr. Doolittle')
D pos             S               5U 0
CL0N01Factor1+++++++Opcode&ExtExtended-factor2+++++++++++++++++++++++++++
C                 EVAL      pos = %scan('oo' : source)
 * After the EVAL, pos = 6 because 'oo' begins at position 6 in
 * 'Dr. Doolittle'.

C                 EVAL      pos = %scan('D' : source : 2)
 * After the EVAL, pos = 5 because the first 'D' found starting from
 * position 2 is in position 5.

C                 EVAL      pos = %scan('abc' : source)
 * After the EVAL, pos = 0 because 'abc' is not found in
 * 'Dr. Doolittle'.

C                 EVAL      pos = %scan('Dr.' : source : 2)
 * After the EVAL, pos = 0 because 'Dr.' is not found in
 * 'Dr. Doolittle', if the search starts at position 2.
```

Figure 105. %SCAN Example

%SIZE (Get Size in Bytes)

```
%SIZE(variable)
%SIZE(literal)
%SIZE(array{:*ALL})
%SIZE(table{:*ALL})
%SIZE(multiple occurrence data structure{:*ALL})
```

%SIZE returns the number of bytes occupied by the constant or field. The argument may be a literal, a named constant, a data structure, a data structure subfield, a field, an array, or a table name. It cannot, however, contain an expression. The value returned is in unsigned integer format (type U).

For a graphic literal, the size is the number of bytes occupied by the graphic characters, not including leading and trailing shift characters. For a graphic field, the size returned is the single-byte length.

For variable-length fields, %SIZE returns the total number of bytes occupied by the field (two bytes longer than the declared maximum length).

The length returned for a null-capable field (%SIZE) is always its full length, regardless of the setting of its null indicator.

If the argument is an array name, table name, or multiple occurrence data structure name, the value returned is the size of one element or occurrence. If *ALL is specified as the second parameter for %SIZE, the value returned is the storage taken up by all elements or occurrences. For a multiple-occurrence data structure containing pointer subfields, the size may be greater than the size of one occurrence times the number of occurrences. The system requires that pointers be placed in storage at addresses evenly divisible by 16. As a result, the length of each occurrence may have to be increased enough to make the length an exact multiple of 16 so that the pointer subfields will be positioned correctly in storage for every occurrence.

%SIZE may be specified anywhere that a numeric constant is allowed on the definition specification and in an expression in the extended factor 2 field of the calculation specification.

```
DName++++++++++ETDsFrom+++To/L+++IDc.Keywords+++++++++++++++++++++++++++
D
D arr1              S              10     DIM(4)
D table1            S               5     DIM(20)
D field1            S              10
D field2            S              9B 0
D field3            S              5P 2
D num               S              5P 0
D mds               DS             20     occurs(10)
D mds_size          C                     const (%size (mds: *all))
D mds_ptr           DS             20     OCCURS(10)
D   pointer                         *
D vCity             S             40A     VARYING INZ('North York')
D fCity             S             40A             INZ('North York')
CL0N01Factor1+++++++Opcode(E)+Extended-factor2+++++++++++++++++++++++++++
C                                                               Result
C                   eval      num = %SIZE(field1)                   10
C                   eval      num = %SIZE('HH')                       2
C                   eval      num = %SIZE(123.4)                      4
C                   eval      num = %SIZE(-03.00)                     4
C                   eval      num = %SIZE(arr1)                      10
C                   eval      num = %SIZE(arr1:*ALL)                 40
C                   eval      num = %SIZE(table1)                     5
C                   eval      num = %SIZE(table1:*ALL)              100
C                   eval      num = %SIZE(mds)                       20
C                   eval      num = %SIZE(mds:*ALL)                 200
C                   EVAL      num = %SIZE(mds_ptr)                   20
C                   EVAL      num = %SIZE(mds_ptr:*ALL)             320
C                   eval      num = %SIZE(field2)                     4
C                   eval      num = %SIZE(field3)                     3
C                   eval      n1 = %SIZE(vCity)                      42
C                   EVAL      n2 = %SIZE(fCity)                      40
```

Figure 106. %SIZE Example

%STATUS (Return File or Program Status)

%STATUS{(file_name)}

%STATUS returns the most recent value set for the program or file status. %STATUS is set whenever the program status or any file status changes, usually when an error occurs.

If %STATUS is used without the optional file_name parameter, then it returns the program or file status most recently changed. If a file is specified, the value contained in the INFDS *STATUS field for the specified file is returned. The INFDS does not have to be specified for the file.

%STATUS starts with a return value of 00000 and is reset to 00000 before any operation with an 'E' extender specified begins.

%STATUS is best checked immediately after an operation with the 'E' extender or an error indicator specified, or at the beginning of an INFSR or the *PSSR subroutine.

```
*...1....+....2....+....3....+....4....+....5....+....6....+....7...+....
CL0N01Factor1+++++++Opcode(E)+Factor2+++++++Result++++++++Len++D+HiLoEq....
 * The 'E' extender indicates that if an error occurs, the error
 * is to be handled as though an error indicator were coded.
 * The success of the operation can then be checked using the
 * %ERROR built-in function.  The status associated with the error
 * can be checked using the %STATUS built-in function.
C                   EXFMT(E)  INFILE
C                   IF        %ERROR
C                   EXSR      CheckError
C                   ENDIF
C ...
 *------------------------------------------------------------------
 * CheckError: Subroutine to process a file I/O error
 *------------------------------------------------------------------
C     CheckError    BEGSR
C                   SELECT

C                   WHEN      %STATUS < 01000
 * No error occurred

C                   WHEN      %STATUS = 01211
 * Attempted to read a file that was not open
C                   EXSR      InternalError

C                   WHEN      %STATUS = 01331
 * The wait time was exceeded for a READ operation
C                   EXSR      TimeOut

C                   WHEN      %STATUS = 01261
 * Operation to unacquired device
C                   EXSR      DeviceError

C                   WHEN      %STATUS = 01251
 * Permanent I/O error
C                   EXSR      PermError

C                   OTHER
 * Some other error occurred
C                   EXSR      FileError

C                   ENDSL

C                   ENDSR
```

Figure 107. %STATUS and %ERROR with 'E' Extender

```
DName+++++++++++ETDsFrom+++To/L+++IDc.Keywords+++++++++++++++++++++++++++
D Zero             S               5P 0 INZ(0)
CL0N01Factor1+++++++Opcode(E)+Factor2++++++Result++++++++Len++D+HiLoEq....

 * %STATUS starts with a value of 0
 *
 * The following SCAN operation will cause a branch to the *PSSR
 * because the start position has a value of 0.
C     'A'          SCAN         'ABC':Zero   Pos
C     BAD_SCAN     TAG

 * The following EXFMT operation has an 'E' extender, so %STATUS will
 * be set to 0 before the operation begins.  Therefore, it is
 * valid to check %STATUS after the operation.
 * Since the 'E' extender was coded, %ERROR can also be used to
 * check if an error occurred.
C                  EXFMT(E)  REC1
C                  IF        %ERROR
C                  SELECT
C                  WHEN      %STATUS = 01255
C ...
C                  WHEN      %STATUS = 01299
C ...
 * The following scan operation has an error indicator.  %STATUS will
 * not be set to 0 before the operation begins, but %STATUS can be
 * reasonably checked if the error indicator is on.
C     'A'          SCAN      'ABC':Zero   Pos              10
C                  IF        *IN10 AND %STATUS = 00100
C ...

 * The following scan operation does not produce an error.
 * Since there is no 'E' extender %STATUS will not be set to 0,
 * so it would return a value of 00100 from the previous error.
 * Therefore, it is unwise to use %STATUS after an operation that
 * does not have an error indicator or the 'E' extender coded since
 * you cannot be sure that the value pertains to the previous
 * operation.

C     'A'          SCAN      'ABC'        Pos
C ...

C     *PSSR        BEGSR
 * %STATUS can be used in the *PSSR since an error must have occurred.
C                  IF        %STATUS = 00100
C                  GOTO      BAD_SCAN
C ...
```

*Figure 108. %STATUS and %ERROR with 'E' Extender, Error Indicator, and *PSSR*

%STR (Get or Store Null-Terminated String)

```
%STR(basing pointer{: max-length})(right-hand-side)
%STR(basing pointer : max-length)(left-hand-side)
```

%STR is used to create or use null-terminated strings, which are commonly used in C and C++ applications.

The first parameter must be a basing-pointer variable. The second parameter, if specified, must be a numeric value with zero decimal positions. If not specified, it defaults to 32767.

The first parameter must point to storage that is at least as long as the length given by the second parameter.

Error conditions:

1. If the length parameter is not between 1 and 32767, an error will occur.

2. If the pointer is not set, an error will occur.

3. If the storage addressed by the pointer is shorter than indicated by the length parameter, either:

    a. An error will occur

    b. Data corruption will occur.

%STR Used to Get Null-Terminated String

When used on the right-hand side of an expression, this function returns the data pointed to by the first parameter up to, but not including, the first null character (x'00') found within the length specified. This built-in function can be used anywhere that a character expression is valid. No error will be given at run time if the null terminator is not found within the length specified. In this case, the length of the resulting value is the same as the length specified.

```
D String1        S              *
D Fld1           S              10A

C                EVAL      Fld1 = '<' + %str(String1) + '>'
 * Assuming that String1 points to '123,' where ',' represents the
 * null character, after the EVAL, Fld1 = '<123>      '.
```

Figure 109. %STR (Right-Hand-Side) Example 1

The following is an example of %STR with the second parameter specified.

```
D String1        S              *
D Fld1           S              10A

C                    EVAL     Fld1 = '<' + %str(String1 : 2) + '>'
* Assuming that String1 points to '123,' where ',' represents the
* null character, after the EVAL, Fld1 = '<12>     '.
* Since the maximum length read by the operation was 2, the '3' and
* the ',' were not considered.
```

Figure 110. %STR (Right-Hand-Side) Example 2

In this example, the null-terminator is found within the specified maximum length.

```
D String1        S              *
D Fld1           S              10A

C                    EVAL     Fld1 = '<' + %str(String1 : 5) + '>'
* Assuming that String1 points to '123,' where ',' represents the
* null character, after the EVAL, Fld1 = '<123>    '.
* Since the maximum length read by the operation was 5, the
* null-terminator in position 4 was found so all the data up to
* the null-terminator was used.
```

Figure 111. %STR (Right-Hand-Side) Example 3

%STR Used to Store Null-Terminated String

When used on the left-hand side of an expression, %STR(ptr:length) assigns the value of the right-hand side of the expression to the storage pointed at by the pointer, adding a null-terminating byte at the end. The maximum length that can be specified is 32767. This means that at most 32766 bytes of the right-hand side can be used, since one byte must be reserved for the null-terminator at the end.

The length indicates the amount of storage that the pointer points to. This length should be greater than the maximum length the right-hand side will have. The pointer must be set to point to storage at least as long as the length parameter. If the length of the right-hand side of the expression is longer than the specified length, the right-hand side value is truncated.

Note: Data corruption will occur if *both* of the following are true:

1. The length parameter is greater than the actual length of data addressed by the pointer.

2. The length of the right-hand side is greater than or equal to the actual length of data addressed by the pointer.

If you are dynamically allocating storage for use by %STR, you must keep track of the length that you have allocated.

```
D String1        S              *
D Fld1           S             10A
...
C                    EVAL      %str(String1:25) = 'abcdef'
 * The storage pointed at by String1 now contains 'abcdef,'
 * Bytes 8-25 following the null-terminator are unchanged.

D String1        S              *
D Fld1           S             10A
...
C                    EVAL      %str(String1 : 4) = 'abcdef'
 * The storage pointed at by String1 now contains 'abc,'
```

Figure 112. %STR (Left-Hand-Side) Examples

%SUBST (Get Substring)

`%SUBST(string:start{:length})`

%SUBST returns a portion of argument string. It may also be used as the result of an assignment with the EVAL operation code.

The start parameter represents the starting position of the substring.

The length parameter represents the length of the substring. If it is not specified, the length is the length of the string parameter less the start value plus one.

The string must be character or graphic data. Starting position and length may be any numeric value or numeric expression with zero decimal positions. The starting position must be greater than zero. The length may be greater than or equal to zero.

When the string parameter is varying length, the values of the other parameters are checked against the current length, not the maximum length.

When specified as a parameter for a definition specification keyword, the parameters must be literals or named constants representing literals. When specified on a free-form calculation specification, the parameters may be any expression.

%SUBST Used for Its Value

%SUBST returns a substring from the contents of the specified string. The string may be any character or graphic field or expression. Unindexed arrays are allowed for string, start, and length. The substring begins at the specified starting position in the string and continues for the length specified. If length is not specified, then the substring continues to the end of the string. For example:

```
The value of  %subst('Hello World': 5+2) is  'World'
The value of  %subst('Hello World':5+2:10-7) is 'Wor'
The value of  %subst('abcd' + 'efgh':4:3) is 'def'
```

For graphic characters the start position and length is consistent with the two-byte character length (position 3 is the third two-byte character and length 3 represents three two-byte characters to be operated on).

%SUBST Used as the Result of an Assignment

When used as the result of an assignment, this built-in function refers to certain positions of the argument string. Unindexed arrays are not allowed for start and length.

The result begins at the specified starting position in the variable and continues for the length specified. If the length is not specified, then the string is referenced to its end. If the length refers to characters beyond the end of the string, then a run-time error is issued.

When %SUBST is used as the result of an assignment, the first parameter must refer to a storage location. That is, the first parameter of the %SUBST operation must be one of the following:

- Field

- Data structure

- Data structure subfield

- Array name

- Array element

- Table element

Any valid expressions are permitted for the second and third parameters of %SUBST when it appears as the result of an assignment with an EVAL operation.

```
CL0N01Factor1+++++++Opcode(E)+Extended-factor2+++++++++++++++++++++++++++++
 *
 * In this example, CITY contains 'Toronto, Ontario'
 * %SUBST returns the value 'Ontario'.
 *
C        ' '          SCAN      CITY          C
C                     IF        %SUBST(CITY:C+1) = 'Ontario'
C                     EVAL      CITYCNT = CITYCNT+1
C                     ENDIF
 *
 * Before the EVAL, A has the value 'abcdefghijklmno'.
 * After the EVAL A has the value 'ab****ghijklmno'
 *
C                     EVAL      %SUBST(A:3:4) = '****'
```

Figure 113. %SUBST Examples

%TRIM (Trim Blanks at Edges)

%TRIM(string)

%TRIM returns the given string less any leading and trailing blanks.

The string can be character or graphic data.

When specified as a parameter for a definition-specification keyword, the string parameter must be a constant.

```
DName+++++++++++ETDsFrom+++To/L+++IDc.Keywords+++++++++++++++++++++++++++++
D
D LOCATION        S              16A
CLON01Factor1+++++++Opcode(E)+Factor2+++++++Result++++++++Len++D+HiLoEq..
CLON01Factor1+++++++Opcode(E)+Extended-factor2+++++++++++++++++++++++++++++
 *
 * LOCATION will have the value 'Toronto, Ontario'.
 *
C                   EVAL      LOCATION = %TRIM('  Toronto, Ontario  ')
 *
 * Name will have the value 'Chris Smith'.
 *
C                   MOVE(P)   'Chris'     FIRSTNAME        10
C                   MOVE(P)   'Smith'     LASTNAME         10
C                   EVAL      NAME =
C                             %TRIM(FIRSTNAME) +' '+ %TRIM(LASTNAME)
```

Figure 114. %TRIM Examples

%TRIML (Trim Leading Blanks)

%TRIML(string)

%TRIML returns the given string less any leading blanks.

The string can be character or graphic data.

When specified as a parameter for a definition-specification keyword, the string parameter must be a constant.

```
CLON01Factor1+++++++Opcode(E)+Extended-factor2+++++++++++++++++++++++++++
 *
 * LOCATION will have the value 'Toronto, Ontario  '.
 *
C                   EVAL      LOCATION = %TRIML('  Toronto, Ontario  ')
```

Figure 115. %TRIML Examples

%TRIMR (Trim Trailing Blanks)

%TRIMR(string)

%TRIMR returns the given string less any trailing blanks.

The string can be character or graphic data.

When specified as a parameter for a definition-specification keyword, the string parameter must be a constant.

```
DName++++++++++ETDsFrom+++To/L+++IDc.Keywords+++++++++++++++++++++++++++
D
D LOCATION        S             18A
CL0N01Factor1+++++++Opcode(E)+Factor2+++++++Result++++++++Len++D+HiLoEq..
CL0N01Factor1+++++++Opcode(E)+Extended-factor2++++++++++++++++++++++++++
 *
 * LOCATION will have the value '  Toronto, Ontario'.
 *
C                   EVAL      LOCATION = %TRIMR('  Toronto, Ontario  ')
 *
 * Name will have the value 'Chris Smith'.
 *
C                   MOVEL(P)  'Chris'    FIRSTNAME        10
C                   MOVEL(P)  'Smith'    LASTNAME         10
C                   EVAL      NAME =
C                             %TRIMR(FIRSTNAME) +' '+ %TRIMR(LASTNAME)
```

Figure 116. %TRIMR Examples

%UNS (Convert to Unsigned Format)

%UNS(numeric expression)

%UNS converts the value of the numeric expression to unsigned format. Any decimal digits are truncated. %UNS can be used to truncate the decimal positions from a float or decimal value, allowing it to be used as an array index.

%UNSH (Convert to Unsigned Format with Half Adjust)

%UNSH(numeric expression)

%UNSH is like %UNS, except that if the numeric expression is a decimal or a float value, half adjust is applied to the value of the numeric expression when converting to unsigned type. No message is issued if half adjust cannot be performed.

```
DName+++++++++++ETDsFrom+++To/L+++IDc.Keywords++++++++++++++++++++++++++
D p7              s              7p 3 inz (8236.567)
D s9              s              9s 5 inz (23.73442)
D f8              s              8f   inz (173.789)
D result1         s             15p 5
D result2         s             15p 5
D result3         s             15p 5
D array           s              1a   dim (200)
D a               s              1a
CLON01Factor1+++++++Opcode&ExtExtended-factor2++++++++++++++++++++++++++
C                 eval       result1 = %uns (p7) + 0.1234
C                 eval       result2 = %uns (s9)
C                 eval       result3 = %unsh (f8)
 * The value of "result1" is now 8236.12340.
 * The value of "result2" is now   23.00000
 * The value of "result3" is now  174.00000.

C                 eval       a = array (%unsh (f8))
 * %UNS and %UNSH can be used as array indexes
```

Figure 117. %UNS and %UNSH Examples

Appendixes

Appendix A. Solutions

Given below are the solutions to the exercises presented in Part 1. Where a coding example is shown, there is a corresponding source member in the source file WKBKANS in WKBKLIB.

Note: For many of the exercises, more than one correct answer is possible.

Solution to Exercise 1

The RPG IV source member EMPPAY illustrates many of the key features of RPG IV, including:

1. Blank lines

2. Expanded fields

3. Mixed-case entry

4. Underscore in names

5. H spec keywords

6. New D spec

7. New P spec

8. Stand-alone fields (on D spec)

9. New unsigned integer data type

10. Opcode extender now next to opcode and new extender E

11. New opcodes -- IF and EVAL

12. New built-in functions -- %FOUND, %ERROR

13. Free-form expression in extended factor 2 on C spec

14. CalcPay function call

15. Subprocedure CalcPay definition

16. Continuation on the O spec

Solution to Exercise 2

Note that the parameter for the DECEDIT keyword could be either ',' or '0,'. With the first specification, no leading zeros are printed; with the second one, they are.

```
H DECEDIT(',')  FORMSALIGN(*YES) DFTNAME(TEST)
H DFTACTGRP(*NO) ACTGRP('TESTAG')
```

Solution to Exercise 3

```
FRAF      IR  F              TDISK   RAFDATA(CTLD)
FCTLD     IP  F   30         DISK
```

Solution to Exercise 4

```
FQSYSPRT  O   F   132        PRINTER OFLIND(*INOF)
F                                    FORMLEN(60)
F                                    FORMOFL(56)
```

Solution to Exercise 5

This solution takes the liberty of using longer field names, although these are not required for a correct solution.

```
D DS1            DS

D  Array                     5     DIM(100)

D  Name                     31     INZ
D   FirstName               15     OVERLAY(Name)
D   MidInitial               1     OVERLAY(Name:15)
D   LastName                15     OVERLAY(Name:16)

D Temp          S            3  0 INZ

D SaveName      S                  LIKE(Name)
C               SETON                                        LR
```

Note the following about the above code sample:

- The field names make use of mixed case for readability
- Subfields are indented to show their relationship to the main field
- The subfields of Name are defined using the length notation

Solution to Exercise 6

Note how the length of the subfields is much clearer in the length notation than in the positional notation.

```
*   Data Structure defined using positional notation
D Address1        DS
D   StreetNo1           1      3P 0
D   StreetNam1          4     23
D   City1              24     38
D   State1             39     53

*   Same data structure defined using length notation
D Address2        DS
D   StreetNo2                  5P 0
D   StreetNam2                20
D   City2                     15
D   State2                    15

C                 SETON                                          LR
```

Solution to Exercise 7

```
C                 READE(N)  FILE1                        10
C                 MOVE      ARR3(3)    FIELD1
```

Solution to Exercise 8

Note that the specs that define the data structure precede the program-described record definition.

If you compare these RPG IV specs with the corresponding RPG III specs given in Part 1, you can see how the RPG IV representation is easier to read and understand.

```
D DS1             DS
D   F1                  1      5P 0
D   F2                 11     12B 0
D   F3                 21     24B 0
D   F4                 31     35  0
D   F5                  1     80
D                      76     80   INZ(*ALL'*')
** Note that field ZZZ1 was only created so that an initialization
** could be done.  Since we do not need to use the name ZZZ1,
** we can leave the field unnamed.
IFILE1     NS 01
I                          1    5  FIELD1
I                          6   10 2BIN1
```

Solution to Exercise 9

```
FQSYSPRT   O   F   80        PRINTER OFLIND(*INOA)
C                   EXCEPT
C                   SETON                                        LR
OQSYSPRT   H   1PNOA            3 2100
O                                      24 'This is an RPG testcase '
O                                      36 'DATE:'
O                   UDATE        Y     45
O          E                        2
O                                      24 'Record number 1 has been'
O                                      48 ' identified as corrupted'
O                                      66 'Check your file'.
```

Solution to Exercise 10

```
FOUT       O   F   80        DISK
D PAR          S       50    DIM(4) CTDATA TOFILE(OUT) PERRCD(1)
D PAR#         C             CONST(4)
D DFTADR       C             CONST('00000Unknown')
C     1              DO    PAR#        X              5 0
C     PAR(X)         IFEQ  *BLANKS
C                    MOVEL DFTADR      PAR(X)
C                    ENDIF
C                    ENDDO
C                    SETON                             LR
**CTDATA PAR
00003Cowslip Street      Toronto      Ontario
01150Eglinton Avenue     North York   Ontario
00012Jasper Avenue       Edmonton     Alberta
00027Avenue Road         Sudbury      Ontario.
```

Solution to Exercise 11

Answer to Question 1: Prototype

```
 * Main Source Section
 * Prototype for subprocedure Fmtcust and return value
D FmtCust       PR        25A
 * Prototyped parameters
D   FirstName             10A
D   LastName              15A
D   ValidRec               N
```

Answer to Question 2: Procedure Interface and Begin- and End-P specs:

```
      * Subprocedure Section
      * --------------------
      * Begin-procedure
      P FmtCust         B
      * Procedure-interface (same as the prototype)
      D FmtCust         PI            25A
      D   FirstName                   10A
      D   LastName                    15A
      D   ValidRec                      N
      * End-procedure
      P                 E
```

Look at the following example to see how the subprocedure you defined can be used:

```
      * Main Source Section
      * -------------------
      * The following source shows the prototype, procedure interface
      * and subprocedure definition for FmtCust. This solution also shows
      * a small example of how you would use this subprocedure.
      * See Exercise 16 in stage 10 for the DDS for PAYROLL.
      *
      H DFTACTGRP(*NO) ACTGRP('MyActGrp')
      FPAYROLL    IF   E           DISK
      * Prototype for subprocedure Fmtcust and return value
      D FmtCust         PR            25A
      * Prototyped parameters
      D   FirstName                   10A
      D   LastName                    15A
      D   ValidRec                      N
      * +++++  Define field for concatenated first and last name
      D FLname          S             25
      * Read a record
      C                 DOW       *IN20 = '0'
      C                 READ      PAYREC                             20    EOF
      *
      * Since the subprocedure returns a value, it is called in an expression.

      C                 EVAL      FLname = FmtCust(Fname:Lname:*IN20)
      C     'FLname =   'DSPLY              FLname
      C                 ENDDO                                              Loop back
      ***
      C                 SETON                               LR             Set LR
      C                 RETURN                                             Return
```

```
 * Subprocedure Section
 * --------------------
 * Begin-procedure
P FmtCust         B
D FmtCust         PI          25A
 * Procedure-interface (same as the prototype)
D   FirstName                 10A
D   LastName                  15A
D   ValidRec                    N

 * Calculations
 * Return value must be compatible with return type in definition
C                 IF        ValidRec = '0'                          If not EOF
C                 RETURN    %TRIMR(FirstName) + ' ' + LastName
C                 ENDIF
C                 RETURN    'Last Customer'
 * End-procedure
P                 E
```

Solution to Exercise 12

```
H DATFMT(*MDY) TIMFMT(*HMS) DATEDIT(*MDY/)
D MyDate        S           D    DATFMT(*YMD/) INZ(D'02/01/98')
D CurDate       S           D    DATFMT(*USA) INZ(*JOB)
D ThisDate      S           D
D MyTime        S           T    INZ(T'12:00:00')
```

Solution to Exercise 13

```
     * PRTOBJ  - Print program modified to use a date field
     *
     * DSPOBJ is the outfile from DSPOBJD - Create manually
     FDSPOBJ   IF   E           DISK
     FQPRINT    O   F 132        PRINTER OFLIND(*INOF)
     * +++++ Need to define the date field and its internal format +++++
     DLSTUSD         S           D    DATFMT(*YMD)
     * +++++ End of added code section
     *****************************************************************
     C                 EXCEPT    HDG                                  Prt heading
     *****************************************************************
     * Read a record
     * QLIDOBJD is the format name of the QADSPOBJ file
     C                 READ      QLIDOBJD                      20     Read
     *****************************************************************
     * Continue reading until EOF
     C     *IN20       DOWEQ     '0'                                  Not EOF
     *
     * +++ Convert Date Subroutine is deleted
     *
     * Convert the date from MMDDYY to YYMMDD
     * +++ Move the character field to date field.  Since the character field
     * +++ does not have separators - it must be moved by specifying
     * +++ the format in factor 1 followed by a 0 (zero).
     * +++ Length removed for LSTUSD.
     * +++ Test if date is valid (blanks means not used) and move it.
     C     *MDY0       Test(D)             ODUDAT            10
     C                 IF        NOT(*IN10)
     C     *MDY0       MOVE      ODUDAT    LSTUSD
     C                 ENDIF
     * +++ End of added code section
     C                 EXCEPT    DETAIL                               Print detail
     C   OF            EXCEPT    HDG                                  Prt heading
     C                 READ      QLIDOBJD                      20     Read
     C                 ENDDO                                          Loop Back
     * End the program
     C                 SETON                               LR         Set LR
     * +++ Convert Date Subroutine is deleted
```

```
OQPRINT     E           HDG         2 06
O                                      25 'Objects '
O                                         'in Library'
O           E           HDG         2
O                                       6 'Object'
O                                      18 'Obj type'
O                                      30 'Attribute'
O                                      42 'Last used'
O           E           DETAIL      1
O                       ODOBNM         10
O                       ODOBTP         19
O                       ODOBAT         33
O           N10         LSTUSD         42
O           10                         42 'Not used'
*   +++++                  The Y edit code has to be removed
*   +++++                  as a date field contains delimiters.
*   +++++                  If date is blank, means not used
```

Solution to Exercise 14

```
H DATFMT(*MDY)
D MyDate          S             D    DATFMT(*YMD/) INZ(D'02/01/98')
D CurDate         S             D    DATFMT(*USA) INZ(*JOB)
C     CurDate      SUBDUR   MyDate      NoDays:*D       3 0
C     'NoDays      'DSPLY              NoDays
C                  SETON                               LR
```

Solution to Exercise 15

```
     * PRTOBJ  - Print program modified to use a date field
     * Note: Must compile with FIXNBR(*ZONED) - added on H spec
     * DSPOBJ is the outfile from DSPOBJD - Create it manually
    H DATEDIT(*MDY) FIXNBR(*ZONED)
    FDSPOBJ    IF   E            DISK
    FQPRINT    O    F 132        PRINTER OFLIND(*INOF)
    DLSTUSD         S            D   DATFMT(*YMD)
     * +++++ Need to define a date field to hold current date ++++
     * +++++ plus a field to hold result in number of days    ++++
    DCurDate        S            D   INZ(*JOB)
    DNoDays         S            5 0
     * +++++ End of added code section
     ****************************************************************
    C                   EXCEPT    HDG                              Prt heading
     ****************************************************************
     * Read a record
     * QLIDOBJD is the format name of the QADSPOBJ file
    C                   READ      QLIDOBJD                   20    Read
     * Continue reading until EOF
    C     *IN20         DOWEQ     '0'                              Not EOF
     ****************************************************************
     * Convert the date from MMDDYY to YYMMDD
    C     *MDY0         TEST(D)             ODUDAT           10
    C                   IF        NOT(*IN10)
    C     *MDY0         MOVE      ODUDAT    LSTUSD
     *
     * +++ Subtract the last-used date from the current date
     * +++ CurDate initialized to *JOB
    C     CurDate       SUBDUR    LSTUSD         NoDays:*D
     * +++ End of added code section
    C                   ENDIF
    C                   EXCEPT    DETAIL                           Print detail
    C  OF               EXCEPT    HDG                              Prt heading
    C                   READ      QLIDOBJD                   20    Read
    C                   ENDDO                                      Loop Back
     * End the program
    C                   SETON                            LR        Set LR
     *
     * +++ End of added code section
```

```
OQPRINT      E           HDG            2 06
O                                        25 'Objects '
O                                           'in Library'
O            E           HDG            2
O                                         6 'Object'
O                                        18 'Obj type'
O                                        30 'Attribute'
O                                        42 'Last used'
  *  +++++                      Add the heading
O                                        60 'Days Since Used'
O            E           DETAIL         1
O                        ODOBNM            10
O                        ODOBTP            19
O                        ODOBAT            33
O            N10         LSTUSD            42
O            10                            42 'Not used'
O            N10         NoDays        L   56
O            10                            56 'Not used'
  *  +++++                      Add the field and edit
```

Solution to Exercise 16

Compare the code within each RPG IV subroutine to the corresponding RPG III subroutines. Note how much easier it is to read the calculation code.

```
      * RPGPAY   - Pay check program with new EVAL statement
      *
     FPAYROLL   IF   E            DISK
     FQPRINT    O    F   132      PRINTER OFLIND(*INOF)
      * +++++  Define the Tax and Pay fields based on the database
     D Pay          S              +2    Like(Rate)
     D Tax          S              +2    Like(Rate)
     D Net          S              +2    Like(Rate)
      *
     C              EXCEPT    Heading                              Prt Heading
      * Read a record
     C    *IN20     DOWEQ     '0'
     C              READ      PAYREC                        20     EOF
      *
     C    *IN20     IFEQ      '0'                                  If not EOF
      ***
      * Calculate pay and tax
     C              EXSR      PayCalc                              Calc pay
     C              EXSR      TaxCalc                              Calc tax
     C              EVAL      Net = Pay - Tax
     C              EXCEPT    Detail                               Prt record
     C    OF        EXCEPT    Heading                              Prt Heading
     C              ENDIF                                          EndIf EOF
     C              ENDDO                                          Loop back
      ***
     C              SETON                             LR           Set LR
     C              RETURN                                         Return
      ********* Insert Payment calculation here  ***********
     C    PayCalc   BEGSR
      *
     C              IF        Hours <= 35
     C              EVAL      Pay  = Hours * Rate
     C              ELSE
     C              EVAL(H)   Pay  = (35 * Rate)
     C                           + ((Hours - 35) * (Rate * 1.75))
     C              END
     C              ENDSR
      ********* Insert Tax calculation here  *************
     C    TaxCalc   BEGSR
      *
     C              EVAL      Tax = 0
     C              IF        Pay > 200
     C              EVAL(H)   Tax = (Pay - 200) * (Taxd / 100)
     C              END
     C              ENDSR
```

```
OQPRINT    E         Heading        2 06
O                                        25 'Pay and tax calculation '
O                    UDATE        Y      36
O          E         Heading        2
O                                        19 'First and Last name'
O                                        36 'Earned'
O                                        46 'Pay tax'
O                                        56 'Net pay'
O          E         Detail         1
O                    FNAME                10
O                    LNAME                26
O                    PAY          3       36
O                    TAX          3       46
O                    NET          3       56
```

Solution to Exercise 17

```
       * RPGPAY   - Pay check program with subprocedures
       *
      H DFTACTGRP(*NO) ACTGRP('MyActGrp')
      FPAYROLL   IF   E           DISK
      FQPRINT    O    F  132      PRINTER OFLIND(*INOF)
       * +++++  Prototypes for subprocedures PayCalc and TaxCalc
       * +++++  Define the Pay and Tax return values based on the database
      D PayCalc         PR            +2    Like(Rate)
      D TaxCalc         PR            +2    Like(Rate)
       * Global data
      D Pay             S             +2    Like(Rate)
      D Tax             S             +2    Like(Rate)
      D Net             S             +2    Like(Rate)
       *
      C                 EXCEPT    Heading                          Prt Heading
       * Read a record
      C     *IN20       DOWEQ     '0'
      C                 READ      PAYREC                    20     EOF
       *
      C     *IN20       IFEQ      '0'                              If not EOF
      ***
       * Calculate pay and tax
      C                 EVAL      Pay = PayCalc
      C                 EVAL      Tax = TaxCalc
      C                 EVAL      Net = Pay - Tax
      C                 EXCEPT    Detail                           Prt record
      C     OF          EXCEPT    Heading                          Prt Heading
      C                 ENDIF                                      EndIf EOF
      C                 ENDDO                                      Loop back
      ***
      C                 SETON                             LR       Set LR
      C                 RETURN                                     Return
```

```
OQPRINT      E           Heading        2 06
O                                        25 'Pay and tax calculation '
O                        UDATE         Y  36
O            E           Heading        2
O                                        19 'First and Last name'
O                                        36 'Earned'
O                                        46 'Pay tax'
O                                        56 'Net pay'
O            E           Detail         1
O                        FNAME            10
O                        LNAME            26
O                        PAY            3 36
O                        TAX            3 46
O                        NET            3 56
 * Subprocedure Section
 * --------------------
 * Begin-procedure
P PayCalc       B
 * Procedure-interface (same as the prototype)
D PayCalc       PI            +2    Like(Rate)

 ********* Insert Payment calculation here  ***********
 *
C                 IF        Hours <= 35
C                 RETURN(H) Hours * Rate
C                 ELSE
C                 RETURN(H) (35 * Rate)
C                               + ((Hours - 35) * (Rate * 1.75))
C                 END
 * End-procedure
P               E


 * Begin-procedure
P TaxCalc       B
 * Procedure-interface (same as the prototype)
D TaxCalc       PI            +2    Like(Rate)

 *********   Insert Tax calculation here  *************
 *
C                 EVAL      Tax = 0
C                 IF        Pay > 200
C                 RETURN(H) (Pay - 200) * (Taxd / 100)
C                 END
 * End-procedure
P               E
```

Solution to Exercise 18

```
     * RPGPAY  - Pay check program with subprocedures
     *
     H DFTACTGRP(*NO) ACTGRP('MyActGrp')
     FPAYROLL   IF   E            DISK
     FQPRINT    O    F  132        PRINTER OFLIND(*INOF)
     * +++++  Prototypes for subprocedures PayCalc and TaxCalc
     * +++++  Define the Pay and Tax return values based on the database
     D PayCalc         PR           +2    Like(Rate)
     D TaxCalc         PR           +2    Like(Rate)
     * Global data
     D Pay             S            +2    Like(Rate)
     D Tax             S            +2    Like(Rate)
     D Net             S            +2    Like(Rate)
     * +++++  Define field for concatenated first and last name
     D FLname          S            25
     *
     C                 EXCEPT    Heading                             Prt Heading
     * Read a record
     C     *IN20       DOWEQ     '0'
     C                 READ      PAYREC                        20    EOF
     *
     C     *IN20       IFEQ      '0'                                 If not EOF
     ***
     * Calculate pay and tax
     C                 EVAL      Pay = PayCalc
     C                 EVAL      Tax = TaxCalc
     C                 EVAL      Net = Pay - Tax
     * +++++  Concatenate first and last name
     C                 EVAL      FLname = %TRIMR(Fname) + ' ' + Lname
     C                 EXCEPT    Detail                              Prt record
     C     OF          EXCEPT    Heading                             Prt Heading
     C                 ENDIF                                         EndIf EOF
     C                 ENDDO                                         Loop back
     ***
     C                 SETON                             LR          Set LR
     C                 RETURN                                        Return
     OQPRINT    E            Heading       2 06
     O                                     25 'Pay and tax calculation '
     O                       UDATE       Y 36
     O          E            Heading       2
     O                                     19 'First and Last name'
     O                                     36 'Earned'
     O                                     46 'Pay tax'
     O                                     56 'Net pay'
     O          E            Detail        1
     * +++++  Delete the FNAME field and write FLname instead of LNAME
     O                       FLname          26
     O                       PAY         3   36
     O                       TAX         3   46
     O                       NET         3   56
```

```
* Subprocedure Section
* --------------------
* Begin-procedure
P PayCalc        B
* Procedure-interface (same as the prototype)
D PayCalc        PI            +2    Like(Rate)

********** Insert Payment calculation here  ***********
*
C                  IF        Hours <= 35
C                  RETURN(H) Hours * Rate
C                  ELSE
C                  RETURN(H) (35 * Rate)
C                               + ((Hours - 35) * (Rate * 1.75))
C                  END
* End-procedure
P                E

* Begin-procedure
P TaxCalc        B
* Procedure-interface (same as the prototype)
D TaxCalc        PI            +2    Like(Rate)

********** Insert Tax calculation here  *************
*
C                  EVAL      Tax = 0
C                  IF        Pay > 200
C                  RETURN(H) (Pay - 200) * (Taxd / 100)
C                  END
* End-procedure
P                E
```

Solution to Exercise 19

The following list shows the main actions needed for each exercise instruction.

1. Change the call statement in DSPOBJMOD to:

   ```
   CALLPRC    PRC(PRTOBJILE)
   ```

2. CRTCLMOD MODULE(YourLib/DSPOBJMOD) SRCFILE(YourLib/WKBKSRC)

3. Change the call statement in PRTOBJILE to:

   ```
   CALLB      'DAYSSINCE'
   ```

4. CRTRPGMOD MODULE(YourLib/PRTOBJILE) SRCFILE(YourLib/WKBKSRC)

5. CRTRPGMOD MODULE(YourLib/DAYSSINCE) SRCFILE(YourLib/WKBKSRC)

6. CRTPGM PGM(YourLib/PRTOBJPGM) MODULE(DSPOBJMOD PRTOBJILE DAYSSINCE)

7. CALL PRTOBJPGM <library name>

8. WRKSPLF

Solution to Exercise 20

1. CRTSRVPGM SRVPGM(YourLib/MYSRVPGM) MODULE(DAYSSINCE) EXPORT(*ALL)

2. CRTPGM PGM(YourLib/PRTOBJPGM2) MODULE(DSPOBJMOD PRTOBJILE) BNDSRVPGM(MYSRVPGM)

3. CALL PRTOBJPGM2 <library name>

Solution to Exercise 21

Answer to Question 1: 41

```
D Question       S             25    INZ('Are BIFs Great?')
D Answer         S             15
D AnArray        S              5    DIM(5)
D X              S             3P 0
C                EVAL      Answer = %Trim(%Subst(Question:4))
 ** Answer = 'BIFs Great?'
C        ' '     CHECKR    Answer        X
 ** When factor one is a blank character, CHECKR returns the
 ** the length of Answer.  So X = 11.
C                EVAL      X = X + %Elem(AnArray)
 ** The number of elements in AnArray is 5.
C                          + %Size(AnArray:*ALL)
 ** The size of all elements in AnArray is 25.
 ** So X = 11 + 5 + 25 = 41.
C                SETON                              LR
```

Answer to Question 2:

```
D Question       C                     CONST('Are BIFs Great?')
 **                                  1   5    10
D Answer         S             15
D AnArray        S              5    DIM(5)
D X              S             3P 0
C                EVAL      Answer = %Subst(Question:5:5)
C                          + %Subst(Question:1:4)
C                          + %Subst(Question:10:5) + '!'
C                SETON                              LR
```

Answer to Question 3: Result = Yes

Answer to Question 4:

```
       FOUT         O  F  80        DISK
       D PAR             S         50    DIM(4) CTDATA TOFILE(OUT) PERRCD(1)
       D PAR#            C               CONST(%ELEM(PAR))
       D DFTADR          C               CONST('00000Unknown')
       C      1          DO        PAR#        X                5 0
       C      PAR(X)     IFEQ      *BLANKS
       C                 MOVEL     DFTADR       PAR(X)
       C                 ENDIF
       C                 ENDDO
       C                 SETON                                LR
     **CTDATA PAR
     00003Cowslip Street    Toronto      Ontario
     01150Eglinton Avenue   North York   Ontario
     00012Jasper Avenue     Edmonton     Alberta
     00027Avenue Road       Sudbury      Ontario
```

Solution to Exercise 22

```
       *
       * This program uses a lookup routine which locates the product code
       * and corresponding description from the user spaces without the
       * overhead of opening the product file and doing database I/O.
       *
     FPRODDSP   CF   E            WORKSTN
     D ProdCode      S         5    DIM(32767) BASED(ProdPtr)
     D                              ASCEND
     D ProdDesc      S              DIM(32767) BASED(DescPtr)
     D                              LIKE(DESC)

     D ProdSpcNam   DS
     D   ProdName              10   INZ('PRODCODE')
     D   ProdLib               10   INZ('*CURLIB')
     D DescSpcNam   DS
     D   DescName              10   INZ('PRODDESC')
     D   DescLib               10   INZ('*CURLIB')
     D Indx          S         5  0 INZ(1)
     D Error         C              'Invalid Product Code'
```

```
C* Obtain a pointer (ProdPtr) to the Product Code space
C                    CALL      'QUSPTRUS'
C                    PARM                    ProdSpcNam
C                    PARM                    ProdPtr

C* Obtain a pointer (DescPtr) to the Product Description space
C                    CALL      'QUSPTRUS'
C                    PARM                    DescSpcNam
C                    PARM                    DescPtr

C* Now Search ProdCode array for a product code and
C* display either the product's description (if found) or
C* "Invalid Product Code" if not found

C                    DOW       NOT *IN03
C                    EXFMT     ProdFmt
 * Exit loop if the user has pressed PF3
C                    IF        *IN03
C                    LEAVE
C                    ENDIF

C                    EVAL      Indx = 1
C        Prod        LookUp    ProdCode(Indx)              12  10
C                    IF        *IN10
C                    EVAL      Desc = ProdDesc(Indx)
C                    ELSE
C                    EVAL      Desc = Error
C                    ENDIF

C                    ENDDO
C                    SETON                                 LR
```

Solution to Exercise 23

The following sequence of commands represent one possible solution to the debugging exercise. Note that the numbers correspond to the steps listed in the exercise.

1. STRDBG YourLib/PRTOBJPGM2

2. CRTCLMOD MODULE(YourLib/DSPOBJMOD) SRCFILE(YourLib/WKBKSRC)

   CRTRPGMOD MODULE(YourLib/PRTOBJILE) SRCFILE(YourLib/WKBKSRC)

   CRTRPGMOD MODULE(YourLib/DAYSSINCE) SRCFILE(YourLib/WKBKSRC)

3. CRTSRVPGM SRVPGM(YourLib/MYSRVPGM) MODULE(DAYSSINCE) EXPORT(*ALL)

   CRTPGM PGM(YourLib/PRTOBJPGM2) MODULE(DSPOBJMOD PRTOBJILE)

4. STRDBG WKBKLIB/PRTOBJPGM2 UPDPROD(*YES)

5. Move cursor to line 9 and press F6, or enter "break 9".

6. Press F14 (Work with module list).

7. Enter '5' next to PRTOBJILE and press Enter.

8. Move your cursor to one of the D specs and press F6.

9. Press F6 again.

10. BREAK 19 WHEN NoDays >= 0.

11. Press F3, enter 'CALL PRTOBJPGM Yourlib'.

12. Move cursor to any line with and press F6.

13. Press F22 (Step Into) or enter STEP INTO on the debug command line.

14. Press F12 (Resume) or enter STEP n, where n is the number of statements before the statement with the conditional breakpoint.

15. Press F11 (Display variable) for each field, or enter EVAL field name on the debug command line.

16. Press F10 (Step) the number of times needed, and then F22 (Step into).

17. Press F3 followed by ENDDBG on the system command line.

Solution to Exercise 24

The following sequence of commands represent one possible solution to the debugging exercise. Note that the numbers correspond to the steps listed in the exercise.

1. CRTRPGMOD MODULE(YourLib/PRTOBJILEA) SRCFILE(YourLib/WKBKSRC) DBGVIEW(*ALL) REPLACE(*YES)

2. UPDPGM PGM(PRTOBJPGM2) MODULE(PRTOBJILE)

3. STRDBG YourLib/PRTOBJPGM2 UPDPROD(*YES)

4. Move cursor to line 9 and press F6, or enter "break 9".

5. Press F14 (Work with module list). Enter '1', 'MYSRVPGM', 'WKBKLIB', '*SRVPGM' and press Enter to add the service program.

6. Enter '5' next to PRTOBJILE and press Enter.

7. Press F15 (Select view). Enter '1' next to the first choice, Listing View, and then press Enter.

8. Press F6 on the line with the CALLB operation. The precise line number depends on the listing options. For the supplied source it was line 112.

9. Press F21, enter 'CALL PRTOBJPGM Yourlib'.

10. Press F22 (Step into).

11. Press F12 (Resume), followed by F22.

12. Press F21, enter 'WRKJOB OPTION(*PGMSTK)'. Then press F11 to see the activation groups associated with the programs in the call stack.

13. Press F3 followed by ENDDBG on the system command line.

Solution to Exercise 25

1. Whatever command you need.

2. See the source shown below.

3. CRTBNDRPG PGM(Yourlib/EMPPAY) (Yourfile/EMPPAY) DFTACTGRP(*NO) DBGVIEW(*ALL)

4. STRDBG EMPPAY

5. STEP 1. Press F3 to end the program, then call it from the system command line, by entering CALL EMPPAY.

6. Use F11 or EVAL as desired.

7. Press F3 and then ENDDBG.

```
 *--------------------------------------------------------------------*
 * Revised EMPPAY --  This program                                    *
 *      1) creates a printed output of employee's pay for the week.   *
 *      2) handles overflow for file QSYSPRT.                         *
 *      3) computes overtime pay and lists it in the output report.   *
 *--------------------------------------------------------------------*

H DATEDIT(*DMY/)

 *--------------------------------------------------------------------*
 * File Definitions                                                   *
 *--------------------------------------------------------------------*
FTRANSACT  IP   E            K DISK
FEMPMST    IF   E            K DISK
FQSYSPRT   O    F 132          PRINTER oflind(*inoa)

 *--------------------------------------------------------------------*
 * Variable Declarations                                              *
 *--------------------------------------------------------------------*
D Pay             S              8P 2
D Regular         S              8P 2
D Overtime        S              8P 2

 *--------------------------------------------------------------------*
 * Constant Declarations                                              *
 *--------------------------------------------------------------------*
D Heading1        C               'NUMBER  NAME               RATE   H-
D                                 OURS  REGULAR     OVERTIME    BONUS -
D                                      TOTAL PAY '
D Heading2        C               ' _____  _____   _____   _-
D                                  ___  _____   _____   ____-
D                                   _  _____'

 *--------------------------------------------------------------------*
 * For each record in the transaction file (TRANSACT), if the employee*
 * is found, compute the employee's pay and print the details.        *
 * When computing pay, break out pay in regular, overtime, and total  *
 * amounts.                                                           *
 *--------------------------------------------------------------------*
C     TRN_NUMBER    CHAIN     EMP_REC                          99
C                   IF        NOT *IN99
C                   IF        trn_hours > 40
C                   EVAL      regular = emp_rate * 40
C                   EVAL(H)   overtime = emp_rate * 1.5
C                                * (trn_hours - 40)
C                   ELSE
C                   EVAL(H)   regular = emp_rate * trn_hours
C                   EVAL      overtime = 0
C                   ENDIF
C                   EVAL      pay = regular + overtime + trn_bonus
C                   ENDIF
```

```
      *------------------------------------------------------------------*
      * Report Layout                                                     *
      *  -- print the heading lines if 1P or OA is on                     *
      *  -- if the record is found (indicator 99 is off) print the payroll*
      *     details otherwise print an exception record                   *
      *  -- print 'END OF LISTING' when LR is on                          *
      *------------------------------------------------------------------*
OQSYSPRT   H    1P                      2  3
O          or   oa
O                                           35 'PAYROLL REGISTER'
O                         *DATE      Y      80
O          H    1P                      2
O          or   oa
O                                           85 Heading1
O          H    1P                      2
O          or   oa
O                                           85 Heading2
O          D    N1PN99                  2
O                         TRN_NUMBER          5
O                         EMP_NAME           24
O                         EMP_RATE    L      33
O                         TRN_HOURS   L      40
O                         Regular            51 '$     0. '
O                         Overtime           63 '$     0. '
O                         TRN_BONUS          73 '$   0. '
O                         Pay                85 '$     0. '
O          D    N1P 99                  2
O                         TRN_NUMBER          5
O                                           35 '** NOT ON EMPLOYEE FILE **'
O          T    LR
O                                           33 'END OF LISTING'
```

Appendix B. *Experience RPG IV Tutorial* Code Samples

This appendix lists the RPG IV source which is included in the save file TUTORIAL. The source corresponds to the code samples given in the *Experience RPG IV Tutorial*. The source members listed below are the ones used to test that the samples in the tutorial compile correctly. Because these samples are, for the most part, code fragments, it was necessary to add some code so that the source member would compile without errors. For example, the samples showing the D spec required a C spec with a SETON opcode to show how the so-called program would end.

Note that no source is provided for stages 1, 5, 6, 11, or 14, either because the sample consisted of one line only, or because there are no code samples in that stage.

Stage 2

```
* Sample code for Stage 2, screen 3
* NOTE: This source member will not compile as is, without the
* necessary compile-time data.
H ALTSEQ(*SRC) CURSYM('$') DATEDIT(*MDY/) DATFMT(*MDY/)
H DEBUG DECEDIT(',') FORMSALIGN FTRANS DFTNAME(MYPGM)
H TIMFMT(*ISO)
```

Stage 3

```
* Sample code for Stage 3, screen 11
* NOTE: This source member will not compile as is, without an
* externally described file DBFILE available.
FDBFile    UF   E              DISK    PREFIX(DB) INCLUDE(Fmt2)
F                                      COMMIT(Sometimes)
```

Stage 4

```
* Sample code for Stage 4, screen 3
D Personal       DS                   INZ
D  Name                        30
D   FirstName            1      15
D   LastName            16      30
D  Phone_No                     10
D Array1                        5  0 DIM(10)
D AnyField        S             7  2
C                 SETON                                            LR
* Sample code for Stage 4, screen 4
D Personal       DS                   INZ
D  Name                        30
D   FirstName            1      15
D   LastName            16      30
D  Phone_No                     10
D   Area_Code                    3     OVERLAY(Phone_No)
D   Local_No                     7     OVERLAY(Phone_No:4)
D Status                         1     INZ('I')
C                 SETON                                            LR
```

```
* Sample code for Stage 4, screen 5
D Work_Field     S              10
D Init_Field     S               3 0 INZ(999)
D MyArray        S               5   DIM(5)
C                    SETON                                        LR

* Sample code for Stage 4, screen 9
D                DS                  INZ
D  Name                         30
D  Hrs_Array                     3 0 DIM(7)
D  Name_Array                    1   DIM(30) OVERLAY(NAME)
C                    SETON                                        LR

* Sample code for Stage 4, screen 10
D                DS
D Subfield1                    10
D Subfield2                     3 0
D Upper          C                 CONST('ABCDEFGHI-
D                                  JKLMNOPQRSTUVWXYZ')
D Lower          C                 'abcdefghijklmnopqrs+
D                                  tuvwxyz'
D BigNumber      C                 CONST(23456
D                                  789)
C                    SETON                                        LR
```

Stage 5

```
* Sample code for Stage 5, screen 3
DSalesTotal      S              10S 2
DDisc_Rate       S              10S 2
DDisc_Total      S              10S 2
C      SalesTotal    MULT(H)  Disc_Rate      Disc_Total      10 2
C                    SETON                                        LR

* Source for Stage 5, screen 8
D Rating         S               1A
D FirstName      S               8A
D Salary         S              10S 2
D Field1         S               1A
D Field2         S               1A
C                    MOVE     *OFF          *IN(03)
C                    IF       (Rating = 'A' OR FirstName = 'Susan')
C                    EVAL     Salary = Salary * 1.25
C                    ENDIF
C                    EVAL     *IN01 = (Field1 > Field2) OR *IN03
C                    SETON                                        LR
```

```
* Source for Stage 5, screen 9
D Status          S             1A
D Quantity        S            10S 0
D Price           S            10S 4
D Amount          S            10S 2
C                 MOVE      *OFF          *IN(03)
C                 DOW       *IN03 = *OFF
C                 IF        (Status = 'S') AND Quantity < 1000
C                 EVAL(H)   Amount = Quantity * Price
C                 ELSE
C                 EVAL(H)   Amount = (Price * 0.90) * Quantity
C                 ENDIF
C                 ENDDO
C                 SETON                                        LR
```

Stage 7

```
* Sample code for Stage 7, screen 8
*
* Main Source Section
H DFTACTGRP(*NO)
* Prototype for subprocedure CalcProcedure
D CalcProcedure    PR            10I 0
* Prototyped parameters
D   TERM1                        5I 0
D   TERM2                        5I 0 VALUE
D   TERM3                        5I 0 CONST
* Global data definitions
D Var1             S             5I 0 INZ(1)
D Var2             S             5I 0 INZ(1)
D Var3             S             5I 0 INZ(1)
D Ans              S            10I 0
* Since the subprocedure returns a value, it is called in an expression.
C                 EVAL      Ans = CalcProcedure(Var1:Var2:Var3)
C     'Ans =      'DSPLY                 Ans
* The subprocedure CalcProcedure returns the value 20.
* Ans = 20
C                 RETURN
*
* Subprocedure Section
* Begin-procedure
P CalcProcedure    B
* Procedure-interface (same as the prototype)
D CalcProcedure    PI            10I 0
D   Term1                        5I 0
D   Term2                        5I 0 VALUE
D   Term3                        5I 0 CONST
* Local data definitions
D Result           S            10I 0
* Calculations
C                 EVAL      Result = Term1 ** 2 * 2
C                                 + Term2 * 7
C                                 + Term3
* Return value must be compatible with return type in definition
C                 RETURN    Result * 2
* End-procedure
P                 E
```

```
* Sample code for Stage 7, screen 10
*
* Main Source Section
H DFTACTGRP(*NO)
* Prototype for subprocedure CalcProcedure
D CalcProcedure   PR
* Prototyped parameters
D    TERM1                         5I 0
* Global data definitions
D Var1            S                5I 0 INZ(1)
* Since the subprocedure does not return a value,
* it is called using CALLP.
C                   CALLP     CalcProcedure(Var1)
C       'Var1 =     'DSPLY                    Var1
C                   RETURN
*
* Subprocedure Section
* Begin-procedure
P CalcProcedure   B          .
* Procedure-interface (same as the prototype)
D CalcProcedure   PI
D    Term1                         5I 0
* Calculations
C                   EVAL      Term1 = Term1 * 2
C       'Term1 =    'DSPLY                    Term1
* Term1 = 2
* Return to main procedure
C                   RETURN
* End-procedure
P                 E
```

```
* Sample code for Stage 7, screen 11
*
* Main Source Section
H DFTACTGRP(*NO)
* Prototype for subprocedure CalcProcedure
D CalcProcedure   PR            10I 0
* Prototyped parameters
D   TERM1                        5I 0
* Global data definitions
D Var1            S             5I 0 INZ(1)
D Ans             S            10I 0
* Since the subprocedure returns a value, it is called in an expression.
C                   EVAL      Ans = CalcProcedure(Var1)
C     'Var1 =      'DSPLY                Var1
C     'Ans =       'DSPLY                Ans
* The subprocedure CalcProcedure returns the value 2.
* Var1 = 1
* Ans = 2
C                   RETURN
*
* Subprocedure Section
* Begin-procedure
P CalcProcedure   B
* Procedure-interface (same as the prototype)
D CalcProcedure   PI            10I 0
D   Term1                        5I 0
* Calculations
* Return value must be compatible with return type in definition
C                   RETURN    Term1 * 2
* End-procedure
P               E
```

```
 * Sample code for Stage 7, screen 13
 *
 * Main Source Section
H DFTACTGRP(*NO)
 * Prototype for subprocedure CalcProcedure
D CalcProcedure    PR
 * Prototyped parameters
D    TERM1                      5I 0
D    TERM2                      5I 0 VALUE
D    TERM3                      5I 0 CONST
 * Global data definitions
D Var1            S             5I 0 INZ(1)
D Var2            S             5I 0 INZ(1)
D Var3            S             5I 0 INZ(1)
 * Call to subprocedure without a return value.
 * Since the subprocedure does not return a value,
 * it is called using CALLP.
C                   CALLP     CalcProcedure(Var1:Var2:Var3)
C     'Var1 =      'DSPLY                  Var1
C     'Var2 =      'DSPLY                  Var2
C     'Var3 =      'DSPLY                  Var3
 * Var1 = 21
 * Var2 = 1
 * Var3 = 1
C                   RETURN
 *
 * Subprocedure Section
 * Begin-procedure
P CalcProcedure    B
 * Procedure-interface (same as the prototype)
D CalcProcedure    PI
D    Term1                      5I 0
D    Term2                      5I 0 VALUE
D    Term3                      5I 0 CONST
 * Local data definitions
D Result          S            10I 0 INZ(20)
 * Calculations
C                   EVAL      Term1 = Result + Term3
C                   EVAL      Term2 = Result + Term3
C                   EVAL      Result = Term3
 * Term3 cannot be modified in the subprocedure
 * because it was passed as a constant.
 * The Result-Field entry for DSPLY must be a
 * field that can be modified.
C     'Term1 =     'DSPLY                  Term1
C     'Term2 =     'DSPLY                  Term2
C     'Term3 =     'DSPLY                  Result
 * Term1 = 21
 * Term2 = 21
 * Term3 = 1
 * Return to main procedure
C                   RETURN
 * End-procedure
P                   E
```

Stage 8

```
* Source for Stage 8, screen 4
H DATFMT(*MDY) TIMFMT(*HMS)
D DateFld          S               D   INZ(D'03/01/98')
D TimeFld          S               T   INZ(T'13:00:00')
D TimeStamp        S               Z   INZ(Z'1997-10-05-15.25.33.000008')
C     'DateFld   'DSPLY                     DateFld
C     'TimeFld   'DSPLY                     TimeFld
C     'TimeStamp 'DSPLY                     TimeStamp
C                SETON                                              LR
```

Stage 9

```
* Sample code for Stage 9, screen 3
H DATFMT(*MDY) TIMFMT(*HMS)
*
D OrderDate        S               D   INZ(D'10/01/97')
D ShipDate         S               D
D WarntyDate       S               D
D StartTime        S               T   INZ(T'16:52:33')
D EndTime          S               T
D MyTimeStmp       S               Z   INZ(Z'1997-10-05-15.25.33.000008')
D NoYrs            S              1S 0 INZ(3)
D microSec         S              6S 0 INZ(999990)
*
* Add 7 days to a date field
* Should see 10/08/94 displayed
*
C     OrderDate    ADDDUR    7:*Days     ShipDate
C     'ShipDate   'DSPLY                 ShipDate
*
* Add 1 month to a date field
* Should see 11/08/94 displayed
*
C                  ADDDUR    1:*M        ShipDate
C     'ShipDate   'DSPLY                 ShipDate
*
* Add a number of years to a date field
* Should see 11/08/97 displayed
*
C     ShipDate     ADDDUR    NoYrs:*Y    WarntyDate
C     'WarntyDate 'DSPLY                 WarntyDate
```

```
 *
 * Add 8 hours to a time field
 * Should see 00:52:33 displayed
 *
C      StartTime      ADDDUR    8:*Hours     EndTime
C      'EndTime     'DSPLY                    EndTime
 *
 * Add 20 minutes to a time field
 * Should see 01:12:33 displayed
 *
C                     ADDDUR    20:*MN       EndTime
C      'EndTime     'DSPLY                    EndTime
 *
 * Add 59 seconds to a time field
 * Should see 01:13:32 displayed
 *
C                     ADDDUR    59:*Seconds  EndTime
C      'EndTime     'DSPLY                    EndTime
 *
 * Add a number of microseconds to a timestamp field
 * Should see 1994-10-05-15.25.33.999998 displayed
 *
C                     ADDDUR    microSec:*MS MyTimeStmp
C      'MyTimeStmp  'DSPLY                    MyTimeStmp
 *
C                     SETON                                LR
```

```
* Sample code for Stage 9, screen 4
H DATFMT(*MDY) TIMFMT(*HMS)
*
D DueDate         S               D   INZ(D'10/01/97')
D LoanDate        S               D
D HireDate        S               D   INZ(D'12/03/92')
D CurDate         S               D
*
D StartTime       S               T
D EndTime         S               T   INZ(T'16:52:33')
D GetUpTime       S               T   INZ(T'07:15:00')
D BedTime         S               T   INZ(T'22:30:00')
*
D MyTimeStmp      S               Z   INZ(Z'1997-10-05-15.25.33.000123')
*
D NoYrs           S             1S 0 INZ(8)
D YrsEmp          S             2S 0
D NumDays         S             4S 0
D AwakeHrs        S             2S 0
D NumHrs          S             2S 0
D microSec        S             6S 0 INZ(000012)
D StartBlink      S               Z   INZ(Z'1997-10-05-15.25.33.000300')
D StopBlink       S               Z   INZ(Z'1997-10-05-15.25.33.008920')
*
* Subtract a duration from a date field
* Should see 10/01/86 displayed
*
C     DueDate       SUBDUR    NoYrs:*Y      LoanDate
C     'LoanDate     'DSPLY                  LoanDate
*
* Subtract a duration from a date field
* Should see 09/01/86 displayed
*
C                   SUBDUR    1:*M          LoanDate
C     'LoanDate     'DSPLY                  LoanDate
*
* Subtract a duration from a time field
* Should see 08:52:33 displayed
*
C     EndTime       SUBDUR    8:*Hours      StartTime
C     'StartTime    'DSPLY                  StartTime
*
* Subtract a duration from a timestamp field
* Should see 1997-10-05-15.25.33.000111 displayed
*
C                   SUBDUR    microSec:*MS  MyTimeStmp
C     'MyTimeStmp   'DSPLY                  MyTimeStmp
*
* Calculate a duration between two date fields
* Should see 2952 displayed
*
C     DueDate       SUBDUR    LoanDate      NumDays:*D
C     'NumDays      'DSPLY                  NumDays
*
* Calculate a duration between two date fields
* Should see 5 displayed
C     *USA          MOVE      *DATE         CurDate
C     CurDate       SUBDUR    HireDate      YrsEmp:*Y
C     'YrsEmp       'DSPLY                  YrsEmp
```

```
    *
    * Calculate a duration between two time fields
    * Should see 15 displayed
    *
C       BedTime        SUBDUR     GetUpTime    AwakeHrs:*H
C       'AwakeHrs      'DSPLY                  AwakeHrs
    *
    * Calculate a duration between two timestamp fields
    * Should see 8620 displayed
    *
C       StopBlink      SUBDUR     StartBlink   microSec:*MS
C       'microSec      'DSPLY                  microSec
    *
    * Calculate a duration between a date and a timestamp field
    * Should see 4 displayed
    *
C       MyTimeStmp     SUBDUR     DueDate      NumDays:*days
C       'NumDays       'DSPLY                  NumDays
    *
    * Calculate a duration between a time and a timestamp field
    * Should see 7 displayed
    *
C       BedTime        SUBDUR     MyTimeStmp   NumHrs:*H
C       'NumHrs        'DSPLY                  NumHrs
    *
C                      SETON                                        LR

    * Sample code for Stage 9, screen 5
H DATFMT(*MDY) TIMFMT(*HMS)
D LoanDate         S              D
D MyTimeStmp       S              Z   INZ(Z'1998-10-05-15.25.33.000123')
    * Extract portion of a date or timestamp field
C                      EXTRCT     LoanDate:*Y   LoanYear       4 0
C                      EXTRCT     MyTimeStmp:*M MyMonth        2 0
C                      SETON                                        LR

    * Sample code for Stage 9, screen 7
H DATFMT(*YMD-) TIMFMT(*ISO)
    *
D Date1            S              D   DATFMT(*MDY/) INZ(D'98-04-01')
D Time1            S              T   TIMFMT(*HMS) INZ(T'13.00.00')
D CharDate         S              8   INZ('95-01-01')
D DateHire         S              D   DATFMT(*USA)
D UpdDate          S              D   DATFMT(*ISO)
D UpdTime          S              T   TIMFMT(*USA)
    *
C                      MOVE       Date1        UpdDate
    ** UpdDate now = '1998-04-01'
C                      MOVE       Time1        UpdTime
    ** UpdTime now = '01:00 PM'
C       *YMD-          MOVE       CharDate     DateHire
    ** *YMD- refers to the format of CharDate.  DateHire is *USA/
    ** DateHire now = '01/01/1995'
C       *JUL.          MOVEL(P)   DateHire     CharDate
    ** *JUL. refers to the format that CharDate should receive.
    ** CharDate now = '95.001  '
C                      SETON                                        LR
```

```
* Sample code for Stage 9, screen 9
D Date1           S               D    DATFMT(*MDY) INZ(D'1998-04-01')
D CharDate        S               8    INZ('95-10-01')
C     *YMD-       TEST(D)              CharDate              20
** *IN20=*OFF; CharDate contains a valid *YMD value.
C     *YMD        TEST(D)              CharDate              21
** *IN21=*ON; CharDate uses - separator, not / (the default for *YMD)
C                 TEST                 Date1                 22
** *IN22=*OFF; no Factor 1 or extender because Date1 is a Date field.
C                 SETON                                     LR
```

Stage 10

```
* Sample code for Stage 10, screen 5
D Hours           S             5  2
D WeeklyPay       S             9  2
D Rate            S             7  2
*
C                 IF        (Hours <= 40)
C                 EVAL(H)   WeeklyPay = Rate * Hours
C                 ELSE
C                 EVAL(H)   WeeklyPay = ((Hours - 40) * (Rate * 1.5))
C                                        + (Rate * 40)
C                 ENDIF
*
C                 SETON                                     LR

* Sample code for Stage 10, screen 9
*
* Main Source Section
H DFTACTGRP(*NO)
* Prototype for subprocedure CircleArea
D CircleArea      PR            5P 2
* Prototyped parameters
D  Radius                       5P 2 VALUE
* Global data definitions
D TotalArea       S             5P 2
*
C                 EVAL      TotalArea = 10 * 5 + CircleArea (5/2) / 2
C     'TotalArea = 'DSPLY                 TotalArea
C                 RETURN
*
* Subprocedure Section
*    User-Defined Function: CircleArea
*
*    Subprocedure CircleArea is used to find the
*    circle area.
*
P CircleArea      B
D CircleArea      PI            5P 2
D  Radius                       5P 2 VALUE
C                 RETURN    3.14159 * Radius ** 2
P CircleArea      E
```

Note that the value of the float field in the next example is initialized to 3.14159 but its value is 3.1415899999999. This happens because float variables can sometimes only hold an approximation of a decimal value. As long as you use half-adjust when you assign the float value to a non-float variable, you should not experience any problems with this.

```
*=================================================================*
* This is a simple program which allows you to experiment with    *
* %ABS.                                                           *
*=================================================================*
H DFTACTGRP(*NO)

D FltFld          S              8f   INZ(-3.14159)
D IntFld          S             10i 0 INZ(-280)
D PackFld         S              7p 3 INZ(8562.456)
 * Prototype for Display Subprocedure
 * Used to edit DSPLY opcode output
D Display         PR
D   Comment                     10A   VARYING VALUE
 * Call to Display Subprocedure
C                 CALLP     Display('Before')
 * DSPLY  Before
 * DSPLY  FltFld  =      -3.141589999999999E+000
 * *N
 * DSPLY  IntFld  =      -280
 * *N
 * DSPLY  PackFld =       8562.456
 * *N
C                 EVAL                FltFld = %ABS(FltFld)
C                 EVAL                IntFld = %ABS(IntFld)
C                 EVAL                PackFld = %ABS(PackFld)

C                 CALLP     Display('After')
 * DSPLY  After
 * DSPLY  FltFld  =      +3.141589999999999E+000
 * *N
 * DSPLY  IntFld  =       280
 * *N
 * DSPLY  PackFld =       8562.456
C                 SETON                                        LR

P Display         B
D Display         PI
D   Comment                     10A   VARYING VALUE
D   PrtRes        S             20a
C     Comment     DSPLY
C     'FltFld = ' DSPLY                FltFld
C                 EVAL      PrtRes = %TRIML(%EDITC(IntFld : 'P'))
C     'IntFld = ' DSPLY                PrtRes
C                 EVAL      PrtRes = %TRIML(%EDITC(PackFld : 'P'))
C     'PackFld = ' DSPLY               PrtRes
P Display         E
```

The following RPG IV built-in functions can be used to convert data:

```
*=====================================================================*
* This is a simple program which allows you to experiment with        *
* %CHAR.                                                              *
*=====================================================================*
*
H DATFMT(*MDY) TIMFMT(*HMS)
*
D GraphicFld     S              20G   VARYING INZ(G' XXYYZZ ')
D DateFld        S               D    INZ(D'04/01/98')
D TimeFld        S               T    INZ(T'13:00:00')
D TimeStamp      S               Z    INZ(Z'1998-10-05-15.25.33.000008')
D CharFld        S              40A   VARYING
*
C     'GraphicFld ='DSPLY                  GraphicFld
C     'DateFld    ='DSPLY                  DateFld
C     'TimeFld    ='DSPLY                  TimeFld
C     'TimeStamp  ='DSPLY                  TimeStamp
 **N
 *DSPLY  GraphicFld =     XXYYZZ
 **N
 *DSPLY  DateFld    =     04/01/98
 **N
 *DSPLY  TimeFld    =     13:00:00
 **N
 *DSPLY  TimeStamp  =     1998-10-05-15.25.33.000008
 *
C                   EVAL      CharFld = 'The customer''s name is '
C                             + %CHAR(GraphicFld) + '.'
C     'CharFld =    'DSPLY               CharFld
C                   EVAL      CharFld = 'The time is ' + %CHAR(TimeFld)
C                             + ' on ' + %CHAR(DateFld) + '.'
C     'CharFld =    'DSPLY               CharFld
C                   EVAL      CharFld = 'The time is now '
C                             + %SUBST(%CHAR(TimeStamp):12:5) + '.'
C     'CharFld =    'DSPLY               CharFld
 *DSPLY  CharFld =       The customer's name is   XXYYZZ .
 **N
 *DSPLY  CharFld =       The time is 13:00:00 on 04/01/98.
 **N
 *DSPLY  CharFld =       The time is now 15.25.
 *
C                   SETON                                        LR
```

```
 *===================================================================*
 * This is a simple program which allows you to experiment with      *
 * %DEC & %DECH.                                                     *
 *===================================================================*
 *
D FltFld          S              8f   INZ(9.17)
D IntFld          S             10i 0 INZ(529)
D PackFld         S              7p 3 INZ(8562.756)
D ZoneFld         S              9s 5 INZ(23.84212)
D ResFld          S             15p 4
D PrtRes          S             20a
C     'FltFld  = ' DSPLY                     FltFld
C                  EVAL      PrtRes = %TRIML(%EDITC(IntFld : 'P'))
C     'IntFld  = ' DSPLY                     PrtRes
C                  EVAL      PrtRes = %TRIML(%EDITC(PackFld : 'P'))
C     'PackFld = ' DSPLY                     PrtRes
C                  EVAL      PrtRes = %TRIML(%EDITC(ZoneFld : 'P'))
C     'ZoneFld = ' DSPLY                     PrtRes
 *DSPLY  FltFld  =      +9.169999999999999E+000
 **N
 *DSPLY  IntFld  =      529
 **N
 *DSPLY  PackFld =      8562.756
 **N
 *DSPLY  ZoneFld =      23.84212
 *
C                  EVAL      ResFld = %DEC(FltFld:4:1)
C                  EVAL      PrtRes = %TRIML(%EDITC(ResFld : 'P'))
C     'ResFld = '  DSPLY                     PrtRes
C                  EVAL      ResFld = %DEC(IntFld)
C                  EVAL      PrtRes = %TRIML(%EDITC(ResFld : 'P'))
C     'ResFld = '  DSPLY                     PrtRes
C                  EVAL      ResFld = %DECH(PackFld:5:0)
C                  EVAL      PrtRes = %TRIML(%EDITC(ResFld : 'P'))
C     'ResFld = '  DSPLY                     PrtRes
C                  EVAL      ResFld = %DECH(ZoneFld:6:3)
C                  EVAL      PrtRes = %TRIML(%EDITC(ResFld : 'P'))
C     'ResFld = '  DSPLY                     PrtRes
 *
 *DSPLY  ResFld =      9.1000
 **N
 *DSPLY  ResFld =      529.0000
 **N
 *DSPLY  ResFld =      8563.0000
 **N
 *DSPLY  ResFld =      23.8420
 *
C                  SETON                                        LR
```

```
 *=====================================================================*
 * This is a simple program which allows you to experiment with        *
 * %FLOAT.                                                             *
 *=====================================================================*
 *
D IntFld          S              10i 0 INZ(529)
D PackFld         S               7p 3 INZ(8562.756)
D ZoneFld         S               9p 5 INZ(23.84212)
D ResFld          S              15p 4
D PrtRes          S              20a
 *
C                   EVAL      PrtRes = %TRIML(%EDITC(IntFld : 'P'))
C     'IntFld  = '  DSPLY                   PrtRes
C                   EVAL      PrtRes = %TRIML(%EDITC(PackFld : 'P'))
C     'PackFld = '  DSPLY                   PrtRes
C                   EVAL      PrtRes = %TRIML(%EDITC(ZoneFld : 'P'))
C     'ZoneFld = '  DSPLY                   PrtRes
 *DSPLY   IntFld  =      529
 **N
 *DSPLY   PackFld =      8562.756
 **N
 *DSPLY   ZoneFld =      23.84212
C                   EVAL                 ResFld = %FLOAT(IntFld)
C                   EVAL      PrtRes = %TRIML(%EDITC(ResFld : 'P'))
C     'ResFld = '   DSPLY                   PrtRes
C                   EVAL                 ResFld = %FLOAT(PackFld)
C                   EVAL      PrtRes = %TRIML(%EDITC(ResFld : 'P'))
C     'ResFld = '   DSPLY                   PrtRes
C                   EVAL                 ResFld = %FLOAT(ZoneFld)
C                   EVAL      PrtRes = %TRIML(%EDITC(ResFld : 'P'))
C     'ResFld = '   DSPLY                   PrtRes
 *
 *DSPLY   ResFld =      529.0000
 **N
 *DSPLY   ResFld =      8562.7559
 **N
 *DSPLY   ResFld =      23.8421
C                   SETON                                        LR
```

```
 *===================================================================*
 * This is a simple program which allows you to experiment with      *
 * %INT & %INTH.                                                     *
 *===================================================================*
 *
D FltFld          S              8f   INZ(9.17)
D PackFld         S              7p 3 INZ(8562.756)
D ZoneFld         S              9p 5 INZ(23.84212)
D ResFld          S             15p 4
D PrtRes          S             20a

C     'FltFld = '  DSPLY                     FltFld
C                  EVAL      PrtRes = %TRIML(%EDITC(PackFld : 'P'))
C     'PackFld = ' DSPLY                     PrtRes
C                  EVAL      PrtRes = %TRIML(%EDITC(ZoneFld : 'P'))
C     'ZoneFld = ' DSPLY                     PrtRes
 *DSPLY  FltFld =      +9.169999999999999E+000
 **N
 *DSPLY  PackFld =     8562.756
 **N
 *DSPLY  ZoneFld =     23.84212
C                  EVAL                      ResFld = %INT(FltFld)
C                  EVAL      PrtRes = %TRIML(%EDITC(ResFld : 'P'))
C     'ResFld = '  DSPLY                     PrtRes
C                  EVAL                      ResFld = %INTH(PackFld)
C                  EVAL      PrtRes = %TRIML(%EDITC(ResFld : 'P'))
C     'ResFld = '  DSPLY                     PrtRes
C                  EVAL                      ResFld = %INTH(ZoneFld)
C                  EVAL      PrtRes = %TRIML(%EDITC(ResFld : 'P'))
C     'ResFld = '  DSPLY                     PrtRes
 *DSPLY  ResFld =      9.0000
 **N
 *DSPLY  ResFld =      8563.0000
 **N
 *DSPLY  ResFld =      24.0000
C                  SETON                                          LR
```

```
 *=====================================================================*
 * This is a simple program which allows you to experiment with        *
 * %UNS & %UNSH.                                                       *
 *=====================================================================*
 *
D FltFld          S               8f   INZ(9.17)
D IntFld          S              10i 0 INZ(529)
D PackFld         S               7p 3 INZ(8562.756)
D ZoneFld         S               9p 5 INZ(23.84212)
D ResFld          S              15p 4
D PrtRes          S              20a
 *
C     'FltFld = '  DSPLY                         FltFld
C                  EVAL          PrtRes = %TRIML(%EDITC(IntFld : 'P'))
C     'IntFld = '  DSPLY                         PrtRes
C                  EVAL          PrtRes = %TRIML(%EDITC(PackFld : 'P'))
C     'PackFld = ' DSPLY                         PrtRes
C                  EVAL          PrtRes = %TRIML(%EDITC(ZoneFld : 'P'))
C     'ZoneFld = ' DSPLY                         PrtRes
 *DSPLY  FltFld =      +9.169999999999999E+000
 **N
 *DSPLY  IntFld =      529
 **N
 *DSPLY  PackFld =     8562.756
 **N
 *DSPLY  ZoneFld =     23.84212
C                  EVAL                  ResFld = %UNS(FltFld - 8.1)
C                  EVAL          PrtRes = %TRIML(%EDITC(ResFld : 'P'))
C     'ResFld = '  DSPLY                         PrtRes
C                  EVAL                  ResFld = %UNS(IntFld)
C                  EVAL          PrtRes = %TRIML(%EDITC(ResFld : 'P'))
C     'ResFld = '  DSPLY                         PrtRes
C                  EVAL                  ResFld = %UNSH(PackFld)
C                  EVAL          PrtRes = %TRIML(%EDITC(ResFld : 'P'))
C     'ResFld = '  DSPLY                         PrtRes
C                  EVAL                  ResFld = %UNSH(ZoneFld)
C                  EVAL          PrtRes = %TRIML(%EDITC(ResFld : 'P'))
C     'ResFld = '  DSPLY                         PrtRes
 *DSPLY  ResFld =      1.0000
 **N
 *DSPLY  ResFld =      529.0000
 **N
 *DSPLY  ResFld =      8563.0000
 **N
 *DSPLY  ResFld =      24.0000
C                  SETON                                       LR
```

The following RPG IV built-in functions can be used to get data information:

```
*=================================================================*
* This is a simple program which allows you to experiment with    *
* %DECPOS.                                                        *
*=================================================================*
*
D IntFld          S              10i 0 INZ(529)
D PackFld         S               7p 3 INZ(8562.756)
D ZoneFld         S               9s 5 INZ(23.84212)
D ResFld          S               5i 0
*
C                 EVAL      ResFld = %DECPOS(IntFld)
C     'ResFld = ' DSPLY                  ResFld
C                 EVAL      ResFld = %DECPOS(PackFld)
C     'ResFld = ' DSPLY                  ResFld
C                 EVAL      ResFld = %DECPOS(ZoneFld)
C     'ResFld = ' DSPLY                  ResFld
*
*DSPLY  ResFld =        0
**N
*DSPLY  ResFld =        3
**N
*DSPLY  ResFld =        5
C                 SETON                                           LR


*=================================================================*
* This is a simple program which allows you to experiment with    *
* %ELEM.                                                          *
*=================================================================*
*
D AnArray         S              5    DIM(10)
D ADS             DS                  OCCURS(10)
D   DSField1                     5
D   DSField2                     5
D AnotherAry      S                   LIKE(AnArray)
D                                     DIM(%ELEM(AnArray))
D ArrayElem       S              5P 0
D DSOccurs        S              5P 0
D Counter         S              5P 0 INZ(1)
D Diff            S              5P 0 INZ(1)

C                 EVAL      ArrayElem = %ELEM(AnArray)
* ArrayElem = 10
C                 EVAL      DSOccurs = %ELEM(ADS)
* DSOccurs = 10
C                 DOU       Counter >= %ELEM(AnotherAry)
* Control loop based on # elements in AnotherAry (10)

C                 IF        AnArray(Counter) <> AnotherAry(Counter)
C                 EVAL      Diff = Diff + 1
C                 ENDIF
C                 EVAL      Counter = Counter + 1
C                 ENDDO
C     'Dif =    ' DSPLY                  Diff
C     'Counter =' DSPLY                  Counter

C                 RETURN
```

```
 *=====================================================================*
 * This is a simple program which allows you to experiment with        *
 * %LEN.                                                               *
 *=====================================================================*
H DATFMT(*MDY) TIMFMT(*HMS)
D FltFld          S              8f   INZ(9.17)
D IntFld          S             10i 0 INZ(529)
D PackFld         S              7p 3 INZ(8562.756)
D ZoneFld         S              9p 5 INZ(23.84212)
D DateFld         S               D   INZ(D'04/01/98')
D TimeFld         S               T   INZ(T'13:00:00')
D TimeStamp       S               Z   INZ(Z'1998-10-05-15.25.33.000008')
D CharFld         S             40A   VARYING INZ('Toronto Ontario')
D GraphicFld      S             20G   VARYING INZ(G' XXYYZZ ')
D ResFld          S             15p 4
D PrtRes          S             20a
C                   EVAL      ResFld = %LEN(FltFld)
C                   EVAL      PrtRes = %TRIML(%EDITC(ResFld : 'P'))
C     'ResFld = '   DSPLY                   PrtRes
 *DSPLY  ResFld =      8.0000
C                   EVAL      ResFld = %LEN(IntFld)
C                   EVAL      PrtRes = %TRIML(%EDITC(ResFld : 'P'))
C     'ResFld = '   DSPLY                   PrtRes
 *DSPLY  ResFld =     10.0000
C                   EVAL      ResFld = %LEN(PackFld)
C                   EVAL      PrtRes = %TRIML(%EDITC(ResFld : 'P'))
C     'ResFld = '   DSPLY                   PrtRes
 *DSPLY  ResFld =      7.0000
C                   EVAL      ResFld = %LEN(ZoneFld)
C                   EVAL      PrtRes = %TRIML(%EDITC(ResFld : 'P'))
C     'ResFld = '   DSPLY                   PrtRes
 *DSPLY  ResFld =      9.0000
C                   EVAL      ResFld = %LEN(DateFld)
C                   EVAL      PrtRes = %TRIML(%EDITC(ResFld : 'P'))
C     'ResFld = '   DSPLY                   PrtRes
 *DSPLY  ResFld =      8.0000
C                   EVAL      ResFld = %LEN(TimeFld)
C                   EVAL      PrtRes = %TRIML(%EDITC(ResFld : 'P'))
C     'ResFld = '   DSPLY                   PrtRes
 *DSPLY  ResFld =      8.0000
C                   EVAL      ResFld = %LEN(TimeStamp)
C                   EVAL      PrtRes = %TRIML(%EDITC(ResFld : 'P'))
C     'ResFld = '   DSPLY                   PrtRes
 *DSPLY  ResFld =     26.0000
C                   EVAL      ResFld = %LEN(CharFld)
C                   EVAL      PrtRes = %TRIML(%EDITC(ResFld : 'P'))
C     'ResFld = '   DSPLY                   PrtRes
 *DSPLY  ResFld =     15.0000
C                   EVAL      %LEN(CharFld) = 11
C     'ResFld = '   DSPLY                   CharFld
 *DSPLY  ResFld =     Toronto Ont
C                   EVAL      ResFld = %LEN(GraphicFld)
C                   EVAL      PrtRes = %TRIML(%EDITC(ResFld : 'P'))
C     'ResFld = '   DSPLY                   PrtRes
 *DSPLY  ResFld =      3.0000
C                   EVAL      %LEN(GraphicFld) = 2
C     'ResFld = '   DSPLY                   GraphicFld
 *DSPLY  ResFld =     XXYY
C                   SETON                                        LR
```

```
 *=================================================================*
 * This is a simple program which allows you to experiment with    *
 * %SIZE.                                                          *
 *=================================================================*
D SmallField     S              5P 2
D BigField       S             30     INZ('Mary had a little lamb. +
D                                         Baaaa')
D
D MyDS           DS
D   MyField                     5
D   MyArray                     5      DIM(%SIZE(BigField))
 * MyArray has 30 elements

D Sizes          DS
D   SizeSmall                  5P 0
D   SizeDS                     5P 0
D   ArraySize                  5P 0

D Count          S             5P 0 INZ(1)
 *
C                   EVAL      SizeSmall = %SIZE(SmallField)
 *      SizeSmall = 3
C                   EVAL      SizeDS = %SIZE(MyDS)
 *      SizeDS = 155
C                   EVAL      ArraySize = %SIZE(MyArray)
 *      ArraySize = 5
C                   EVAL      ArraySize = %SIZE(MyArray:*all)
 *      ArraySize = 150
C                   DOU       Count >= %SIZE(BigField)
 *      Control loop based on size of Field
C                   EVAL      MyArray(Count)
C                               = %SUBST(BigField:Count:1)
C     'MyArray =    'DSPLY                 MyArray(Count)

C                   EVAL      Count = Count + 1
C                   ENDDO
C     'Count =      'DSPLY                 Count

C                   RETURN
```

The following RPG IV built-in functions can be used to edit data:

```
*=====================================================================*
* This is a simple program which allows you to experiment with        *
* %EDITC.                                                             *
*=====================================================================*

D FltFld          S              8f   INZ(12098)
D PackFld         S              7p 3 INZ(12.098)
D ZoneFld         S              9p 5 INZ(-0.12098)
D ResFld          S             40a
 *
C                   EVAL      ResFld = %EDITC(%DEC(FltFLD:6:1) : '4')
C         'ResFld = '  DSPLY                 ResFld
C                   EVAL      ResFld = %EDITC(PackFld : 'A')
C         'ResFld = '  DSPLY                 ResFld
C                   EVAL      ResFld = %EDITC(ZoneFld : '1' : *ASTFILL)
C         'ResFld = '  DSPLY                 ResFld
C                   EVAL      ResFld = %EDITC(ZoneFld : '1' : *CURSYM)
C         'ResFld = '  DSPLY                 ResFld
C                   EVAL      ResFld = %EDITC(ZoneFld : 'A')
C         'ResFld = '  DSPLY                 ResFld
C                   EVAL      ResFld = %EDITC(ZoneFld : 'K')
C         'ResFld = '  DSPLY                 ResFld
C                   EVAL      ResFld = %EDITC(ZoneFld : 'O')
C         'ResFld = '  DSPLY                 ResFld
C                   EVAL      ResFld = 'The date is ' +
C                                      %EDITC(*date : 'Y') + '.'
C         'ResFld = '  DSPLY                 ResFld
 *
*DSPLY  ResFld =        12098.0
**N
*DSPLY  ResFld =         12.098
**N
*DSPLY  ResFld =        *****.12098
**N
*DSPLY  ResFld =            $.12098
**N
*DSPLY  ResFld =         .12098CR
**N
*DSPLY  ResFld =         .12098-
**N
*DSPLY  ResFld =        -.12098
**N
*DSPLY  ResFld =        The date is  1/07/1998.
C                   SETON                                        LR
```

```
*====================================================================*
* This is a simple program which allows you to experiment with       *
* %EDITFLT.                                                          *
*====================================================================*
*
D FltFld          S              8f   INZ(3E3)
D IntFld          S             10i 0 INZ(12098)
D PackFld         S              7p 3 INZ(1209.891)
D ZoneFld         S              9p 2 INZ(-120.98)
D ResFld          S             40a
 *
C                   EVAL      ResFld = %EDITFLT(FltFLD - 2E3)
C     'ResFld = '   DSPLY                     ResFld
C                   EVAL      ResFld = %EDITFLT(IntFld)
C     'ResFld = '   DSPLY                     ResFld
C                   EVAL      ResFld = %EDITFLT(PackFld)
C     'ResFld = '   DSPLY                     ResFld
C                   EVAL      ResFld = %EDITFLT(ZoneFld)
C     'ResFld = '   DSPLY                     ResFld
 *
 *DSPLY  ResFld =       +1.000000000000000E+003
 **N
 *DSPLY  ResFld =       +1.209799999999999E+004
 **N
 *DSPLY  ResFld =       +1.209891000000000E+003
 **N
 *DSPLY  ResFld =       -1.209799999999999E+002
C                   SETON                                        LR
```

```
 *=================================================================*
 * This is a simple program which allows you to experiment with    *
 * %EDITW.                                                         *
 *=================================================================*
 *
D FltFld          S              8f   INZ(12098)
D IntFld          S             10i 0 INZ(12098)
D PackFld         S              7p 3 INZ(1209.891)
D ZoneFld         S              9p 2 INZ(-120.98)
D ResFld          S             40a
 *
C                 EVAL      ResFld = %EDITW(%DEC(FltFLD:6:0) :
C                                                   '0       ')
C     'ResFld = ' DSPLY                   ResFld
C                 EVAL      ResFld = %EDITW(IntFld : '   0 & & ')
C     'ResFld = ' DSPLY                   ResFld
C                 EVAL      ResFld = %EDITW(PackFld : '0(   )-  ')
C     'ResFld = ' DSPLY                   ResFld
C                 EVAL      ResFld = %EDITW(ZoneFld : ',   , *. ')
C     'ResFld = ' DSPLY                   ResFld
C                 EVAL      ResFld = %EDITW(ZoneFld : ' ,   , $0. ')
C     'ResFld = ' DSPLY                   ResFld
C                 EVAL      ResFld = %EDITW(ZoneFld : '$ ,   , 0. ')
C     'ResFld = ' DSPLY                   ResFld
C                 EVAL      ResFld = %EDITW(ZoneFld : ' ,   , 0. &CR')
C     'ResFld = ' DSPLY                   ResFld
C                 EVAL      ResFld = %EDITW(ZoneFld : ' ,   , 0. -')
C     'ResFld = ' DSPLY                   ResFld
C                 EVAL      ResFld = %EDITW(ZoneFld : '0        &Add')
C     'ResFld = ' DSPLY                   ResFld
 *
 *DSPLY  ResFld =      12098
 **N
 *DSPLY  ResFld =       12 0 98
 **N
 *DSPLY  ResFld =      (1209)-891
 **N
 *DSPLY  ResFld =      ******120.98
 **N
 *DSPLY  ResFld =          $120.98
 **N
 *DSPLY  ResFld =      $     120.98
 **N
 *DSPLY  ResFld =          120.98 CR
 **N
 *DSPLY  ResFld =          120.98-
 **N
 *DSPLY  ResFld =      00012098 Add
C                 SETON                                        LR
```

The following RPG IV built-in functions can be used for exception/error handling:

```
 *=================================================================*
 * This is a simple program which allows you to experiment with    *
 * %ERROR & %STATUS.                                               *
 *=================================================================*
 *
D Ptr1           S               *
D Ptr2           S               *
D Msg            S             52
D BigLen         S             10I 0  INZ(*HIVAL)
 *
C                   ALLOC(E)  7          Ptr1
C                   EVAL      Msg = '%STATUS is '
C                             + %EDITC(%STATUS : 'X')
C                             + ' %ERROR is '''
C                             + %ERROR + '''.'
C     Msg           DSPLY
 *
 * DSPLY  %STATUS is 00000 %ERROR is '0'.
 *
 * This is an invalid (too large) amount of storage, and sometimes
 * it may be unavailable.
 * %ERROR will return '1', the status is set to 00425, and
 * %STATUS will return 00425.
C                   ALLOC(E)  BigLen     Ptr1
C                   EVAL      Msg = '%STATUS is '
C                             + %EDITC(%STATUS : 'X')
C                             + ' %ERROR is '''
C                             + %ERROR + '''.'
C     Msg           DSPLY
 *
 * DSPLY  %STATUS is 00425 %ERROR is '1'.
 *
C                   DEALLOC              Ptr1
C                   DEALLOC              Ptr2
C                   SETON                          LR
```

The following RPG IV built-in functions can be used to get feedback information:

```
 *=================================================================*
 * This is a simple program which allows you to experiment with    *
 * %EQUAL & %FOUND.                                                 *
 *=================================================================*
D Table           S             10A    DIM(5) CTDATA ASCEND
D SearchFor       S             10A    DIM(3) CTDATA
D NumSearch       C                    %ELEM(SearchFor)
D Result          S             30A
 * Position the table at or near SearchFor(X)
 * Here are the results of this program for different values
 * of SearchFor(X):
 * SearchFor(X) | DSPLY
 * ------------+-----------------------------
 * 'Catherine' | 'Next greater is Martha'
 * 'Andrea'    | 'Exact match'
 * 'Susan'     | 'Not found'
C                   DO        NumSearch     X             5 0
C     SearchFor(X)  LOOKUP    Table                         10 10
C                   SELECT
C                   WHEN      %EQUAL
 * An exact match was found
C                   EVAL      Result = 'Exact match'
C                   WHEN      %FOUND
 * A name was found greater than search argument
C                   EVAL      Result = 'Next greater is ' + Table
C                   OTHER
 * Not found.  SearchFor(X) is greater than all the names in the table
C                   EVAL      Result = 'Not found'
C                   ENDSL
C     SearchFor(X)  DSPLY                   Result
C                   ENDDO
C                   RETURN
**CTDATA Table
Alexander
Andrea
Bohdan
Martha
Samuel
**CTDATA SearchFor
Catherine
Andrea
Susan
```

```
 *=====================================================================*
 * This is a simple program which allows you to experiment with       *
 * %PARMS.                                                            *
 *=====================================================================*
H DFTACTGRP(*NO)
 * The following prototype describes a procedure that expects
 * either one or two parameters.
D FormatAddress   PR            45A
D   City                        20A   CONST
D   Province                    20A   CONST OPTIONS(*NOPASS)
D A               S             30A
 * The first call to FormatAddress only passes one parameter. The
 * second call passes both parameters.
C                   EVAL      A = FormatAddress('North York')
C     'A = '        DSPLY                 A
C                   EVAL      A = FormatAddress('Victoria' : 'B.C.')
C     'A = '        DSPLY                 A
C                   RETURN
 *---------------------------------------------------------------------
 * FormatAddress:
 * This procedure must check the number of parameters since the
 * second was defined with OPTIONS(*NOPASS).
 * It should only use the second parameter if it was passed.
 *---------------------------------------------------------------------
P FormatAddress    B
D FormatAddress    PI            45A
D   City                        20A   CONST
D   ProvParm                    20A   CONST OPTIONS(*NOPASS)
D Province         S             20A   INZ('Ontario')
 * Set the local variable Province to the value of the second
 * parameter if it was passed. Otherwise let it default to
 * 'Ontario' as it was initialized.
C                   IF        %PARMS > 1
C                   EVAL      Province = ProvParm
C                   ENDIF
 * Return the city and province in the form City, Province
 * for example 'North York, Ontario'
C                   RETURN    %TRIMR(City) + ', ' + Province
P FormatAddress    E
```

The following RPG IV built-in function can be used to get address of a variable or procedure:

```
*=====================================================================*
* This is a simple program which allows you to experiment with        *
* %ADDR.                                                              *
*=====================================================================*
*
H DATEDIT(*YMD)
*
D DayValues       DS
D   Mon                           9    INZ('Monday')
D   Tue                           9    INZ('Tuesday')
D   Wed                           9    INZ('Wednesday')
D   Thu                           9    INZ('Thursday')
D   Fri                           9    INZ('Friday')
D   Sat                           9    INZ('Saturday')
D   Sun                           9    INZ('Sunday')

* DayName is an array that will "overlay" DayValues.
* DayName is a based field that has storage based on the
* pointer DayPtr.
D DayName         S             9    BASED(DayPtr) DIM(7)

* DayPtr is set to the address of DayValues and allows
* access to the day names as elements of the above array.
D DayPtr          S             *    INZ(%ADDR(DayValues))

D Today           S             D    DATFMT(*ISO)
D BaseDate        S             D    DATFMT(*ISO) INZ(D'1997-12-29')
D Days            S           5P 0
D DayString       S                  LIKE(DayName)
* BaseDate is a Monday

* Calculate the day number for today by getting the number of days
* between today and a date known to be a Monday
C     *ISO          MOVE      *DATE        Today
C     'Today is:    'DSPLY                 Today
C     Today         SUBDUR    BaseDate     Days:*D
C     Days          DIV       7            X              5 0
C                   MVR                    DayNum         5 0
C                   EVAL      DayString = DayName(DayNum + 1)
C     'Which is a: 'DSPLY                  DayString
C                   RETURN
* A sample output could be:
*
*DSPLY  Today is:      1998-03-19
**N
*DSPLY  Which is a:    Thursday
*
```

The following RPG IV built-in functions can be used to perform string functions:

```
*====================================================================*
* This is a simple program which allows you to experiment with       *
* %REPLACE.                                                          *
*====================================================================*
*
D FirstName      S             30A   INZ('Name: Susan') VARYING
D Name           S             30A   INZ('Jake') VARYING
D result         S             40A   VARYING
*
* %REPLACE used to replace string:
C                   EVAL      result = %REPLACE(Name:
C                                         FirstName:
C                                         7:5)
C     'Result =    'DSPLY                 result
* result = 'Name: Jake'

* %REPLACE used to insert string:
C                   EVAL      result = %REPLACE(' (first)':
C                                         FirstName:
C                                         5:0)
C     'Result =    'DSPLY                 result
* result = 'Name (first): Susan'

C                   SETON                                      LR

*====================================================================*
* This is a simple program which allows you to experiment with       *
* %SCAN.                                                             *
*====================================================================*
*
D FirstName      S             30A   INZ('Name (first)') VARYING
D Name           S             30A   INZ('Doolittle') VARYING
D result         S             40A   VARYING
*
* Use %SCAN to find the start position of the specified text:
C                   EVAL      result = %REPLACE(' (last) : ' + Name:
C                                         FirstName:
C                                         %SCAN(' (':FirstName):
C                                         %LEN(FirstName) -
C                                         %SCAN(' )':FirstName))
C     'Result =    'DSPLY                 result
* %SCAN returns the value 5.
* result = 'Name (last): Doolittle'
*
C                   SETON                                      LR
```

```
*=================================================================*
* This is a simple program which allows you to experiment with    *
* %SUBST                                                          *
*=================================================================*
*
D Comment          S              16    INZ('It''s a great day')
D NameField        S              20    INZ('Susan Gantner')
D FirstName        S              10
D ReverseNm        S              20
*
C                   EVAL      %SUBST(Comment:8:5) = 'lousy'
C* Comment = 'It's a lousy day'
C         ' '       SCAN      NameField     X             5 0
C                   EVAL      FirstName = %SUBST(NameField:1:X-1)
C* FirstName = 'Susan       '
C                   EVAL      ReverseNm = %TrimR(%Subst(NameField:X+1))
C                                 + ', ' + %Subst(NameField:1:X -1)
C* ReverseNm = 'Gantner, Susan      '
*
C                   RETURN

*=================================================================*
* This is a simple program which allows you to experiment with    *
* %TRIM, %TRIML, and %TRIMR.                                      *
*=================================================================*
*
D AString          s              12a
D Another          s              11a
D YetAnother       s              11a
D OneMore          s              10a
D BigOne           s              22a
C*0N01Factor1+++++++Opcode(E)+Extended-factor2++++++++++++++++++++++++++
C                   EVAL      AString = ' This is it '
C                   EVAL      Another = %TRIML(AString)
 * Another = 'This is it '
C                   EVAL      YetAnother = %TRIMR(AString)
 * YetAnother = ' This is it'
C                   EVAL      OneMore = %TRIM(AString)
 * OneMore = 'This is it'
C                   EVAL      BigOne = %TRIMR(AString) + %TRIML(AString)
 * BigOne = ' This is itThis is it '
 *
C                   RETURN
```

```
*=================================================================*
* This is a simple program which allows you to experiment with    *
* RPG IV features and built-in functions. (file DBFILE: QDDSSRC)  *
*=================================================================*
*
D CUSTOMER      E DS                   EXTNAME(DBFILE)
*
D                 DS
D TempName                             LIKE(CUSTNAME)
D NameArray                      1A    OVERLAY(TempName)
D                                      DIM(%SIZE(TempName))
*
D X               S            5P 0 INZ(1)
D NumBlanks       S            5P 0 INZ(0)
*
C                   DOU       X > %ELEM(NameArray)
C                   IF        NameArray(X) = ' '
C                   EVAL      NumBlanks = NumBlanks + 1
C                   ENDIF
C                   EVAL      X = X + 1
C                   ENDDO
C                   RETURN
```

Stage 13

```
*=================================================================*
* This is a simple program which allows you to experiment with    *
* date, time, and timestamp fields.                               *
*=================================================================*

H DATFMT(*MDY) TIMFMT(*HMS)

D DateFld         S             D    INZ(D'04/01/94')
D TimeFld         S             T    INZ(T'13:00:00')
D TimeStamp       S             Z    INZ(Z'1994-10-05-15.25.33.000008')

C     'DateFld   'DSPLY               DateFld
C     'TimeFld   'DSPLY               TimeFld
C     'TimeStamp 'DSPLY               TimeStamp
C                 SETON                                        LR
```

Appendix C. Contents of Sample-Code Save Files

The Experience RPG IV CD contains two sample-code save files: WKBKLIB and TUTORIAL. WKBKLIB includes source for the workbook exercises and solutions. TUTORIAL includes sample code from the *Experience RPG IV Tutorial*.

See the README file in the *SAMPLE* directory for some suggested procedures on how to upload the following save files from your PC onto your AS/400 system.

List of Objects in WKBKLIB Save File

EMPMST	*FILE	PF-DTA	Data file for EMPPAY
PAYROLL	*FILE	PF-DTA	Data file for RPGPAY
PRODFILE	*FILE	PF-DTA	Data file for PRODINQ
TRANSACT	*FILE	PF-DTA	Data file for EMPPAY
WKBKANS	*FILE	PF-SRC	Source file for Exercises
	CSPEC1	RPGLE	Solution to Ex. 7
	DAYSSINCE	RPGLE	Solution to Ex. 19
	DSPOBJMOD	CLLE	Solution to Ex. 19
	EMPPAY	RPGLE	Solution to Ex. 25
	ESPEC1	RPGLE	Solution to Ex. 3 - Raf file Declaration
	ESPEC2	RPGLE	Solution to Ex. 10 - Compile-time array
	EX11	RPGLE	Solution to Ex. 11 - P Spec, Subprocedure Example
	EX11Q1	RPGLE	Solution to Ex. 11 - P Spec, Question 1
	EX11Q2	RPGLE	Solution to Ex. 11 - P Spec, Question 2
	EX12	RPGLE	Solution to Ex. 12
	EX14	RPGLE	Solution to Ex. 14
	EX15	RPGLE	Solution to Ex. 15, revised PRTOBJ
	EX17	RPGLE	Solution to Ex. 17, revised PRTOBJ
	EX18	RPGLE	Solution to Ex. 18, revised RPGPAY
	EX2	RPGLE	Solution to Ex. 2 - H spec
	EX21Q1	RPGLE	Solution to Ex. 21, Question 1
	EX21Q2	RPGLE	Solution to Ex. 21, Question 2
	EX21Q4	RPGLE	Solution to Ex. 21, Question 4
	EX5	RPGLE	Solution to Ex. 5 - D spec
	EX6	RPGLE	Solution to Ex. 6
	FSPEC1	RPGLE	Solution to Ex. 4 - Line counter specs
	ISPEC1	RPGLE	Solution to Ex. 8 - D spec created
	OSPEC1	RPGLE	Solution to Ex. 9 - SkipB/A SpaceB/A
	PRODINQ	RPGLE	Solution to Ex. 22
	PRTOBJ	RPGLE	Solution to Ex. 13
	PRTOBJILE	RPGLE	Solution to Ex. 19
	RPGPAY	RPGLE	Solution to Ex. 16

WKBKSRC	*FILE	PF-SRC	**Source file for Exercises**
	CSPEC1	RPG	Source for Ex. 7
	DAYSSINCE	RPGLE	Source for Ex. 19
	DSPOBJMOD	CLLE	Source for Ex. 19
	EMPMST	PF	DDS for file EMPMST; used by EMPPAY
	EMPPAY	RPGLE	Source for Ex. 25
	EMPPAY1	RPGLE	Source for Ex. 1
	ESPEC1	RPG	Source for Ex. 3 - Raf file Declaration
	ESPEC2	RPG	Source for Ex. 10 - Compile-time array
	EX12	RPGLE	Source for Ex. 12
	EX21Q1	RPGLE	Source for Ex. 21, Question 1
	EX21Q2	RPGLE	Source for Ex. 21, Question 2
	EX21Q3	RPGLE	Source for Ex. 21, Question 3
	EX5	RPG	Source for Ex. 5
	FILLSPACE	RPGLE	Source for Ex. 22
	FSPEC1	RPG	Source for Ex. 4 - Line counter specs RO
	ISPEC1	RPG	Source for Ex. 8 - D spec created
	OSPEC1	RPG	Source for Ex. 9 - SkipB/A SpaceB/A
	PAYROLL	PF	DDS for file PAYROLL; used by RPGPAY
	PRODDSP	DSPF	DDS for display file PRODDSP; used by PRODINQ
	PRODFILE	PF	DDS for file PRODFILE; used by PRODDSP
	PRODINQ	RPGLE	Source for Ex. 22
	PRTOBJ	RPGLE	Source for Ex. 13
	PRTOBJILE	RPGLE	Source for Ex. 19
	RPGPAY	RPGLE	Source for Ex. 16
	TRANSACT	PF	DDS for file TRANSACT: used by EMPPAY

List of Objects in TUTORIAL Save File

DBFILE	*FILE	PF-DTA	**File for sample program for LIKE**
QDDSSRC	*FILE	PF-SRC	**DDS source file**
	DBFILE	PF	File for sample program for LIKE
QRPGLESRC	*FILE	PF-SRC	**RPG IV source file**
	BIFABS	RPGLE	Stage 12 - Example 1, %ABS
	BIFCHAR	RPGLE	Stage 12 - Example 2, %CHAR
	BIFDEC	RPGLE	Stage 12 - Example 3, %DEC & %DECH
	BIFFLOAT	RPGLE	Stage 12 - Example 4, %FLOAT
	BIFINT	RPGLE	Stage 12 - Example 5, %INT & %INTH
	BIFUNS	RPGLE	Stage 12 - Example 6, %UNS & %UNSH
	BIFDECP	RPGLE	Stage 12 - Example 7, %DECP
	BIFELEM	RPGLE	Stage 12 - Example 8, %ELEM
	BIFLEN	RPGLE	Stage 12 - Example 9, %LEN
	BIFSIZE	RPGLE	Stage 12 - Example 10, %SIZE
	BIFEDITC	RPGLE	Stage 12 - Example 11, %EDITC
	BIFEDITF	RPGLE	Stage 12 - Example 12, %EDITFLT
	BIFEDITW	RPGLE	Stage 12 - Example 13, %EDITW
	BIFERR	RPGLE	Stage 12 - Example 14, %ERROR & %STATUS
	BIFEQL	RPGLE	Stage 12 - Example 15, %EQUAL & %FOUND
	BIFPARMS	RPGLE	Stage 12 - Example 16, %PARMS
	BIFADDR	RPGLE	Stage 12 - Example 17, %ADDR
	BIFREPL	RPGLE	Stage 12 - Example 18, %REPLACE
	BIFSCAN	RPGLE	Stage 12 - Example 19, %SCAN
	BIFSUBST	RPGLE	Stage 12 - Example 20, %SUBST
	BIFTRIM	RPGLE	Stage 12 - Example 21, %TRIM, %TRIML, & %TRIMR
	BIFLIKE	RPGLE	Stage 12 - Example 22, (file DBFILE: QDDSSRC)

```
ST10SCR5    RPGLE    Stage 10 - screen 5
ST10SCR9    RPGLE    Stage 10 - screen 9
ST13DBG     RPGLE    Stage 13 - screen 3,8,12
ST2SCR3     RPGLE    Stage 2 - screen 3
ST3SCR11    RPGLE    Stage 3 - screen 11
ST4SCR10    RPGLE    Stage 4 - screen 10
ST4SCR3     RPGLE    Stage 4 - screen 3
ST4SCR4     RPGLE    Stage 4 - screen 4
ST4SCR5     RPGLE    Stage 4 - screen 5
ST4SCR9     RPGLE    Stage 4 - screen 9
ST5SCR3     RPGLE    Stage 5 - screen 3
ST5SCR8     RPGLE    Stage 5 - screen 8
ST5SCR9     RPGLE    Stage 5 - screen 9
ST7SCR10    RPGLE    Stage 7 - screen 10
ST7SCR11    RPGLE    Stage 7 - screen 11
ST7SCR13    RPGLE    Stage 7 - screen 13
ST7SCR8     RPGLE    Stage 7 - screen 8
ST8SCR4     RPGLE    Stage 8 - Screen 4
ST9SCR3     RPGLE    Stage 9 - screen 3
ST9SCR4     RPGLE    Stage 9 - screen 4
ST9SCR5     RPGLE    Stage 9 - screen 5
ST9SCR7     RPGLE    Stage 9 - screen 7
ST9SCR9     RPGLE    Stage 9 - screen 9
```

Bibliography

This is a partial list of IBM AS/400 publications that provide additional information about topics related to RPG IV programming on the AS/400 system.

- *Java for RPG Programmers*, by Phil Coulthard and George Farr, GK2T-9890, ISBN number 1-889671-23-1. Now RPG programmers can leverage their skills with this practical guide to Java. You will learn Java by example covering a wide range of RPG IV and Java topics including: syntax, data types, classes and objects, user interface design, database access, and much more. To order this book, see the most current information available on the World Wide Web at: http://www.advice.com/ibm

- *ADTS/400: Programming Development Manager*, SC09-1771, provides information about using the Programming Development Manager (PDM) to work with lists of libraries, objects, members, and user-defined options to easily do such operations as copy, delete, and rename. Contains activities and reference material to help the user learn PDM. The most commonly used operations and function keys are explained in detail using examples.

- *ADTS/400: Source Entry Utility*, SC09-2605, provides information about using the Application Development ToolSet for AS/400 Source Entry Utility (SEU) to create and edit source members. The manual explains how to start and end an SEU session and how to use the many features of this full-screen text editor. The manual contains examples to help both new and experienced users accomplish various editing tasks, from the simplest line commands to using predefined prompts for high-level languages and data formats.

- *CL Reference*, SC41-5722, provides a description of the AS/400 control language (CL) and its OS/400 commands. (Non-OS/400 commands are described in the respective licensed program publications.) Also provides an overview of *all* the CL commands for the AS/400 system and describes the syntax rules needed to code them.

- *DDS Reference*, SC41-5712, provides detailed descriptions for coding the data description specifications (DDS) for file that can be described externally. These files are physical, logical, display, print, and intersystem communication function (ICF) files.

- *ILE Concepts*, SC41-5606, explains concepts and terminology pertaining to the Integrated Language Environment (ILE) architecture of the OS/400 licensed program. Topics covered include creating modules, binding, running programs, debugging programs, and handling exceptions.

- *ILE RPG for AS/400 Programming Guide*, SC09-2507, provides information about the ILE RPG for AS/400 programming language, which is an implementation of the RPG IV language in the Integrated Language Environment (ILE) on the AS/400 system. It includes information on creating and running programs, with considerations for procedure calls and interlanguage programming. The guide also covers debugging and exception handling, and explains how to use AS/400 files and devices in RPG programs. Appendixes include information on migration to RPG IV and sample compiler listings. It is intended for people with a basic understanding of data processing concepts and of the RPG language.

- *ILE RPG for AS/400 Reference*, SC09-2508, provides information about the ILE RPG for AS/400 programming language. This manual describes, position by position and keyword by keyword, the valid entries for all RPG IV specifications, and provides a detailed description of all the operation codes and built-in functions. This manual also contains information on the RPG logic cycle, arrays and tables, editing functions, and indicators.

- *System API Reference*, SC41-5801, provides information for the experienced programmer on how to use the application programming interfaces (APIs) to such OS/400 functions as:
  - Dynamic Screen Manager
  - Files (database, spooled, hierarchical)
  - Message handling
  - National language support
  - Network management
  - Objects
  - Problem management
  - Registration facility
  - Security
  - Software products
  - Source debug
  - UNIX-type APIs
  - User-defined communications
  - User interface
  - Work management

Experience RPG IV

CHECKPOINT SCORES

As you work through the Experience RPG IV Tutorial, use this page to keep track of the rally points you acquire at each checkpoint.

1 ☐   7 ☐   13 ☐

2 ☐   8 ☐   14 ☐

3 ☐   9 ☐

4 ☐   10 ☐

5 ☐   11 ☐

6 ☐   12 ☐   ☐

TOTAL POINTS

Total Points Possible = 120

- If you got a score of 110 or higher, then you must be Susan.

- If you got a score between 100 and 109, then you are ready to program using RPG IV.

- If you got a score between 80 and 99, then you may want to review the stages of the tutorial in which you got the lowest number of points.

- If you got a score between 60 and 79, then you should review the RPG manuals.

- If you got a score between 0 and 59, then you should stop programming in ASSEMBLER and learn RPG!